Port of Guaymas.—The key to Sonora and Arizona

T. ROBINSON WARREN.

My little Maria signalizing her consort the Caroline.

NEW YORK:
CHARLES SCRIBNER, 124 GRAND STREET.
LONDON:
SAMPSON LOW, SON & CO., 47 LUDGATE HILL.

DUST AND FOAM;

OR,

THREE OCEANS AND TWO CONTINENTS;

BEING

TEN YEARS' WANDERINGS IN MEXICO, SOUTH AMERICA, SANDWICH ISLANDS,
THE EAST AND WEST INDIES, CHINA, PHILIPPINES,
AUSTRALIA AND POLYNESIA.

BY T. ROBINSON WARREN.

NEW YORK:
CHARLES SCRIBNER, 124 GRAND STREET.
LONDON: SAMPSON LOW, SON & CO.,
47 LUDGATE HILL.
M DCCC LIX.

W. H. Tinson, Stereotyper.

Geo. Russell & Co., Printers.

WHATEVER MERIT

THE FOLLOWING PAGES MAY POSSESS,

I RESPECTFULLY DEDICATE TO

MY FATHER.

PREFACE.

THE following pages are a compilation from desultory notes made ashore and afloat, generally under disadvantageous circumstances. In them I pretend to no literary merit; happy indeed will I be, if among the many tongues in which I have been in the habit of expressing my ideas during the last ten years—Spanish, French, English, Kanaka, and half a dozen other idioms common to the South Sea Islands—I have retained the power of even writing correctly my own native language.

A winter's cruising in the Gulf of Mexico, and a year in Europe, had instilled within me a strong taste for travel and nautical adventure, and I hailed with delight the opportunity offered by the California emigration for indulging in my propensities.

Like the Kanaka, sporting in his native surf, I at once plunged headlong among the foaming billows of excitement, and after many a struggle, gained the outmost breaker, when, poising myself upon its crest, I was hurled forward with it in its mad career; now, wrestling in its seething foam, then drawn downward by its relentless undertow; again, gliding onward in its lightning course, bruised amidst the coral rocks of misfortune—a friendly comber cast me at last in safety upon my native shore.

Few lands have I left unvisited, few waters have I not ploughed, and consequently I think myself entitled to the traveller's privilege of telling my own story in my own way, leaving my readers to take it for what it is worth.

Claiming to be no authority—nautical, historical, political or statistical—I merely give my views as based upon observation extremely superficial, and beg in the language of our South American cousins, to place my book, and my humble self, at the *feet* of the indulgent reader, "*whose hands I kiss.*"

CONTENTS.

CHAPTER I.

THE VOYAGE.

CHAPTER II.

RIO JANEIRO.

CHAPTER III.

ST. CATHARINE'S.

CHAPTER IV.

STRAITS OF MAGELLAN.

CHAPTER V.

LIMA.

CHAPTER VI.

PANAMA.

CHAPTER VII.

CALIFORNIA.

CHAPTER VIII.

SONORA.

CHAPTER IX.

SANDWICH ISLANDS.

CHAPTER X.

MANILA.

CHAPTER XI.

CHINA.

CHAPTER XII.

SINGAPORE.

CHAPTER XIII.

MELBOURNE.

CHAPTER XIV.

POLYNESIA.

CHAPTER XV.

VOYAGE IN SOUTH PACIFIC.

CHAPTER XVI.

WEST COAST.

CHAPTER XVII.

DUST AND FOAM.

CHAPTER I.

THE VOYAGE.

The Author waxes eloquent upon the Discovery of Gold, and of its Effects upon the People—Is seized with the prevailing Epidemic—Is elected President of a Mining Company—Takes Ship for California—Is enthusiastic upon Things nautical—Reaches the Brazilian Coasts, and describes their magnificent Appearance.

LIKE a revelation burst upon us the news of the discovery of gold in California; all suddenly the astounding fact was simultaneously felt throughout the length and breadth of this broad land, that in our own territory, within our very grasp, the long sought "El Dorado," in search of which thousands of lives, and countless treasures had in vain been expended, had at last been discovered, where it had lain ages upon ages, the golden harvest unheeded and ungarnered, since Nature in her throes had vomited it broadcast over valley and hill, into rivers' bottoms, and on mountains' tops.

An excitement as intense as it was violent, seized upon the whole nation, from North to South, from East to West; like an electric shock it spread, pervading all ranks and conditions of life; the rich saw millions added to their hoards, the poor fancied a millenium, their wants supplied, and a life of ease in prospect. City and village alike poured forth their pilgrims to a common shrine; commerce, agriculture, and the arts were abandoned, and all eyes fixed upon the golden calf; domestic ties were snapped asunder, husbands parted from wives, brothers from sisters, parents from children—all offering up their heart's truest and best affection on that golden altar. Hundreds of vessels crowded with living freight sailed gaily from our shores, upon a long and perilous voyage; over the interminable western plains, caravan after caravan of hardy pioneers pushed forward, regardless alike of burning deserts, of hostile tribes and mighty rivers.

The hitherto impenetrable fastnesses of the isthmus of Panama resounded to the shout of the reckless emigrant, who, braving tropical suns, deadly malarias and the wild beasts of the wilderness, forced his canoe against the swift currents of swollen rivers, over shoals and rapids, until way-worn he reached and looked with delight upon the fair bosom of the Pacific.

Such was the state of things in the month of December, 1848; the excitement became epidemic, and few escaped contagion. I myself was an early victim of the disease in its most virulent form, and at once determined to join the ranks of the vast phalanx, then forming, whose rallying cry was, "Westward ho!"

On looking about for the best and safest means of getting to the land of promise, and after carefully weighing the advantages and disadvantages of the different routes, I finally concluded to join some one of the many companies then forming, with a view to mining and trading, and who purposed sailing around Cape Horn. For the accomplishment of this end, a vessel was to be bought fully equipped with everything necessary to the success of the undertaking, and which would in case of need serve as a home on our arrival at our destination; for, like prudent generals, we would in this way reserve to our ourselves a means of retreat should our advance have been premature.

I resolved upon this mode of prosecuting my journey for various cogent reasons. I judged the voyage by sea to be the most healthy, the least expensive, and attended with less risk than either the route by the isthmus of Panama, or by the Indian trails of the western prairies. The accounts we were then receiving from the isthmus were of the most distressing character. The hardships endured by the emigrants crossing it uninured to a tropical climate were terrible in the extreme, and the cholera, and fevers had already found many victims. The news from the plains was scarcely less disastrous. Hundreds had succumbed to the unusual hardships of the deserts; cholera had there too thinned the ranks; and loss of animals, and attacks of hostile Indians had turned homeward many a one disheartened. In view of all this I decided upon a voyage by sea, and joined a company consisting of some thirty young men, who associated themselves together for mutual defence and support, each of whom contributed as his quota, the sum of five hundred dollars, therewith creating a fund with which we purchased a fine bark of 300 tons burden, together with an outfit and mining materials necessary for the prosecution of our voyage.

Of this association I was chosen President, and after maturing all our plans, we set sail for San Francisco, on the — day of Feb., A.D. 1849.

To many, the idea of a long sea voyage would be disagreeable in the extreme, but to me it conveyed a feeling of positive delight; and here, at the outset of my journey, I must confess myself an enthusiastic admirer of all pertaining to the ocean. Upon its fickle bosom I have spent the greater part of nine long years.

I have battled with the West Indian hurricane, the Brazilian pampero, and the typhoon of the China seas, and have passed days, yes, weeks, under sweltering suns in equatorial calms. I have been stinted in provisions and half mad for want of water, yet still I love the life; there is an excitement in it, which, while it is pleasurable, is inspiring. It's glorious to cut along the blue rippling sea of the tropics, impelled by a trade-wind which, untiring, fills your sails, speeds you onward, and invigorates you with its refreshing temperature. It's glorious to feel that though your bark is but a speck upon the mighty waste of waters, that in her you rest secure, let the storm rage never so fiercely, let the waves run never so high, and that you, trusting in your own skill, can confidently cope with them. While there is something terribly sublime in a hurricane at sea, when the deafening roar stuns, and the mighty waves are surging and breaking around you—still, even then, one soars above the littleness of fear, with the feeling that he, in his weakness, is successfully contending against such fearful odds.

To me, every trifling incident connected with the sea is fraught with interest, and I luxuriate in the endless vicissitudes of a sailor's life; thus it will not seem strange that I selected the route around Cape Horn in preference to all others. But, alas! all in this world do not think alike, and before our little bark had been twenty days at sea, the enthusiasm of my thirty co-adventurers had oozed from their fingers' ends, and home-sickness and despondency had usurped its throne. Curses loud and deep were unsparingly bestowed upon the sea and all "that go down thereto," and I will venture to say, that there were scarce ten men on board that vessel, who would not have forfeited their interest in the expedition to have been once more on terra firma.

The voyage, for the first thirty days, was to me a peculiarly pleasant one. Once escaped from the cold blasts of our own coast, the northeast trade-winds bore us pleasantly onward on our course, our little vessel proving herself swift and true.

On approaching the line, however, we lost our favoring breezes, and became entangled within the belt of equatorial calms, where we were held prisoners for the space of sixteen days. The weather was intensely hot, the thermometer standing, during night and day, at an average of ninety degrees Fahrenheit, the sails hanging heavily against the masts, as we lazily rolled over the long Atlantic swell. Oh! the tediousness of those long, long days. No ripple stirred the glassy surface of the water; day after day the sun arose bright and burning from the sea, and night after night sunk fiery red below the horizon. The tar oozed from the deck-seams, the furniture in the cabins cracked asunder, and the water, heated and foul, became thick and stringy in the casks, too nauseous for Christian man to drink. No place was there to escape the heat; the cabins were insupportable, and a vertical sun gave no shade. One could not jump overboard without a long, green, shovel-nosed shark making his appearance, with an ogreish look which banished all idea of the pleasures of a bath.

We whistled our lips to African dimensions; we stuck our

knife blades deep into the mast ; and, in a word, conformed to every extravagance of a sailor's superstition. But all in vain ; no breeze would come ; so we bided our time, and in pure despair cursed old Boreas for a recreant knight, in leaving sweet little " St. Mary" in such a dire predicament. But all things have an end, as did our calm, and somewhere about the sixteenth day of our sufferings, a gentle breeze sprang up, which, gradually assuming the type of the southeast trades, sent us dancing merrily across the South Atlantic.

One of the most remarkable and beautiful of the ocean phenomena, is that of the phosphorescent light produced by small animalculæ, of a gelatinous nature, which appear to bear the same relation to the water as do the fire-flies to the air. They abound more in some parts of the ocean than in others, and I think that I have observed them to be more luminous in the vicinity of the Cape de Verde Islands than in any other part of the world. Never shall I forget the startlingly beautiful effect produced by our little craft, as with a spanking breeze she skirted along this group. Every plunge she made was as into a molten mass of silver, and the spray flew like silver stars against the black, dark sky ; and astern, as far as eye could penetrate, the gloom was a broad, bright wake glittering with dazzling stars ; every wavelet that broke into the gloom discharging a precious freight of glistening jewels.

I had often read of flying-fish, and had pictured to myself some awkward member of the finny tribe, half bird, half fish. How different the reality ! Hour after hour have I watched with delight these bright-winged sprites, as in shoals of hundreds they have shot from crest to crest, like feathered arrows from a bow, their silvery wings glistening in the bright sunshine, as pursued by their relentless enemy, the dolphin, they dart into the air and sail upon the wing, until exhausted they again sink into the sea. These little water-fairies are scientifically classified as the "Exocœtus Exiliens," and have fins nearly as long as their bodies (from five to nine inches), placed behind the gills, and these are used as wings; they shoot from beneath the surface of the water and sail for a distance of from eighty to one hundred yards upon the wing, and then suddenly drop into the sea. From this we would infer, that as soon as the fins lose their moisture they likewise lose their buoyancy. "A delicate species of this fish is found in the Mediterranean, having four wings. The body is of a delicate bluish tint, and the bone of the head so transparent that the brain is quite perceptible."

The dolphin is also found in great abundance in this part of the ocean; indeed, cannibal that he is, and living upon his own species, he displays to the greatest advantage the grace and swiftness for which he is so celebrated, when in pursuit of the flying-fish. His length is from twenty-five to forty inches, with an oval head, and his body tapering off to the tail, gives the idea of perfect symmetry. As he swims along just beneath the surface of the water, he appears of a bright green hue, varying in shade according to his depth, but as he darts from wave to wave, the eye is delighted by ever-varying flashes of green, gold, and silvery tints.

To those for the first time sailing in the southern hemisphere, the brightness of the constellations, their novelty, and the clearness of the atmosphere, is a source of wonder and delight. Preëminent among them stands the constellation of the "Southern Cross;" early Christian voyagers regarded it with unspeakable awe as a symbol of their faith. Its beauty has been sung by poets of every tongue, and it was the first constellation noticed and named south of the equator. It is composed of four bright stars, the two which form the top and bottom of the cross having the same right ascension ; consequently the figure of the cross is perpendicular when on the meridian.

In the same field of view the constellation of the Magellan Clouds is descried, consisting of two small white patches always maintaining their relative positions, and without changing in shape or appearance. They probably derive their name from having first been described by Magellan, or perhaps from the fact that when within the straits of that name the constellation appears directly overhead, as if a standing beacon for those entering. They are two nebulous masses of light conspicuously visible, and appear to be portions of the milky way. When examined through a telescope they present a singular appearance, and are found to be composed of an infinite variety of small clustering stars.

During the voyage, I had an opportunity of witnessing something of rare occurrence—a Lunar Bow. The moon was at its full ; a heavy mass of dark black clouds suddenly arising, obscured the firmament ; a torrent of rain began to fall, and the moon, struggling through the clouds, threw her bright rays upon the falling drops, forming a perfect silver arc extending from horizon to horizon. The effect was grand, the deep background of those inky clouds being in strange contrast with the splendor of that broad, bright bow.

After once taking the southeast trades, they rarely leave you until you are on the Brazilian coast, and they generally blow with great uniformity, usually veering but two or three points during the twenty-four hours. We were at this time favored with a steady breeze, and with studding-sails drawing, went kiteing away before wind and sea, and on the —— day from New York our observations showed us to be within one hundred miles of the entrance to Rio Janeiro harbor.

The approach of dawn on the morning following, found the decks of our little craft covered with eager expectants, all anxiously awaiting a first glance at the coast of Brazil, and the breaking day revealed to our delighted gaze the bold and lofty headlands of Cape Frio. This cape is the extremity of a high mountainous promontory, rising abruptly from the sea until lost in the misty clouds which hover round its summit, and is a spur of the long range running northerly up the coast. This is the first land that is made in coming from the eastward, and is to the mariner a well-known and unmistakable landmark. On its summit has recently been erected a lighthouse, which may be seen a long way sea-ward on a clear night. It was a matter of speculation to us as to how the light-keeper ever scaled his eyrie, and whether or not he held his office for life, as it seemed that after once arriving at the scene of his labors, he would have no desire again to brave the perils of a descent.

The coast running north and south up to this point, here turns abruptly off to the westward, and sixty miles distant lies the Port of Rio Janeiro. The land from the Cape, westward, is a huge mountain wall rising perpendicularly from the sea. Its jagged peaks shooting upward in bold relief against the sky, a luxuriant and eternal verdure covering them from base to summit, while the light and shade produced by projecting crag and deep ravine, with water leaping from precipice to precipice, makes a grand perspective.

A few hours' sail along this granite barrier brought us abreast the harbor, and towering high above us frowned the lofty summit of the Sugar Loaf. Here the breeze deserted us, and we lay the livelong night rolling heavily on the bar awaiting impatiently the light and wind enough to carry us in. About ten o'clock the next morning the breeze came in from the sea and filled our sails, and as we neared the entrance, a world of natural beauty fascinated our delighted gaze.

CHAPTER II.

RIO JANEIRO.

Describes the Entrance to Rio Janeiro—Its splendid Harbor—Gives a slight Historical Sketch of it—General Description of the City, its Churches, Palaces, its Hospitals and its Villas—Touches upon Slavery and its Abuses — Gives Ideas of Catholicism as existing in Brazil and the Depravity of its Priests—Treats of the State of Society—Gives Descriptions of the Emperor, the Empress, and of the Brazilian Court.

THE only ingress to this magnificent harbor leads through a narrow cleft of that granite mountain on whose sides bristle fortresses which, ably defended, would defy the navies of the world. As we swung close under the precipice a sentinel hailed us, demanding our name and nation, and bade us pass on. Now fully before us stretched away the harbor of the "Hidden Water."

Terrace upon terrace, dressed in loveliest verdure; islet upon islet, resting in the deep shade of overhanging hills; turretted fortresses, spires and domes ; hamlets peeping through groves of orange trees, crafts of novel structure, with the graceful lateen sail, scudding swiftly by ; stately ships of war, with the colors of every nation at their peak, and the city rambling o'er valley and hill, formed a coup d'œil which it does not often fall to the lot of man to gaze upon—too lovely as a whole for the eye, yet unsatisfied, to attempt to discriminate its individual beauties. With shortened sail we glided slowly to an anchorage. Cheer after cheer arising from the California-bound ships as we slowly picked our way among them, when suddenly luffing in the wind, we let go our anchor abreast the fort.

The anchor down, I went aloft and took a lengthened view of the surrounding scenery. About a league from us lay the town of Rio Janeiro, and few cities show to better advantage. Built without regard to regularity, running along the beach, up the sides of hills, through ravines, its suburbs stretching away, circling around coves and capes, an idea is given of a place far larger than it really is. Abounding in churches, convents and fortifications, for the most part located on commanding elevations, with a high mountain range for a background, the whole forms a *tout ensemble* at once picturesque, romantic and imposing.

The suburbs of the Gloria and Botofogo, running along the base of the mountains, now hiding in an orange grove, now circling an intruding indentation of the bay, now disappearing altogether behind some chapel-crowned hill, and now running half way up the mountain side, with its gardens and its towers, present a sweet piece of natural coquetry to the admiring gaze; the houses, built in the Italian style, bright with the prevailing gilt, green and white, which add greatly to the charming scene.

To the northward the bay stretches away many miles into the interior, white with glistening sails and studded with islets, until, it seems at last to wash the very feet of the mighty Organ mountains. Opposite the city, across the bay, lies the beautiful village of Praya Grande, consisting principally of the residences of merchants doing business in the city. Like the Gloria and Botofogo it revels among secluded nooks, and courts the shady orange grove, and, like its sisters, hiding coquetishly behind hedges of flowering shrubs.

Half an hour after our arrival, the Custom House barge came alongside, pulled by twenty negroes, who at every stroke rose on their feet, and then throwing their whole weight upon the oar, fell back into their seats. The boat was a very large one, and the stern sheets woofed over with an arched awning made of bamboo, and was also furnished with a writing table, and cane sofas on which the officers reclined.

The captain of the port first came over the side, followed by a lieutenant, an interpreter and a secretary. The captain and his aid were dressed in most elaborate uniforms, glittering with gold-lace and stars; the former had evidently a high opinion of his own importance, but was, nevertheless, quite affable, and inclined to be accommodating; the interpreter (as is generally the case in South American ports) knew nothing of the language beyond a few ordinary phrases, which he kept continually repeating with great volubility; when addressed, he became very dignified, and like Punch's dog, contented himself with looking very wisely. The captain of the port's boat was followed by that of the health officer, who, with his attendants, was likewise ostentatious in his uniform. After examining our bill of health, he retired, not, however, before giving us leave to visit shore at our pleasure.

Before going ashore, let us take a retrospective glance at the history of the empire. In the year 1775, Nicolas de Villegagnon, an officer of distinction in the French navy, formed an expedition under the sanction of Henri II., then reigning monarch, for the purpose of founding a colony on the coast of Brazil; the ostensible object of this project being to establish an asylum for persecuted Protestants. He obtained the connivance and patronage of the venerable Admiral Coligny, and through his instrumentality succeeded in collecting a goodly number of followers.

After encountering countless perils, he entered the bay of "Nitherhoy" or Hiddenwater, and proceeded at once to build a fortress, which was called after his patron, Coligny, on an island named after himself, "Villegagnon." This colony was unfortunate, however, from the very outset, and to crown all, its leader apostatized, and commenced in the New World the persecutions they had flown from in the Old.

Accessions were being made at this time in considerable numbers in Europe, when, on hearing of the treachery of Villegagnon, and of the various mishaps which had, in consequence, befallen the colonists, they decided on abandoning their designs, and thus the colony receiving no aid or support from home, soon dwindled into insignificance. Who can say what might have not been the destiny of this magnificent country, had Villegagnon been true to the cause? When we look and wonder at the rapid strides she has made in civilization and in the arts under the narrow and crooked policy of designing Jesuits; knowing as we do the blighting influence of Romanism upon a young nation, crippling her energies and fettering her development with fanaticism and superstition, does not the thought suggest itself, that, had that infant colony been permitted to flourish—had favorable accounts been received of its progress in Europe—had those emigrants, on the eve of setting forth, not been deterred by disastrous news, and in fine, had the colony gradually merged into a nation, entertaining the Protestant faith, and holding all the liberal views incidental thereto, is it not possible that the Brazilian nation might have fulfilled as happy a destiny as has the republic of the United States of America? Both colonies were founded in the same "terra incognita," having the same advantages as regards fertility of soil, and very nearly the same diversity of climate. Colonized within but a few years of each other, the English Pilgrim and the French Huguenot held a common faith. The one was successful in his scheme, and now behold the glory of the nation sprung from the seed sown by the Covenanters; foremost in the ranks of nations, she stands the exponent of a successful scheme! On the other hand, behold a nation reared upon the ashes of the Huguenot, whose progress has been impeded at every step by ignorance and superstition, and the narrow policy of designing men, many of whom were of a high order of intellect, but whose talents were neutralized, and whose convictions were gagged by the invisible influence of their unholy religion.

In the year 1760, Rio superseded Balhia as the vice-regal residence. In 1808, John the Sixth of Portugal, fearful of falling into the hands of Napoleon, hastily fled from the peninsula with all his family, and arrived at Rio in the month of March of the same year. Up to this period, Brazil had been looked upon as an unimportant colony, and its government had been administered in the most absolute manner. All foreign commerce being strictly prohibited, no foreign vessel had been allowed to enter its waters, but in case of their being obliged to run in from stress of weather, they were only allowed to refit, and no foreigner was permitted, under any pretext, to set foot in the interior.

On the arrival of the prince, the ports were thrown open to commerce, institutions of learning and science were founded, and printing presses introduced ; all this put new life and energy into the colony, and changed the whole aspect of affairs. Each day saw new resources developed, and the young pulse of the colony began to throb with increasing strength. This prosperity begat new ideas, and the Brazilians not being able to endure the thought of being a colony, a decree was published by which the colony became a kingdom. After a few years, the popularity of John VI. began to wane, and in 1821, he appointed his son, Don Pedro, regent of Brazil, and embarked himself for Portugal.

The mother country growing uneasy at the increasing importance of her offspring, issued an order to Don Pedro to present himself before the court at Lisbon, and give an account of his stewardship ; and deported herself so arrogantly and overbearingly, that a revolt was the consequence, and the Brazilians determined upon a separation from her. In September, 1822, Don Pedro was crowned Emperor of Brazil, under the title of Don Pedro I.; he married Leopoldina, archduchess of the house of Austria, and reigned about ten years, but becoming tyrannical and unpopular, he was obliged to abdicate in favor of his son Pedro de Alcantara, and to take refuge in Europe.

Don Pedro II., was declared to have attained his majority on July 23d, 1840, in the sixteenth year of his age, and in 1841 married Teresa, sister of the king of Sicily, and in the same year, his sister married the eldest son of Louis Phillippe, of France, the Prince de Joinville, thus cementing a blood alliance with a powerful nation. * * * *

Jumping into one of the many shore boats hovering around us, I ordered the negro boatman to shove off, and in a moment was clear of the vessel, when loosening the sail, we spun shoreward before a spanking breeze. Having got everything snug, the negro coolly handing me the sheet, and motioning me to take the tiller, stretched himself under the thwarts for a nap. Left to myself, and my own reflections, I gave myself up to the novelty of the scene.

Rio Janeiro.

For the first mile, my track lay through the fleet of California-bound ships, to the number of some eighty or a hundred, their decks filled with emigrants, attired in the most outlandish style, whose shouts, songs, and laughter disturbed the quiet echoes of the bay. Around each ship were grouped native canoes, laden with every variety of fruit, live stock and curiosity from the shore, the owners of which with their wild gesticulations to excite the attention of purchasers, their constant squabbles among themselves for precedence, the chattering of parrots and monkeys, the bleating of sheep and cackling of poultry, formed an amusing feature of the scene. Clearing the fleet, we rapidly neared the guard-boat, when luffing under her stern and being scrutinized, we were permitted to continue our course, and once more easing off the sheet, in a few moments we were in the passage-way between the Isla de Cobra and the city, and shooting a few lengths ahead, the keel grated on the beach. Leaping ashore, I found myself in the palace square; before me rose the imperial palace, for many years the vice-regal residence, but now used for state offices, a suite of rooms, however, being reserved for the court when they visited the city on state occasions.

The building material is of a yellowish stone, and in the style of the old Portuguese and Spanish architecture; it is quite extensive, and flanked on the left with a chapel, whose cloisters are immediately in the rear, and at present attached to the palace. From a balcony fronting the square, the emperor, on gala days, reviews the troops and shows himself to the populace. From this gallery extends a lovely view, and being open to the sea, makes it a peculiarly airy and agreeable lounge.

Occupying the lower side of the square, is a pile of lofty buildings, chiefly pertaining to the Hotel Pharoux, the best inn in Rio, immediately in front of which is a small promenade, jutting into the sea, and here the merchants assemble morning and evening to take the air and view the shipping.

The "Hotel Pharoux," is kept by a Frenchman, and is on a grand scale, the lower floors being occupied by a restaurant of no mean pretensions, as well as by billiard and bath rooms. The chambers are large and airy, and the furniture showy and suited to a warm climate. Those who succeed in getting rooms fronting the bay are fortunate indeed, I myself was one of the favored; every morning as the day dawned, I opened the window, drew my bed across it, and lay quietly gazing on the scene before me. Directly below, was the landing-place for small boats, and at that early hour the market-boats from every vessel in the harbor, numbering at least two hundred, were there assembled, some riding off at a little distance, and others along side the mole—Spanish, English, French, Dutch and Portuguese—all vociferating at the top of their voices, each in his own peculiar dialect. Stewards were rushing to and fro with their market baskets and hailing their respective boats, who were making desperate efforts to penetrate the little flotilla and reach the shore ; chandlers' clerks with stores, tiny midshipmen, with swords as long as themselves, ordering at the top of their little cracked voices ; refractory sailors, who with an eye to grog, were endeavoring to negotiate with the land-sharks, who are always attracted on such occasions, like vultures from afar ; together with negro boatmen, noisily soliciting a fare, fruit venders, and peddlers of every article under the sun, formed a scene of confusion that would have put old Babel itself to the blush.

Further on in the line of view lay the naval fleets of England, France, America and Spain. There they rode in peaceful contiguity, seemingly dull and motionless, but within each hull throbbed a tiny world, Argus-eyed in the interest of the nation they represented, and ever on the alert, like faithful watch-dogs, ready to show their bristling teeth. Over and beyond them, on the other side of the bay, the pretty villas of Praya Grande came peeping forth from the morning's mist, and the mighty Organ mountains looked mightier still through the rising sun's refracted rays.

In front of the palace is a large ornamental fountain, around which is always collected a noisy group of slaves, men and women water-carriers, who, while filling their jars, chattered their incomprehensible jargon. The sea-wall running along the edge of the square is a favorite lounging-place for idlers of all sorts : nurses with their little charges ; female slaves in ther picturesque attire of gaudy turban and calico, with gilt rings around wrist and ankle, bearing on their heads trays piled with sweetmeats, whose virtues they extol with not very melodious voices; lazy policemen, looking more like monkeys than human beings, and about on a par with them in intellect; diseased slaves, turned out as useless and to die, all congregate here to pass the morning hours.

Further along the water's edge extends the market, with as fine an assortment of fish, flesh, and fowl, as is to be seen in any part of the world; the vegetables and fruits being large and most luscious in flavor. Hopping about in their hundred little cages, parrots, and endless varieties of the feathered tribe, give forth their notes, to which monkeys of all descriptions, from the Marmoset to the Ring-tail, chatter an accompaniment.

Leading out of the upper side of the Square is the Rua Direita, the principal street in Rio; wide, and tolerably well paved, it is the central point of all the wholesale business of the city. Here is situated the Custom House, Merchants' Exchange, the National Bank and Post-Office, and, consequently, throughout business hours it is a place of general resort. The absence of horse power for the transportation of goods, strikes a stranger most forcibly, when he sees carts heavily laden dragged by struggling negroes over a ragged pavement. Huge boxes and bales are thus carried from place to place, sometimes in carts, at others on the backs and shoulders of slaves. This, of course, very much retards the speed of business, and has a most unhappy effect upon the unfortunate blacks thus degraded to the vel of the brute.

The Custom House has its principal entrance on the Rua Direita, and runs back to the water, covering an immense space of ground ; but all the different departments centering under a common roof, gives an idea of great confusion in their mode of doing business. The Rotunda (used as the Collector's office) is a very spacious apartment, of a circular form, with a tier of desks running around it, occupied by clerks dispatching goods, etc. In this apartment, under their very noses, is heaped an indiscriminate variety of cases, bales, and boxes, some of which are being hammered open by porters, others under examination by garrulous officers, and others being closed ; the din attendant upon the operation is terrific, as any one who has had to do with Spanish or Portuguese officials may imagine. The rest of the building is occupied by the offices of the captain of the port, inspectors, etc., etc. The scale of duties on all imports is excessive, and on exports scarcely less burdensome, and the restrictions on any business connected with vessels are of the most illiberal character. No boat can go off to a vessel in the harbor without first calling at a guard-boat anchored in the bay, and the same formality must be gone through with on returning on shore. Every possible annoyance is thrown in the way of those attempting to transact business for the first time with the Custom House, and it is only by bleeding freely that you can get along with these officials at all. The number of clerks and employees of different sorts is prodigious, and one can see without difficulty the absolute necessity of this systematized scheme of robbery and extortion, on remarking the number of good-for-nothing hangers-on drawing their maintenance from this one department. These worthies all wear uniform from the highest to the lowest, and are most insolent and vulgar in their bearing.

The Exchange, adjoining the Custom House, is a fine looking building, modern in style, its upper stories fitted up with reading-rooms in which are to be found the newspapers and periodicals of the principal cities of the world, and below is the meeting-place for merchants and strangers, and where the business of the day is discussed. Striking off at right angles from the Rua Direita is the Rua Ouvidor, the principal street of the retail trade; the shop windows are decorated with great taste, and here is displayed for sale every article which taste could suggest or luxury devise; Paris, London, Canton, and Calcutta have all contributed, while the brilliancy of the diamonds and the rich yellow hue of the golden ornaments suggest extravagant ideas of native wealth. This in common with most of the streets in Rio is extremely narrow, the pavements scarcely admitting of two to walk abreast, and the street, gradually inclining towards the centre, forms a large gutter which is invariably full of filth. The water pipes of the houses, instead of leading to the ground, reach only as far as the balconies of the second story, and there discharge their contents; thus on a rainy day, one is continually dodging streams of water rushing down from the roofs of houses by which he may be passing.

The streets being too narrow for two vehicles to pass abreast without encroaching on the sidewalk, one is obliged to keep his eyes open, and on the first intimation of their approach rush for shelter into some friendly doorway, which however does not always save him from being splashed with mud.

Omnibuses have here been introduced, and being drawn by four horses, are driven up and down the streets at full speed by their negro Jehus; their approach can be heard half a mile off, and was always a signal of terror; people flew in every direction for safety, and the looks of dismay of the lazy blacks awakened from their naps were most amusing. The ordinary vehicle in use is an immense gig, poised aloft on a pair of enormous coach springs of the old-fashioned kind; this is drawn by a single horse, ridden by a negro "en postillion," who rushes him at every pile of rubbish and filth he sees, yelling at the same time like a madman; the motion is awful, and many a novice is made sick by it. The houses are generally lofty, the lower part being occupied as stores, and the upper stories as dwellings, while not unfrequently the garret is the kitchen of the establishment. Their color is generally white, which gives them a neat and cheerful appearance, the dazzling effect being obviated by the green blinds of the jalousies. The city proper, from the narrowness of its streets and the loftiness of the houses, has rather a confined air, although boasting of some fine squares; the suburbs extend however three or four miles in three different directions, and their streets being wide and airy and remote from the traffic of the city are exceeding cleanly. The houses bordering on them are handsome and spacious and of elegant exterior, each occupying a large space of ground, generally under a high state of cultivation, producing a most delightful effect. In these suburbs the foreign ministers, consuls, government officers and wealthy merchants reside, where after the turmoil of business they retire from the bustle and heat of the city to enjoy the "far niente" of their domestic paradise. Says a German: "Nothing can be compared to the beauty of these retreats, when the most sultry hours of the day are passed and the gentle breezes, impregnated with balsamic perfumes from neighboring wooded mountains, cool the air; the enjoyment continues to increase as night spreads over the land and the sea, which shines at a distance, and the city where the noises of business have ceased is gradually lighted up. He who has not personally participated in the enjoyment of the tranquil moonlight in these happy latitudes, can never be inspired, even by the most faithful description, with those feelings which scenes of such wondrous beauty excite in the mind of the beholder: a delicate transparent mist hangs over the country, the moon shines brightly amid the singularly grouped clouds, the outlines of the objects which are illuminated by it are clear and well defined, while a magic twilight seems to remove from the eye those which are in the shade. Scarce a breath is stirring, and the neighboring mimosas, which have folded up their leaves to sleep, stand motionless behind the dark crowns of the mango, the iaca and the etherial iambos; or sometimes a sudden wind arises, and the sapless leaves of the acaju rustle, and the richly flowered gramejama and pitanga let fall a fragrant shower of snow white blossoms; shrill cries of the cicada, the grasshopper, and the tree-frog make an incessant hum and produce by their monotonous song a pleasant melancholy.

"A stream gently murmuring descends from the mountain, and the macuc, with its almost human voice, seems to call for help from a distance. Every quarter of an hour different balsamic odors fill the air, and other flowers alternately unfold their leaves to the night, and almost overpower the senses with their perfume; now it is the bowers of the paulinia or the neighboring orange grove, then the thick tufts of the eupatoria or the branches of the flowers of the palm suddenly bursting and disclosing their blossoms, which maintain a constant succession of fragrance. While the silent vegetable world, illuminated by swarms of fire-flies as by thousands of roving stars, charms the night by its delicious effluvia—brilliant lightnings play incessantly in the horizon, and elevate the mind in joyful admiration of the stars, which, glowing in solemn silence in the firmament above, fill us with sentiments of still sublimer wonder."

The finest view of Rio and its harbor is to be obtained from the summit of the Corcovada, a lofty peak of about 2,000 feet, towering above the city and almost overhanging it. This mountain being accessible almost to the summit on horseback, the ascent is not very fatiguing; the first part of the ascent leads through a dense primeval forest with a thick undergrowth of vines and flowering shrubs, and one naturally pauses in mute admiration of the luxuriance and gigantic proportions of tropic vegetation. An extract from the translation of a German work may not be out of place. "Instead of the uniform poverty of species of the European forest, especially in the north, there is here an infinite diversity in form, stem, leaf and blossom. Almost every one of these sovereigns of the forest is distinguished, in the total effect of the picture, from its neighbor. While the silk cotton tree, partly armed with thorns, begins at a considerable height from the ground to spread out its arms, and its dilated leaves are grouped in light and airy masses, the luxuriant lecythis and the Brazilian anda shoot out from a less height many a branch profusely covered with leaves, which unite to form a verdant arcade; the jacanda attracts the eye by the lightness of its double-feathered leaves, and the large, gold-colored flowers of this tree and the ipi dazzle by their splendor contrasted with the dark-green foliage.

The spondia arches its pennated leaves into light oblong forms; a very peculiar and most striking effect in the picture, is that produced by the trumpet tree among the lofty forms of the forest. The smooth, grey stems of the ash, rise slightly bending, to a considerable height, and spread out at the top in verticillated branches, standing at right angles, which have at their extremities large tufts of deeply lobated white leaves; the flowery cæsalpina—the airy laurel—the lofty geoffroca—the soap tree, with its shining leaves—the slender cedar—here and there the dark crown of the Chilian fir, among the lighter green, appears like a stranger among the natives of the tropics, while the towering stems of the palms, with their waving crowns, are an incomparable ornament of the forest, the beauty and majesty of which no tongue can adequately describe. But the animal kingdom which people these ancient forests, are not less distinguishable than the vegetable world.

"Except at high noon, when all living creatures in the torrid zone seek shade and repose, and when a solemn stillness is diffused over the scene, illuminated by the dazzling beams of the sun, every hour of the day calls into action another race of animals; the morning is ushered in by the howling of monkeys, the high and deep tones of the tree-toad and frog, the monotonous chirp of the grasshopper and locust. When the rising sun has dispelled the mists which preceded it, all creatures rejoice in the return of day; the wasps leave their long nests, the ants issue from their dwellings, the gayest butterflies, rivalling in color the splendors of the rainbow, flutter from flower to flower, or collect in separate companies on the sunny banks of the cool streams; the blue, shining menelaus and the large eurytochus, with its oscillated wings, hover like birds in the green bushes of the moist valleys—the foronia, with rustling wings, flies from tree to tree, while the owl, the largest of the moth kind, sits immovably on the trunk, with outspread wings, awaiting the approach of evening. Myriads of brilliant beetles buzz in the air and sparkle like jewels in the fresh green of the leaves or on the odorous flowers; meanwhile, agile lizards, remarkable for form and size and brilliant color, dark-colored poisonous serpents, which exceed in splendor the enamel of the flowers, glide out of the leaves and the hollows of the trees, and creeping up their stems, bask in the sun. Squirrels and troops of monkeys issue inquisitively from the thick woods, and chattering, leap from tree to tree. Birds of the most singular form and superb plumage flutter singly or in companies through the fragrant bushes—green, blue and red parrots filling the air with their screams—the toucan, sitting on the extreme branches, rattles with his large hollow bill in loud and plaintive notes, wailing for rain; the busy oriole announces, with screaming cries, the approach of man; the amorous thrush pours forth a stream of delicious melody; and the delicate humming-bird, rivalling in beauty and lustre diamonds, emeralds and sapphires, hovers around the brightest flowers."

On approaching the summit, the trees become scarce, vegetation, however, reaching the extremest point of elevation. The panorama that bursts upon the view when the summit is gained cannot be exceeded for beauty or diversity in the world; never did the eye rest upon a scene more strikingly fascinating. The view is most comprehensive; the bay with its archipelago of beautiful islets; the long ranges of lofty mountain spurs diverging in every direction; the deep blue sea beyond, whose long swells eternally break and foam at the feet of the hoary-headed

Sugar Loaf, which raises its lofty peak a marked feature in the picture; the fleet at anchor, and hundreds of native craft moving gaily across the line of view; the huge Organ Mountains, blue in the distance; and the city, with its chapel-crowned heights, and flanked by her smiling suburbs, are lovely to behold; and the chimes of the deep-toned bells stealing upward, sweetly breaking the death-like stillness, strike melodiously upon the ear.

Rio is rich in churches, there being about fifty in number, many of which are vast in proportions and imposing in appearance, while the chapels attached to the convents are in some instances more spacious than the churches themselves, and generally more elaborately constructed and richer in ornament; the holy fathers, their founders, dreading the fevers incident to a residence on the lower lands and swamps, chose as the site of their edifices commanding elevations, where, free from malaria, they could at the same time enjoy the delightful sea breezes and an unobstructed view of the surrounding scenery; consequently, almost all the prominent hills in the immediate vicinity of the city are occupied by some chapel or monastery.

The church of the Candellaria is perhaps the most imposing in point of structure; and next, that of the Rosario. These churches are very large, their altars rich in decorations, and the votaries worshipping at their shrines most devout and numerous. The church of our "Lady of Glory," crowns a commanding height, and is most beautifully situated; and here the emperor and empress weekly kneel before her altars. On a lofty island in the middle of the harbor, is the church of "Bom Viagem," or "Good Voyage," here all mariners offer their vows before going to sea; and many are the precious candlesticks which decorate her altars, and which were vowed in the dark hour of shipwreck and despair.

The convent of St. Benedict is the richest, most extensive and interesting of all the convents of Rio ; it is built on an eminence overhanging the sea, and upon its corridors, after the labors of the day are over, the fathers are wont to assemble at eventide, to feast their eyes on the lovely view and refresh themselves with the cooling sea breezes.

This structure is of a massive and gloomy exterior, but on entering and ascending a stone stairway, you gain the corridor, extending the whole length of the building, and terminating at either end in a large hall; these halls are hung with paintings, representing the saints, and portraits of the most prominent of the deceased members of the order. Here also is an extensive library, containing several thousand volumes, which is open to the public ; a most charming retreat for the student or man of literature. The convent of Santa Teresa, also beautifully situated, is at the other extremity of the city, and of a still gloomier exterior, the iron-barred windows and massive moss-grown masonry, giving it rather a repulsive appearance. Opposite to Santa Teresa, is the convent of San Antonio, vying with the others in beauty of location ; its brotherhood are sworn to eternal poverty, but notwithstanding their vows, they are said to be one of the richest in Rio. The building is very extensive, having several large chapels, a library, containing some four thousand volumes, a refectory, a hospital, and likewise spacious cloisters. Nunneries were never favorite institutions with the Brazilians, they never contemplate with patience, that system of shutting up within four walls the maiden just on the threshold of womanhood, understanding too well the importance of an increasing population, to sympathize in an institution which deprives them of wives and mothers.

Independently of this consideration, the Brazilians have a vein of liberal feeling running through their religious ideas, which penetrates the shallow veil of monkish superstition and priestly intrigue, and which convinces them that monastic influence is antagonistic to an advanced state of civilization.

The hospitals reflect great credit upon the city, as well for their commodiousness and cleanliness, as for their liberal support and the disinterested kindness of those connected with them ; they are managed by brotherhoods, who devote themselves to their interests. The most extensive of the hospitals is that of the "Misericordia," on the sea-shore, which is open to all, whatever their nation, rank or color ; it was the first institution of the kind erected in Rio, and dates back as far as 1582. A new building is now nearly completed, its plan being on the most extensive scale, built altogether by private subscription; it is, in fact, a noble charity, and well worthy the support which it receives. There are patients to the amount of six thousand, annually admitted, although there are a very large proportion of deaths. Connected with this institution is a foundling hospital, called "Casa de Roda," or "House of the Wheel," from the fact, that in the wall of the building is constructed a wheel, in which there is a compartment where infants can be deposited from the street ; as it receives its burden, it immediately revolves sufficiently to convey it inside the walls. Thus any one wishing to hide the fruits of their guilt, and wanting to be rid of the care and responsibility of a young babe, may place it in this receptacle, where it will be at once provided for; in spite of all this precaution and care, however, the mortality among the little ones is terrible, for out of four or five hundred yearly taken in, at least one half if not two-thirds die. Auxiliary to this institution is an asylum for female foundlings, who are received at a tender age, brought up with the utmost care, educated, and taught useful accomplishments, and on a certain day of each year, the doors are thrown open to the public; the girls, tastefully dressed, go through their various exercises, and donations are received from those who feel inclined to favor the charity; when, likewise, any young man who may be in want of a wife, is at liberty to choose one of these young girls, to whom, if he prove to be a man of character, he is married by the institution, who gives the bride a dower of three hundred dollars.

The Brazilians possess greater educational advantages than any of the South American nations, and the fruits of the system are everywhere visible; colleges and schools, both public and private, are very numerous; the public schools which contain over a thousand pupils, being barely sufficient to supply the wants of an increasing population.

There is a naval and military academy under government patronage, for the purpose of educating officers for either service, which is open to all possessed of certain acquirements requisite to qualify them for admission. The pupil here enjoys privileges of a high order, and after pursuing his studies for a term of years, is entitled to hold a certain rank in the service to which he belongs; as far as I can learn, the officers of the Brazilian navy, as a body, stand high in their profession, as well for their scientific attainments, as for their nautical qualifications.

The standard of education among the ecclesiastics is not very high, their ability to go through the Latin forms of the Mass book being the only intellectual test required for entering the priesthood, not one in a hundred can speak any language other than his own, and but very few can deliver an intelligible discourse. I met a good many during my stay at Rio, but to a man, they were utterly without any knowledge of the resources of their country, its topography, or productions; in fact, beyond the city of Rio, they neither knew nor cared anything. I was told there was a good deal of cultivated intellect among the monastic orders, but saw none of it; considering the materials at their disposal in their fine libraries, their ignorance would be most culpable. Through their laxity of morals, and their ignorance, and want of energy, the clergy have greatly lost caste, principally, however, among the better classes; indeed, the priestly garb is in such bad odor, that few of the higher class care to take orders, and consequently their ranks are filled from the lower walks of life. Entering into the holy office from motives of expediency, redolent of vulgar superstition and prejudice, they tyrannize over the poor, and truckle to the rich, using every effort to exclude all light, and frowning down all innovation, as tending to subvert their influence; thus their superiors look upon them with contempt, and though they adhere to the tenets of the church, they despise their ignorance. To this feeling may be attributed the astonishing advances made by this nation in civilization, the arts and sciences, within a few years, leading them to a general intercourse with foreigners, and free exercise of their intellectual faculties untrammelled by priestly interference.

The climate of Rio is delightfully mild and regular, perfectly free from extremes of heat or of cold. During the months of January and February (mid-summer) the heat at noon is frequently oppressive, but the evenings and mornings are always cool and refreshing ; in the months of July and August (mid-winter) the air is elastic and bracing, being peculiarly suited to invalids. Rain is frequent at all seasons of the year, refreshing the heated atmoshere of mid-summer, and rendering vegetation bright and beautiful all the year round. The thermometer shows an average temperature for mid-day in mid-summer of from 76° to 86° Fahrenheit. Up to the year 1850, the climate of Rio was considered to be one of the healthiest on the globe, and up to that period free from all epidemics, and in fact from all diseases beyond a few simple fevers, which yielded readily to medical treatment ; but in the year 1850, the black vomit, in all its horror, there established its throne, and claimed thousands for its victims ; consternation seized upon the whole population, and Rio and its environs, that terrestrial paradise, became a very charnel house. The fever attacked all indiscriminately, but was more fatal to the whites, and there are few families there who do not mourn a member, a victim to the scourge. The pure air of the cool season dissipates the malaria, but each returning summer brings with it the fatal poison.

To the slaver can be traced this dread malady, in form more malignant and deadly than any previously known on this continent ; it was imported in slave ships, which arriving crowded to suffocation with negroes more or less diseased, the poison escaped from their filthy kennels, and disseminating itself into the atmosphere, tainted and blasted whatever came in contact with it. The slave trade, until the year 1850, was carried on with unabated vigor ; many vessels and vast sums of money were employed in this ungodly traffic, and cargo after cargo openly landed on the coast. The English took every precaution to guard against it, but with small success ; armed vessels cruised outside the harbor, and steamers were ready at a moment's warning to pursue ; still it seemed as if this very opposition only served to increase the profits of the slaver by enhancing the value of the slave. Many foreigners are engaged in the traffic, their headquarters being at Rio, and I knew several Americans who were largely interested, and who thought it no shame to avow it ; the natives are large dealers, and immense sums are annually realized by them. The slaves of Rio bear a very large proportion to the free population, and are treated in the most inhuman manner ; half fed, half clothed, without shelter, and frequently no resting-place other than the bare ground, over worked, performing the functions of pack animals, they wear a sullen, despairing look, which sickens the heart to behold. They very often become deformed from being overloaded, and their limbs contorted in the most horrible manner, and diseases are thus brought on, which soon render them useless to their employers, and lingering a year or two, death ensues, putting an end to their sufferings ; if offensive to their masters they are subjected to frightful punishments, from which death often ensues.

Every free person, whatever his color, is the owner of one or more slaves, and many of the poorer classes are maintained by the wages of their servants ; thus anything like labor is held in utter disrepute by the whites, and, consequently, the lower classes lead a life of laziness and sloth, and become early inoculated with all the vices of which idleness is the root. The negroes have an enemy to contend with, in the shape of an insect, from the attack of which they are often lamed for life; the name of this little plague is the Bichu, or, as it is vulgarly called, the "Jigger." Smaller than the head of a pin, it generally inserts itself under the toe-nail, and there deposits its eggs in the perforation; this, in time, produces great inflammation, and if not removed, begets a putrefying sore. They do not confine their attacks to the toe, but burrow into any part of the foot or leg, and these poor devils, by neglecting to remove them, become most terribly maimed. I myself have suffered severely, and on several occasions had them taken from my foot; the negresses are very skillful operators, and extract them with less pain than do the surgeons themselves.

Excepting among those high in rank, there appears to be but little pure white blood in Brazil, and I have been astonished to note in large assemblages the manifold shades of color; even among the better classes there may often be observed in a family of half a dozen as many different tints, from European white to African black. This excites no remark, as the Brazilians appear to have no aversion to amalgamation with negroes so long as they are free and well to do in the world; this feeling is however more prevalent in the country than in cities, and the illegitimate children of a favorite female slave are generally admitted on terms of perfect equality with the legitimate issue of the planter. This being the case, it is not astonishing that there should be so little familiar intercourse between resident foreigners and the native society, for although the former may be inclined to throw aside many of his home prejudices, still he cannot reconcile himself to be on intimate terms with families a portion of whom have black faces and woolly heads.

Although the males of the higher classes are very generally

men of information and in daily intercourse with foreigners, urbane, polite and hospitably inclined, the females are usually uneducated beyond the elementary branches and the lighter accomplishments; jealously guarded and fortified by an impenetrable etiquette, they have nothing to incite them to intellectual exertion. A Brazilian lady before marriage is never seen excepting at a ball or public entertainment; here she appears to great advantage: graceful in figure, with fine eyes, black glossy hair, and an inherent taste in dress, she bounds through the mazes of the dance fascinating all who behold her; but lead her forth to enjoy a quiet promenade on the balcony and engage her in conversation, when after discussing the dresses of the ladies at the last tertulia she is at the end of her rôle, her vivacity vanishes, and anything deeper mystifies and bores her. I deal in generalities, for there are many exceptions; there is as pure blood to be found in Brazil as anywhere in the world, as intellectual and lovely women, but they are sadly in the minority.

Rio enjoys an extensive and select foreign society, made up of the corps diplomatique of different nations and resident merchants with their families, so that a visitor at once finds himself at home without being dependent on that of the natives.

During my stay at Rio, I had an opportunity of seeing the royal family on the occasion of the celebration of the birthday of some one of its members. At about 11 o'clock A.M. the pageant commenced. First came a regiment of horse, five hundred strong, well mounted and showily uniformed; following them were a dozen companies of infantry and artillery, with their bands of music, whose performances were really very fine.

Of these troops the majority were black, yet they were fine soldierly-looking men, and made an imposing appearance, being well equipped in every respect. Next came the emperor and empress in a state coach drawn by eight milk-white mules, magnificently caparisoned, and accompanied by a staff of mounted officers: after them came the coaches of the aristocracy, vying with them in the costliness and elegance of their equipages; a body of 500 men, infantry and artillery, brought up the rear.

On arriving at the Palace Square, the troops took up position on its three sides, the artillery being posted with their pieces directly in front of the palace; the coaches drove up to the palace, and as their occupants alighted, at once withdrew. After the troops were got into position and were pronounced ready for inspection, the emperor and commander-in-chief appeared on the balcony, when the troops filed off and passed before them in review, again taking up their old position. The manœuvring being concluded, a royal salute was fired by the artillery and a feu-de-joie of small arms by the troops; the empress with her maids of honor then made their appearance on the balcony, showing themselves to the populace. I had a fine view of the whole court, standing as I did within a few yards of them. The emperor is a fine commanding-looking man, florid in complexion and light hair. His features, though heavy when not excited, when animated light up with great vivacity. The empress is of the usual height of women, and inclined to embonpoint, her face exceedingly pleasant and intelligent; her light hair, falling in curls upon her cheeks, gave an exceedingly sweet expression to her whole countenance; indeed, from the character given her by her subjects, she must be exceedingly amiable. Her dress was, of course, in full court costume: a robe of white satin with a profusion of the richest gold embroidery, draped with Valenciennes lace and looped with sparkling brilliants; the train was of green velvet, fringed with gold, and she was crowned wth a magnificent tiara of diamonds and emeralds ; the attire of her maids of honor was very similar, and they were all strikingly good-looking women.

The festivities of the day were concluded with an opera at the Theatre Royal, where I went, of course. The house is a large one and well fitted up, the part fronting the stage being wholly appropriated to the royal box, which was luxurious in appointment and lighted with a massive and elegant candelabra. Although arriving at an early hour, I found almost every seat taken and the boxes crowded with the aristocracy of Rio ; the ladies showed to the greatest advantage in their elaborate toilets, and the whole theatre was in a blaze of diamonds. The curtain of the Royal box rose simultaneously with that of the stage, displaying to our gaze the emperor in field-marshal's uniform, beside him the empress, and behind them the members of the royal family and the maids of honor. The national anthem then struck up, during the performance of which the audience stood facing the royal box, after which loud vivas arose from the multitude, which were cordially acknowledged by their majesties; the opera was then performed, which was only passable, followed by a ballet, which was *execrable.*

CHAPTER III.

ST. CATHARINES.

The Author resigns his Presidency—Leaves his Ship and tries Steamboat Navigation—He encounters a Pampero, which he describes—The Steamer is knocked into a Cocked Hat—He gives himself up as lost, but finds he is mistaken—The Gale abates and the Steamboat puts into St. Catharines—A Description of the Harbor—The Vessel is besieged by People of all ranks, ages and sexes, who are lost in wonder at the sight of a River Steamboat in their Waters—The Maidens take forcible possession of the Saloons, converting them into Ball-rooms, and the modest young Men of Steamboats, *Nolens volens*, are made furiously to Polka—The Island is unanimously voted a Paradise, and the Author *lays himself out* in describing it—The Steamboat is pronounced by a Nautical Jury to be "a Lame Duck," and is ordered to be "*Hog Braced*" before again going to Sea—Six weeks are necessary for the administration of the above Swinish Tonic, prescribed by the *Nautical Doctors* —How the young Gentlemen manage to kill Time—Their Functions as Time-killers being performed in the most artistic manner.

After having been some time in Rio, I was informed one morning that an American steamer, the ——, from New York, bound to San Francisco, had been telegraphed outside the port. The news caused great excitement among the Americans, bets having been freely made that she would never reach Rio, being, as all old salts affirmed, utterly unseaworthy, having been built, originally, to run on Long Island Sound, and they

3

consequently argued that she was unfit for ocean navigation—indeed, as she steamed up to her anchorage, even to a landsman's eye, it seemed like tempting Providence to send forth such an "edifice" upon such a voyage. Notwithstanding the prognostications of wise-acres, however, she came in in fine style and in good condition. Strange enough it seemed to see, quietly floating in a port thousands of miles distant from Yankee land, one of our own far-famed river steamboats, looking as saucy as if alongside her pier at the North River, just ready for a start for Boston. The natives were astounded and delighted, and I can see them now as they sat and clapped their hands, as the lofty working-beam see-sawed on its axis; remarking on her huge length, her double-tier of saloons, and her light and fragile appearance, invariably winding up by ejaculating, "Ah, those Yankees, what energy and genius they show in everything they undertake!"

Impatient of the slow progress of a sailing vessel, I, with the approbation of my "company," took passage in this steamer for San Francisco, hoping to arrive there some months sooner than I otherwise would do by remaining in the barque. Many of my friends endeavored to dissuade me from going in the steamer, sneering at her sea-going qualities, and pronouncing me a madman in thus throwing life away. I had, however, no apprehensions on the score of personal safety, being somewhat of a fatalist in faith, firmly convinced that my life was in the hands of Him who would only take it at his own good pleasure; so, notwithstanding the remonstrances of friends and the croakings of many an old shell-back, who denounced the vessel as a "coffin," and by other contemptuous epithets common in nautical parlance, on one of the last days of April I bade adieu to my friends, many of whom, shaking their heads lugubriously, insisted upon it that they would never see me again.

Rendering myself on board just as the anchor was aweigh, I had barely time to arrange some little affairs below, when the wheels commenced revolving, and I hastened on deck to take a parting glance.

Rapidly steaming along, we were soon clear of the shipping, and half an hour brought us to the mouth of the harbor, through which, aided by a strong current, we swiftly shot, and were once more on the heaving bosom of the Atlantic. Gradually the land became indistinct, and before the sun went below the horizon, the Sugar-loaf only appeared in the dim distance.

In the hurry of embarkation, I had not had time to inspect my new home. The steamer, as I have already mentioned, was formerly a passenger boat on Long Island Sound, and although of a stout hull, in nowise suitable for ocean navigation. Although her guards had been sponsoned in order that, when rolling heavily, she might not start her projecting decks, and although several very politic alterations had been made under the eye of her experienced captain, still her immense height out of water, and the amount of surface which she would present to a gale of wind argued very unfavorably to her safety. Her extreme length (280 feet) was also against her, from the fact that she was not sufficiently braced to withstand the strain of long and heavy seas. No material alteration had been made in her upper works; the saloon on her main-deck, and the long saloon on her upper or promenade-deck running almost fore and aft the ship, being suffered to remain, two light masts had been stepped fore and aft, rigged with jib, fore and main-sails, and square-sail to steady her in a beam sea. The cabin furniture remained intact, and as may be imagined, I was luxuriously accommodated, my spacious room with its elegant hangings, etc., contrasting very favorably with the little den I had left aboard the barque. I was the only passenger on board, although there were several gentlemen connected with the enterprise going out in the vessel ; the captain and mate, who were prominent men in our navy, were not only gentlemen, but men of considerable scientific attainments, thus forming a very pleasant little côterie, and many a jovial hour have I passed in their company. In spite however of my luxurious accommodations and pleasant society, I must acknowledge I did not feel quite at my ease regarding the staunchness of the vessel, and while watching the falling barometer and the sharp lightnings along the western horizon, I began to think of the forebodings of my friends and turned into my bunk with a very unpleasant feeling of insecurity. Sometime about the morning watch I was awakened by a series of violent shocks and by the roaring of a gale, when hastily jumping from my berth, I found that I could with difficulty keep my feet, from the unusual and peculiar motion of the vessel. On reaching the deck, I found the wind blowing a hurricane, the sea running wild and high, and that we, being in its trough, were consequently rolling heavily, and at every roll the ship would fetch up with her guards against a sea with a violence that would make everything quiver again. These shocks of course followed each other in rapid succession, producing a thundering, crashing sound with each concussion, which added to the din of the gale, and the strains of the laboring engine were most deafening and bewildering. As the day advanced, the gale increased in violence, the ship working heavily, and evidently making very bad weather of it; as night set in, things began to look squally, the wood-work had started in many places, the heavy hog-frames had given a foot or more, and the pools of water in the gangways, amidships, forced upon us the unwilling conviction that she was badly hogged, and might at any moment, under the heavy pressure of the machinery and weight of the coal, settle and go down!

Thus closed the evening of our second day, a violent Pampero blowing, a falling mercury, and a half wrecked steamboat in which to put our trust in! Little was said regarding our situation, no one allowing the other to imagine that he was in the least anxious as to the result, and indeed few who could have seen us assembled in the cabin quietly puffing our cigars, would have dreamed that there was not one of that group who really believed that the ship beneath him would ride out in safety the gale then blowing. The majority were men who had knocked about the world a good deal, and who either had learned to suppress their feelings, or with a positive indifference to results, to let things take their course. At about eight o'clock in the evening I went on deck, and never have I beheld so wild a sky, a fiercer gale or a more tremendous sea. Squall followed squall with terrific force, sea after sea roared and foamed and dashed madly by, each shock quivering our devoted ship from keel to truck; the whole face of the mighty deep was in a vast chaos of wild confusion, rendered wilder still by the phosphorescent glare of the breaking seas and the lurid lightnings which incessantly played about us. The ship pitched and rolled and labored most distressingly, while the engine, although performing to admiration, with difficulty made its revolutions; altogether the prospect for the night was most gloomy, so much so that I made up my mind that unless the gale subsided at an early hour, there would be but little hope of our living through it—I turned in. My own feelings can better be imagined than described.

A sense of utter despondency pervaded me; on the threshold of life was I to be permitted only thus briefly to gaze through its half open portals? Were all my bright hopes for the future, my ardent anticipations of honors and happiness thus suddenly to be blasted? These and a thousand other thoughts as appalling rapidly suggested themselves to my imagination and produced a state of mind anything but agreeable; nature however soon came to the rescue, and although firmly convinced that the chances were strongly in favor of awakening in another world, I closed my eyes and was quickly in dreamland. Shortly before day, the gale broke, and when I went on deck I found it had almost wholly abated. The vessel was a wreck, started at every point, it seemed almost miraculous that she had withstood the violence of the gale; a consultation was held, and it was unanimously resolved to put into St. Catharines and refit.

The appearance of the Island of St. Catharines to one approaching from the northward is striking, the huge conical rocks rising abruptly from the sea, and the clustering islands, green as emeralds, against the dark and frowning mountains on the main, produce a very fine effect. Passing through the little archipelago we arrived at the entrance of the narrow straits dividing the island from the mainland; here is situated the fortress of Santa-Cruz, and here the larger class of vessels anchor, on account of there not being water sufficient for them to get to the inner harbor. After having been boarded by officials from the port, who gave us the requisite permission, we steamed away for the city. Shooting from under the shore of the mainland came a six-oared whale boat, pulled by negroes. In a moment she was alongside, and from the stern sheets a burly sailor-looking man jumped aboard noisily announcing himself in a breath, as a pilot and as our countryman. The said captain is quite a notable in his way; the proprietor of a small plantation at the mouth of the harbor, by his Yankee energy and knowledge of the world, he has gained a great ascendency over the simple people among whom he lives, and in matters nautical is the oracle of the province. He holds the responsible position of pilot, and at that time was agent of the American Consul to transact the business of vessels who could not get up to the town. Report goes that some twenty years ago he was master of a whale ship, when happening in at St. Catharines and becoming enamored of its quiet seclusion and natural beauties, but more particularly of one of its dark-eyed daughters, he sold his ship and with the proceeds (which he forgot to remit to the owners) bought his little place. Whether the story be true or false I know not, but I do know that he has since been the accredited Consul of the United States of America to the Island of St. Catharines, a glorious representative of the first maritime nation in the world.

An hour's steaming through a narrow channel, winding among lofty hills and islets, covered with luxuriant vegetation, brought us up with the inner harbor, formed merely by a contraction of the channel opposite the town, after passing which, it again widens, giving egress to the sea by the southern end of the island; thus vessels arriving from the northward, bound south, enter through the northern passage and sail out by the southern. Our anchor was scarcely down before we were surrounded by a flotilla of boats, and the beach was lined with people looking with wonder upon the Yankee steamer ; never before had their eyes opened upon such a structure, and young and old, sailors and landsmen, gazed with undisguised amazement upon this "marine anomaly." No sooner had the formalities of the Custom House been gone through with, than the vessel was inundated with visitors who were impatient to inspect her, and for an hour or two we were completely taken by storm ; of pretty girls there were a large proportion on board, who, after satisfying their curiosity regarding the vessel, improvised a waltz in the saloons. We of course being too gallant to allow them, to dance alone, soon joined them, and were quickly upon the most friendly terms with the whole party. After amusing themselves for an hour or so in this way, they invited us to accompany them on shore and finish our first evening with an impromptu ball. Thinking the opportunity a good one, some four or five of us idlers accepted, glad of a chance of making an entrée into St. Catharines "society ;" so jumping into one of the boats and wedging ourselves in among the girls, we pulled gaily for the shore. On reaching the beach we each gallantly caught our neighbor around her waist and bore her out of reach of the surf. The party safely landed, we accompanied our newly-made friends to one of their residences which had been designated for the occasion.

My first impressions of the town were most favorable. Having landed at the foot of the public square, we passed through its entire length in order to gain our destination in the suburbs ;

the church, occupying the upper side, flanked on the one side by the president's palace and on the other by public buildings, all standing in bold relief, their outlines well defined in the bright moonlight, gave the Plaza an imposing appearance ; taking advantage of the beautiful night, hundreds were strolling about the Plaza, while music softly stole through many an open casement.

Arriving at a pretty little country house in the midst of gardens, where the perfumes of flowers as they floated in the evening air were most overpowering, we were ushered in by our kind friends. After resting and partaking of their hospitality, in the shape of luscious fruits and conserves of the country, we resumed our dancing, which we kept up to a late hour, having been, meanwhile, joined by large accessions of the beaux and belles of the town. The young ladies were, without exception, lively and companionable, graceful, and of pleasing appearance, while some of them were exceedingly pretty. At a late hour we bade adieu to our kind entertainers, and with promises of soon repeating our visit, made our way to the ship, much gratified with our first experience in St. Catharines.

A survey of the steamer having been made, she was found to have sustained some very serious damage, and that repairs requiring a month's time to accomplish, would be necessary to put her in a fit condition to proceed on her voyage. This was anything but pleasant news to me, who was so anxious to get to California, and in spite of all perspective pleasures incident to a month's residence among the hospitable inhabitants of this island, I must confess that I received the report in a most rebellious way, but as ill-humor could be of no avail, I came to the conclusion to make the best of it.

The curiosity concerning our steamer continued unabated,

and day after day, from morning till night, she was thronged with visitors ; people came from far and near, and many a party from the interior made a pilgrimage to the bay for no other purpose than to gratify their curiosity respecting her. Among so many people, it would have been strange not to have made some pleasant acquaintances, and many a hospitable invitation we received to visit our friends at their homes ; availing ourselves of these privileges, we had ample means of passing our time pleasantly, and of observing the peculiar customs of the country.

In view of our anticipated temporary residence, those of us who were not attached to the vessel, or took no part in her executive duty, proceeded at once to establish our headquarters at the "Hôtel do Vapor," as snug a little hostelrie as is to be found on the South American continent, and kept by one Hamel, an American, who had resided many years in the country, and who was married to a native ; he was as jovial and liberal a landlord as could be met with anywhere.

The only guests of the establishment, we took formal possession, and made ourselves perfectly at home, being honorably attended in our head waitress, who, though a slave, was a princess in her own right, and daughter of the King Cabenda ; she always appeared perfectly conscious of her noble birth, and was extremely dignified in all her movements. Our male attendant was one of the brightest, most knowing negroes I ever saw, the very life and factotum of the establishment ; he was hideously ugly, and hunchback in the bargain, but notwithstanding his personal defects, was a most valuable and entertaining servant ; he rejoiced in the name of Chico, and the name Chico, Chico, Chico, used to echo through the house morn ing, noon and night, and its ubiquitous owner was always ready to respond to its call.

I was as favorably impressed with the appearauce of the town by daylight as I had previously been by moonlight. Its large square, carpeted with bright green turf, pleasantly contrasted with the dazzling whiteness of the buildings around it ; the streets running irregularly over hill and dale, lined with dwellings generally surrounded with gardens, tastefully planted with flowers and fruit trees, formed a rurally picturesque scene. The little villas in the suburbs were perfect gems of rural beauty ; half hidden among plantations of the orange, the mango, and the fig, they were most delightful retreats from the heat of the tropical sun. Here, each afternoon on returning from our ride, we would drop in upon some one of our suburban friends, who, delighted to see us, would always insist upon our passing the evening, and upon our acceding, would gather together from the neighborhood all the young people to assist in entertaining us. Thus day followed day in rapid succession, when so far from feeling ennui we were continually enjoying ourselves, and in this way managed to get through very pleasantly the three weeks which, in perspective, had appeared so interminable. By the aid of an old French billiard-table, we managed to kill the morning hours, while the afternoon and evening, as I have said before, were devoted to visiting and excursions into the country.

During our stay we made frequent journeys into the interior of the island, and were always charmed by the beauty and luxuriousness of the vegetable kingdom. The air was loaded with almost overpowering perfumes, and musical with the songs of hundreds of birds, whose gay plumage seemed like the transient hues of the prism as they shot across the dark green background of the forest. Trellis-work of vines and parasites, winding and twining around the giant forms of the forest, loaded with flowers of the richest odor and brightest hue, formed natural avenues through which we passed unconscious of a meridian sun, save when some opening permitted its fierce rays to penetrate. Here and there we would stumble upon a secluded plantation, hidden by a banana orchard and hedged by coffee plants, through which unceremoniously forcing our horses, we would invariably be greeted with kind welcomes from the proprietor. We frequently partook of the welcome of these Brazilian farmers, who, although their table appointments were not of the most approved pattern, made up for it by the luxuriance of the fare. Farina is the staff of life with them, ground from the mandioca root, and is made up by the native cooks into an infinite variety of dishes, all of which are exceedingly palatable. The mandioca grows all over tropical Brazil, to the height of from four to five feet, attaining maturity twenty months after planting ; the root produces the farina, and resembles a carrot ; they are first scraped, and then grated and reduced to a pulp, the juices and water pressed out, and are then powdered and put into an iron pan with a fire beneath, and dried, and are then fit for use.

The banana enters largely into the diet of the planter, and is eaten either raw or cooked. As is the case in most tropical countries, the very luxuriousness of the vegetation is the greatest obstacle to its advancement ; for its inhabitants, raising without effort sufficient quantities of food to maintain themselves, do not care to exert themselves for the improvement of their condition.

CHAPTER IV.

STRAITS OF MAGELLAN.

Author leaves St. Catharines and his Sweethearts behind him—Is once more upon old Ocean—Is dubious as to the Staunchness of his Conveyance—Enters the Straits of Magellan—Arrives at Port Famine—Finds no Coal—Does the necessary amount of Swearing, and then becomes resigned—He proceeds to cut Wood for Fuel, with Sailors for Axemen—It begins to Snow, and Snows for thirty Days and thirty Nights, without cessation—Makes Shooting Excursions into unexplored Bays, and slaughters unsuspicious Fowl—Becomes superstitious, sees the Devil, and hears him howl—Experiences Spasmodic Sensations thereat, which are calmed on the idea suggesting itself, that it was only a Sea Lion—He enters the Pacific, and describes his Impressions in strains Poetic—He arrives at Valparaiso—Describes it—Dines with the Consul, and experiences his first Earthquake while at Table—Insecurity of the Harbor—Terrible Gales and Wrecks—We once more Steam along the Coast, remarking upon the Ports of Copiapo, Coquimbo, Iquique, Islay, Arica, and Pisca—Arrive at the Chincha Islands—Theory relating to the Accumulation of Guano—Balls on Shipboard—We touch at Cañete—Are spilt in the Surf.

Our repairs being completed, and the steamer announced once more to be in a seaworthy condition, (the veracity of which statement being deemed most questionable by the writer), we bade adieu to our kind friends, and on the third day of June, passed under a full head of steam through the southern passage, between the island and the main, and in a short time we were again floating on the Atlantic, heading up for Cape Virgin, at the entrance of the Straits of Magellan.

As may be imagined, my previous experience did not tend to reassure me respecting the safety of our vessel, and I must confess myself to have been rather nervous, as to the extent of her ability to resist the gales and heavy seas, which we must almost as a certainty encounter off the mouth of the Rio de la Plata, and the south coast of Patagonia. The captain very prudently determined to hug the coast pretty closely, thus in a measure avoiding the heaviest of the sea, and in the event of a mishap, rendering the chance of making a port more secure. Fortune, however, was with us, and it seemed as if Providence had taken us under his special protection, for although, for ten days we were passing through the stormiest part of the South Atlantic, the sea was calm and quiet, and we glided onward with ease and safety, at the end of each day congratulating ourselves that we had accomplished thus much of the distance without disaster, and hoping for fair weather on the morrow.

While at St. Catharines, the weather had been very warm, but as we got a little more to the southward, we began to feel the cold very sensibly, and heavy woollen clothing took the place of the light summer rig, in which we had been lately accoutred. When off the mouth of the Rio de la Plata, hundreds of Cape pigeons made their appearance, following in our wake, and never leaving us again for several months; these little birds are a species of gull, abounding in the South Seas, and are the very counterpart of our domestic pigeon, both in color and size, and afforded us endless amusement in their graceful circling and wheeling, and diving, as they strove with each other for the bits of refuse from the kitchen. Out of curiosity we caught several, and on close inspection they still maintain their similarity to the domestic bird, but are web-footed, and have a differently shaped bill; after being brought on board, they immediately became very sick, throwing up freely, and are otherwise disagreeable from being overun with vermin. There, too, we made our first acquaintance with the albatross; at first sight I was disappointed, expecting to see a much larger bird, but as they became less shy, and ventured nearer to us, I was astonished at their dimensions, and charmed with their graceful gyrations; or as unconsciously they, with heads beneath their wing, slept peacefully upon the billow; or, rising with the gale, they madly wheeled and shrieked, as if glorying in the elemental strife. Hundreds of miles away from land, when the gale is at its highest, when with difficulty the eye can pierce the atmosphere, thick with driving sleet and foam, suddenly through the contending elements his shrill cry is heard above the storm, and he darts quickly by; then circling about, he hovers around, now skirting over the breaking seas, and through their crests; then settling down on the bosom of some huge wave, he peacefully and gracefully sinks to rest, all unconscious of the fierce tumult raging about him.

On the evening of the 12th of June, our reckoning showed us to be off the mouth of the Straits of Magellan, and we thank heaven for it, for with this nondescript, rickety old affair of a ship, it would be no joke to be caught in one of those Cape Horn snorters, which blow pretty much all the year round in these latitudes. We had bidden adieu to the tropics with a vengeance, for the weather had become horribly cold, the thermometer standing at an average of 35° Fahrenheit, and the raw, piercing southerly winds, made our teeth chatter, so sudden was the change. The days, too, had become very short, and the long evenings of winter were upon us ; however, all this was no great drawback to our comfort, for our Astral lamp once lighted, our great stove red and glowing, the brass teakettle on its top hissing merrily, the whist party made up, and each member of the little circle flanked by a smoking glass of punch, Miss Puss dozing in the corner on the mat, and old Solomon Gills, our venerable monkey, arrayed in a red flannel coat, and duck breeches, snoozing in the coal scuttle, we presented about as true a picture of *marine* comfort, as one would be likely to gaze upon on ship-board in the South Seas.

The breaking day of June 13th, 1849, discovered to us Cape Virgin, the northern headland of the eastern entrance to the Straits of Magellan, their width here being so very great that the southern extremity was not visible.

Steaming rapidly along with a favoring tide, we observed the land to rise perpendicularly from the water to the height of fifty feet, generally level, though occasionally broken by undulating hills. As the day advances, the land on the port hand (Terra del Fuego) comes into view, and we quickly find ourselves between lofty palisades, the distance between either side rapidly lessening, till at mid-day we reached the first narrows ; here the width between shore and shore was but three miles, and the mighty current rushed through with great violence, the water boiling, foaming and roaring terrifically. Through them we shot, and now again we find ourselves in a broad sound, say five miles wide, on either hand tall palisades, the land stretching away in vast plains, covered with innumerable herds of lama and ostriches feeding, who, as we shriek our steam-whistle, fly off like the wind. Attracted by the sound, a band of the far-famed Patagonian Indians, on horseback, make their appearance, and as they stand, statue-like, on the brink of that high eminence, with the clear blue sky for a background, all the marvellous stories of their gigantic stature seem to be verified, for colossal, indeed, seemed their stature. Onward we sped; as we progress, the shores becoming mountainous and barren-looking, more particularly those of Terra del Fuego, the straits now narrowing, now widening, though the average distance from shore to shore would seem to be from six to ten miles, the tides running strong and tumultuously though with great regularity. Somewhere about midnight we reached Port Famine, one hundred and fifty miles within the Straits, and letting go our anchors, awaited daylight to reveal its beauties.

Going on deck the next morning, my attention was attracted by a roaring noise which fairly drowned our voices, when, looking across the strait, its whole surface seemed in tumultuous confusion, the waters tumbling and foaming as if shot from a cascade, reminding me more than anything else of the rapids at the falls of Niagara; all this was caused by the flooding tide met by an opposing wind.

Turning our attention shoreward, we beheld a high, steep bank, ice-covered and rocky, perched on the top of which were a dozen or so of rickety, smoke-stained wooden houses, composing the city of *Port Famine*. This settlement was formed in this remote, God-forsaken locality, for penal purposes by the Chilian government, whither all her criminals are transported, and well it deserves its name, for beyond a little dried venison and pork and a few stinted potatoes, naught else was there to eat, and the inhabitants, as may be supposed, were of the most villainous description, and their appearance, wrapped in their greasy ponchos, with their slouched, chimney-pot hats, was most repulsive. Their governor, likewise a criminal, was, however, a man of a different stamp, polished and well educated, he lived among his books, a broken-hearted man; scarce twenty-five, in an hour of temptation, he had yielded, and was now expiating his crime—poor fellow, he was afterwards murdered by his ungovernable subjects.

On leaving Rio, we had been informed that on our arrival at Port Famine, we would find a deposit of "native coal," which would be all-sufficient to enable us to reach Valparaiso; what was our consternation, then, to hear that not *one pound* of coal was to be had in all that region! We were dumbfounded, and stared at each other in stupid surprise. We were, indeed, in a pretty predicament—midway in the Straits of Magellan, a thousand miles away from civilization, and not more than a few hours' fuel to enable us to reach there! Mid-winter, too, in this high latitude, the day scarce four hours long, and incessant snows in prospect!

What was to be done? An only remedy! and that was, to cut wood enough to carry us to some place where coal could be got. On going into a calculation, it was found that *five days'* steaming would be necessary to reach *St. Carlos*, the nearest inhabited point. Now, furthermore, it was ascertained that we had not one day's fuel, and that the steamer would consume at least twenty-five cords of wood per day, and that, with our men all green as to the use of the axe, at least a fortnight would be required to cut one day's consumption; at which rate, our stay in this delectable region would be, instead of some two or three, of at least *sixty* days duration! This was delightful news indeed—it could not be—we would not believe it—then we swore at, and abused one another—then we got sullen and wouldn't swear—and then—we lit our pipes, and resolved to make the best of it. Heaving up our anchor, and shrieking back through our steam-whistle a parting curse at Port Famine, we moved off to a locality where there was more wood and fewer villains.

Arriving at Bougainville Bay—a little nook scarce large enough to hold us, with a little islet at its mouth for a shelter—we proceeded to take possession, and moored ourselves for a permanent residence. We then proceeded to inspect our ground for wood-cutting. We found it on a mountain side, almost precipitous, the trees extremely wet and filled with sap, and most difficult to be got at, so that, with our green axe-men, our spirits were not very much exhilarated at our discovery. However, we got all ready, hauled the ship in close to the bank, ground our axes, and turned in to refresh ourselves for next day's performances.

June 15*th*.—After a night of fierce gales and driving squalls, the day breaks at about nine o'clock, and going on deck, we find a blinding snow storm raging without, with about a foot of snow already on the ground. All hands on shore to clear it away; no wood-cutting to-day; dark at 4, P.M.; stoves merrily burning; punch-bowl full and simmering, and whist-party formed.

June 16*th*.—Wood-cutting progressing slowly; men unaccustomed to the work; awkward, and easily tire.

17*th*, 18*th*, *and* 19*th*.—Snow, snow, snow—blow, blow, blow—all darkness—men worn out with cutting wood—work progressing slowly.

21st.—Men wounded by a falling tree—snow getting very deep, and cold intense.

22d, 23d, 24th, 25th, and 26th.—Snow, snow—squall following squall—atmosphere so thick, nothing can be seen a hundred feet from the ship.

27th.—To-day, thank God, we leave this miserable, inhospitable hole, and off we strike into the broad strait again. From ten to fifteen miles in width, lofty mountains rise on either side, robed in snow, cold and dreary. Slowly we progress, the wet, green wood burning miserably bad ; all day we puff and blow against rushing tides and driving snow squalls—now through open sounds, then through crooked reaches. Coasting along the shore of Terra del Fuego, a native canoe, filled with those disgusting cannibals, the natives, struck out for us, and we passed near enough to them, as, affrighted, they paddled away for dear life, to distinguish the features of their brutish countenances, less intelligent than that of the African baboon, though closely resembling it in its tout-ensemble of hair and wrinkle. At twilight we anchored in an inhospitable little nook, whose sides were glaciers and whose basin a frozen lake, and were serenaded the livelong night with the bellowings of the sea-cow and the barkings of the otter.

28th.—Again weigh anchor, and find ourselves again puffing along ; to-day the weather is more serene, and we experience but little current ; the features of the land we find the same, bold, mountainous, and snow-covered. Suddenly our attention is attracted towards a little island, close in shore, four or five miles distant. Seizing a glass, we spy upon a tree an American flag—union down—a signal of distress. Steering in, and approaching nearer, we spy a wreck, high and dry, tents erected, and men moving about ; presently a boat comes dancing over the water, and a man springs upon our deck, announcing himself master of the schooner John A. Sutter, gone ashore in a snow-squall, with crew of thirty men, and bound to California, and reports brig Acadian, of Boston, laying alongside rendering him assistance.

We regret we cannot accommodate him, and show him over the side, leaving him to the tender mercies of the Acadian, "and go on our way rejoicing." In the distance we spy Cape Tamar, a mountain promontory, guarding the western entrance to the straits, and beyond it the stormy ocean. But in our situation it would never do to trust to old Ocean, bad enough when we have good fuel and plenty of it; but now it would be madness, and we must fain trust to the intricate navigation through the passages which divide Patagonia from the archipelago of islands, which stud its coast, reaching fairly up to Chili; this is venturesome, but it is our only course; to go outside would be the height of recklessness—besides, we must cut wood as we go along.

Before leaving the straits, it would be as well to remark some of their peculiarities, of wind, tide and current, and of their adaptation to navigation. The distance from their eastern to their western extremity, is about 250 miles, with an average width of about nine miles. The shores are mountainous, running abruptly up from the water; consequently, close alongside of them is oftentimes a depth of two fathoms or more, and the whole coast on either side is indented with little coves, with good anchorage, affording excellent harbors. The tides, until you get some twenty or thirty miles from the western end, run with great regularity, although very strong; wherever the straits narrow, there the tides become furious and rush along with overwhelming impetuosity. The old idea that the Pacific was higher than the Atlantic, and that consequently an irresistible current always rushed through the straits from the westward, has long since been exploded, although, near the western extremity, there is always a slight current setting easterly, caused by the constant westerly winds which continually blow. The winds prevail from the westward and blow at times with frightful violence; the squalls called "Willy Waas," are indeed terrific. To a well-manned ship there would be no insuperable difficulties in her going through either from east to west, or to the contrary. Fore and aft vessels should always go through, and in an easy working vessel, I deem the danger less from going to the westward through the straits than in going round Cape Horn. Bidding adieu to the Straits of Magellan, and heading northerly, we enter Smith's Channel, and as night sets in we anchor in a lovely little nook, without a name, snow hills runinng away up to heaven, and the trees which we so covet, half buried in the drifts.

July 2d.—Here we are once more busily engaged in cutting down trees; Jack is becoming very expert, and goes at it *con amore*; once in a while his axe glances, and slices off a piece of his neighbor's calf, but our doctor is wonderful at cures.

One thing a man has to look out for here, which may seem very comical, but which might result very seriously, and that is, *not* to get suffocated in a snow drift; in many places these drifts are from 30 to 40 feet deep, and arching over small brooks, are by no means compact or solid, easily letting a man through. One or two of our fellows walking unconcernedly along, found themselves clean out of sight, and were only recovered on being missed.

These northern channels being out of the white man's path, and their waters never disturbed by a vessel's prow, are filled with water-fowl of every description, and many a fine day's sport I had in hunting them. Jumping into a boat, and hoisting the sail, with my ducking gun by my side, I would explore the thousand little bays around, and waken with my gun, echoes never before thus given back. Hundreds of black duck, teal, and snipe of various kinds fed among the kelp which lined the shores, while flocks of grey geese and brant, soared within gunshot, and hair and dog-seal poked their ugly noses within oar's length of the boat, and sea-cows and sea-elephants rolled their huge forms from off high rocks, with tremendous splashes into the sea. Some of these seals are most enormous, weighing as much as a good fat ox ; they live together in numbers, in caverns, called by sealers, rookeries, and are entered by them armed only with clubs, without regard to fear ; the only danger is in getting between the seal and the water, which they make for as soon as attacked; in which case, one is liable to get knocked down and crushed.

On one occasion I was scared almost to death by one, and it was the first I ever saw. Having been off in my boat some ten miles from the ship, night overtook me, and although it was moonlight, still a gale was brewing, and the wind swept along in heavy, fitful gusts. Reefing down my sail, and crouching low to avoid the cold blasts, and watching with great anxiety the dark clouds driving over the face of the moon—I was in a nervous and excited mood—when directly before me, the most hideously frightful-looking object I had ever beheld rose out of the water, and from its mouth sent forth a yell, as if from ten thousand demons, and then disappeared ;

As for me, I thought it was the devil, and over I went, head-over-heels into the bottom of the boat; fright had exaggerated both size and sound. Recovering myself in a moment, I ordered the willing men to shake out the reef in spite of the wind, thinking it better to capsize and be drowned, than living to be carried off by Satan.

The characteristics of this channel are the same as those of the straits—lofty, broken mountains, and innumerable islands, all snow-covered to the depth of 20 or 30 feet; we have seen too, many beautiful glaciers, strikingly splendid, as the bright sun shines upon them, while the mers-du-glace stretch away like polished mirrors.

July 4th.—Snowing, cold and dreary, a blue day for us; we consoled ourselves with a game dinner, drank patriotic toasts, and wound up of course in getting gloriously tight, all of us, fore and aft the ship; Jack's allowance being most liberal, grog flowed about forward, and stag-dances were the order of the day.

Slowly progressing to the northward, the weather becomes more moderate, and incessant rains take the place of snow-storms, and the islands and hill sides, doffing their white coats, appear in jockey green, the trees put forth their buds, and during our stationary periods we wander away into the woods, and occasionally bring home a saddle of venison.

Of the Indians and their arrows we are exceeding shy, as the former are of us, but we often catch sight of their filthy forms only partly covered with skins, and their small piercing eyes peering *cannibalistically* at us, so that our fat friends all shudder and instinctively cock their pieces. Their abodes, usually located on a promontory, are nothing more than an immense wicker basket in the form of a bee-hive made of osiers, the inside filled with dry grass and the outside a mass of dry bones, oyster-shells, etc. etc, the filth both inside and out disgusting in the extreme. These tribes live in boats the greater part of the year, and are consequently called "canoe Indians," their only cooking utensil a stone pot, boiled by hot stones thrown in; their food, oysters, muscles, and fish; their dress, when they wear any is of seal skin, a kind of mantle.

After weeks and weeks of rain and hurricane, to our great joy, we reached the island of Chiloe, at the southern extremity of the Republic of Chili, and passing between it and the mainland and driven by a fierce current, on the 8th of August, fifty-three days after leaving the Atlantic, we entered the harbor of San Carlos.

Our arrival caused the greatest excitement, ours being the first steamer that had ever disturbed the waters of this remote bay. Jumping into our boat, we pulled away shoreward, and on reaching the mole found the whole population, some thousands, waiting to receive us; on landing we were surrounded on all sides, and the people gazed upon us very much as they would upon a tame elephant at home; submitting for a while to their scrutiny, we at last, by unequivocal signs of fight, got rid of as ugly a mob of scoundrels as I ever saw collected together. Arrayed in the dark, greasy, villainous-looking ponchos peculiar to the country and the chimney-potted hat pulled down over the eyes, they were as unamiable looking a set of cut throats as I ever saw: few wear shoes, and all appear to be in the most abject poverty. The appearance of the town was as squalid as that of its inhabitants; built entirely of the red-wood of the country, without paint, it seemed gloomy, dark and uninviting. The women are coarse and ugly, and wear no hats; they wear rough shawls, with hair plaited down their backs. The whole population redolent of grease and garlic.

The commerce between this port and Valparaiso is quite important, consisting of large quantities of wheat and other grain, and of various kinds of valuable lumber.

Even in this out of the way place we found a Yankee and a Frenchman, the one a farmer and saw-mill proprietor, and the other of course a barber. The harbor is fine and capacious, with some good sheltered anchorage, but the entrance is exceedingly dangerous, which deters ship-owners from sending their vessels there. Provisions we found exceedingly cheap—magnificent potatoes two rials per bushel, fowls one rial per pair, sheep a dollar, etc.

Having obtained a sufficient supply of fuel, on the 15th of August we steamed out of the harbor, and in short time were floating on the bosom of the Pacific. Leaving far behind us the fierce gales and mountain billows of Cape Horn, onward we sped, merrily dancing o'er the laughing wavelets of the blue Pacific. Away, away in the dim distance, far, far above the misty clouds, the spectral peaks of the mighty Andes chain, in their eternal robe of ice and snow, dazzling and bright, stand forth against the azure sky, a noble landmark to the uncertain mariner. Onward we dash, each hour bringing balmier airs and steadier breezes and with them the practical assurance that at last we had reached that "Paradise of the sailor," the Pacific.

Aug. 18th.—Lovely indeed is this navigation. In full view of the Andes, their snow-capped peaks rising high into the heavens—what can be more sublime than the view now presented to us? The broad ocean stretching away thousands of leagues, calm and placid, its bosom only ruffled by the occasional break of a ripple anxious to discharge its silvery burden, and on the other hand, the mighty chain of everlasting hills seemingly vying with each other which shall nearest approach the heaven of heavens—low down bristling with an armor of evergreen, while on high, mantled in celestial white, as if purified by their nearer approach to the realms of bliss.

The first port made after leaving San Carlos is the Bay of Concepçion, decidedly the finest harbor on the coast. Concepçion is the name of the port itself, while the city, some ten miles distant, is called "Talcahuano." Numbering some five or six thousand inhatitants, it is a place of very considerable trade, and is the rendezvous for all the whalers pursuing their calling in the South Seas; this in itself is a very important branch of trade, and leaves a considerable sum of money annually there.

Large quantities of wheat and flour are likewise brought here from the interior, and shipped hence to California, Peru, and the northern ports of Chili. One feels quite at home on walking through the streets of Talcahuano, being accosted at every turn by his own countrymen, while signs in English tempt him within the many stores. I omitted noticing Valdivia, a small port to the southward of Concepçion; the harbor is, however, difficult of entrance, and its commerce limited to exports of bituminous coal, which is not very extensively used on account of its liability to spontaneous combustion; indeed, many vessels have been burnt at sea while freighted with it. Somewhere about one hundred miles to the northward of Talcahuano is the town of Constituçion, at the mouth of one of the most important rivers in Chili. Here the Rio Maule, a stream of immense volume, empties itself into the ocean. After taking its rise among the eternal snows of the Cordilleras, and traversing a highly fertilized and extensive region of country, at first its course is much obstructed with rapids, but still navigable for flat-boats ; as it approaches the coast, however, it deepens, and becomes navigable for larger vessels. And were it not for its wretched entrance, obstructed by dangerous breakers, Constituçion would be a highly important point, as the products of the line of country through which the river flows are extremely valuable. Charles Minturn, Esq., of New York, has the monopoly for navigating the river by steam for ten years, and several steam-tugs now tow vessels over the bar. A Peruvian steamer which I commanded was afterwards lost among the breakers at the entrance to the port.

As day dawned we beheld spread before us the city of Valparaiso. In the foreground is the harbor, only by courtesy so called, filled with the ships of every nation ; beyond it, and running along the beach, is the principal street, some two miles in length, compact with well-built houses, prominent among which are several churches and the handsome Custom House. Above them, elevated some two hundred feet, and hanging directly over them, is a terrace where are located many neat looking cottages, flanked by a tasty little church, the former the residences of the foreign merchants, and the latter an English Chapel, supported by British residents. Rising abruptly above the southern end of the city are three conical hills, straggling and broken by volcanic action, and named respectively the " Fore, Main and Mizzen Tops "—their terraced sides occupied by sailors, boarding-houses and gambling-hells of the very lowest description. Here Jack retires on the receipt of his wages, from whence after being stupefied with bad liquor and beaten and robbed of his money, he is summarily ejected, lucky not to be sent headlong down some of the steep precipices, as many a poor devil has been before him. These tops are the very St. Giles of the coast and the Alsatian retreat for all criminals and desperadoes. A wild young devil of a naval officer, on being invited on some grand occasion to dine with his admiral "regretted that it would not be in his power, as he had already accepted an invitation from his 'Starboard watch' to dine with them at 'Jones' of the Main top" (one of the most notorious dens in Valparaiso). High above these hills and terraces the Cordillera towers away among the clouds. The harbor is in fact no harbor at all—a mere arm of the sea—the anchorage very insecure and in the winter season very unsafe; a heavy swell rolls in from the sea and breaks into the principal street, making the landing unpleasant as well as dangerous. Northers blow very violently during the winter months and wrecks are frequent, the sea setting in at those times frightfully strong.

On the occasion of a subsequent visit, I was laying with my vessel in the harbor, when a violent Norther sprung up; an enormous sea arose, and ship after ship was swept from its anchorage down upon others, which likewise gave way and went ashore on a reef called "Little Cape Horn." All was confusion, consternation and distress, those on board trusting only to their anchors and chains for life, while those on shore could render no assistance. We held on pretty well, although obliged to cut away our masts, the sea making a clean breach over us. Presently the "—— ——," an American schooner, as beautiful a piece of marine architecture as ever floated and the fleetest vessel in the Pacific, started and came driving down. Passing close to several ships, her crew took advantage of opportunities to escape and save their lives, but the mate steadily refused assistance, having evidently resolved to die with the vessel. I see him now as the fated craft drove by us dismasted, he standing calmly on her deck, his hair streaming in the gale, awaiting his fate. A few fathoms astern of us, a sea struck her, and over she went, bottom upwards, and in a moment was dashed to pieces against the reef. Loss of life is frequent in these gales, and occurs in full view of the inhabitants, who can lend no earthly assistance.

A law exists here for the prevention of smuggling, forbidding any shore boat leaving the beach after sunset under a penalty of $25. One night a heavy norther sprung up, a ship came driving ashore and a living man was seen on the wreck through the moon's pale rays. An American lieutenant prevailed upon some boatmen to risk their lives with him through the boiling surf; after almost superhuman efforts they gain the wreck and triumphantly bring the man ashore; they are immediately arrested and forced to pay the penalty for leaving the beach after sunset, but in the morning the lieutenant was presented by the town with an elegant sword in token of his intrepidity.

Valparaiso is essentially a foreign city, its commerce being in the hands of English, French, and Germans, while over the shop doors signs in every idiom, except the Spanish, give unequivocal proof of the foreign element. With a liberal government, firmly established—the only successful one of all the South American "experiments"—they offer great encouragement to foreign immigration, and make liberal allowance for national peculiarities; toleration is the order of the day, and the absurdly restrictive policy of the other Spanish states has been superseded by the most politic commercial regulations. Even the Protestant faith is looked upon with no unfavorable eye, and one of the most prominent objects on entering the harbor is the pretty little English church, perched high over the town, while each religious procession (Catholic), as it goes chanting through the town, may hear Watts' psalms as they are wafted upward by the voices of a hundred worshippers from the Presbyterian Chapel, near the Custom House.

It is highly interesting to observe how the national prosperity of Chili has increased with the spread of education among the people. But a few years ago her trade was small, her resources undeveloped, and her political state among the lowest of the South American states. She has now a large trade, her exports exceeding her imports, which are very large. Previous to 1832 there were but one or two public schools in the whole republic; two were founded in 1834—one in 1837—one in 1839—two in 1841—and two in 1842. In 1843 the attention of government was directed to the subject of education, and eighteen schools were founded—twenty in 1844—thirteen in 1845—ten in 1847—seven in 1848—and five in 1849. This increase in schools has been followed by an increase of pupils, and female children are now very generally sent to school—Chili having wisely turned her attention to their education—knowing how much a mother's character influences the future life of her citizens. The principle of government is free suffrage to all of twenty five years of age who can read and write and possess $200. Legislation is vested in a chamber of deputies and senate—senators are elected for nine years, and deputies for three years. The president is elected for five years. The bay is two and a half miles wide, circular in form, the southern side being occupied by arsenals, navy-yards, etc. Running along the beach, as I before remarked, is a wide, beautiful street, its southern extremity being devoted to business. Here is the Custom House, a handsome stuccoed building with a clock-tower ; nearly opposite, the Merchants Exchange, filled up with reading-rooms, etc. etc. with a fine view of the bay and shipping ; further along is the Plaza de Victoria, ornamented with a fountain and a theatre capable of containing two thousand people. This section is called the Almendral or Almond Grove, for what reason I cannot imagine, but I suppose on the same principle that Valparaiso is called the "Valley of Paradise," when it should rather have been called the "Valley of the infernal regions."

The retail business is entirely in the hands of the French and Germans, and the shop windows remind one of the "Palais Royal." The wholesale business is carried on by English and Germans ; the principal house is that of Huth, Gruning & Co.; the Americans being represented by Messrs. Alsop & Co., a house of influence and long standing on the coast.

The society of Valparaiso has always been excellent ; the Chilian ladies, noted for their beauty, and looking with lenient eyes upon "outside barbarians," while the ladies on Cerro Alegre, or "Merryhill," as the terraced residence of the foreigners is aptly styled, always were celebrated for their hospitality and amiability.

A great drawback to a residence on this coast is the frequency of earthquakes ; constantly occurring, they keep one in continual dread, and on this very terrace I experienced the first shock that I ever felt.

Dining with our hospitable consul, Mr. Moorhead, while in the act of taking wine with a lady guest, an unaccountable feeling came over me, and without knowing why or wherefore we simultaneously set down our glasses. In an instant Mrs. Moorhead, without a word, rushed from the table and threw open all the doors, and taking her children by the hand, stepped out upon the terrace. The gentlemen remained seated—still the feeling of oppression—the wine glasses and decanters began to dance—and then—it was over—and the oppression passed away. I was rather frightened, but kept my own counsel, but must here confess that on each and every other occasion I was more and more terrified. Some four years afterwards I stood on almost the very identical spot, and experienced one of the most violent shocks ever known there ; the earth yawned, houses tumbled about, and the sea boiled over. I wasn't frightened that time, I was temporarily *insane.*

The climate of Valparaiso is peculiar—the thermometer will average about 40° Fahrenheit in winter, the cold not being sufficiently severe to blight vegetation, although I have seen ice in the streets in July, or mid-winter. The heat of summer is at times intense, but tempered by the sea-breeze.

Its fruits are delicious and various ; the strawberry grows to mammoth size, and I have seen them nearly as large as the bowl of an ordinary wineglass, their flavor is very fine. Currants, gooseberries and cherries likewise abound ; the figs are luscious, as are the nectarines, grapes, and pears and melons of all varieties ; of tropical fruits there are a profusion, such as lemons, oranges, and the indescribable cheremoyas.

Wrapping oneself in a poncho, with a supply of cigars and brandy, the one to neutralize the garlicy odor of the coachman, and the other to keep out the raw, cold air, and seating oneself in a volante, an indescribable kind of gig, with three raw-boned horses harnessed to it, away we go, clickety-clack, over hill and precipice, for a host of hours, through daylight and darkness, until we find ourselves closed in by the Andes and central Cordillera ranges, and rapidly nearing the large and populous city, *Santiago*, the capital of the republic ; and well does a visit to the capital repay one for the unmerciful mountain ride, and hairbreadth escapes which seem to the unsophisticated eye to succeed each other momentarily, from its commencement to his journey's end. Imagine it ! far up in the lap of the Andes mountains ! a huge city ! occupying seven square miles of substantial dwelling houses, fountains and bridges, and a delightful society of beautiful and well informed women and cultivated men ; such is the Santiago of the present day. Divided into squares, an arm of the river traverses each street, cooling it and carrying off the garbage ; the houses are generally low, and roofed with red tiles, which give rather a picturesque air to the city ; they have very thick walls and but few windows, their solidity answering both purposes of security against earthquakes and as non-conductors to the heats of summer. Among the more prominent of the buildings, we find the grand cathedral, constructed of granite, with a front of three hundred and fifty feet, and is quite an imposing structure ; within, it is exceedingly damp and gloomy, and its pictures and altar ornaments are far from striking. The music is however fine, an English organ of exquisite tone having recently been erected, and as there are some good voices in the choir, the chants and symphonies are at times delightful. The Mint is a very attractive and prominent building, in the Grecian style; the coining is now done through the agency of steam; the building is partly occupied by the president, and also by the state officers. The churches and convents boast of but little architectural beauty, and are innumerable, supported by the Dominicans, Mercedarias, Augustines, Franciscans, etc., etc. A pleasant town is this, truly, with its Philadelphia-like squares—its beautiful shrubbery, so delighted in by its fair ladies—its little running streams—its marble fountains—its picturesque bridges over its tumbling torrents—and its sunsets, gorgeously beautiful, as they reflect their hues of gold and orange and purple upon the far off snow-clad mountains. The society of Santiago is delightful, and perhaps the best to be found on the South American continent. Far in the interior, the women still retain a strong nationality of character, and are as yet free from the exactions of Parisian etiquette, which so illy becomes the Spanish maiden; naturally dignified, with an air as fearless and as free from affectation as might be imagined from their remoteness from the world, they charm you with their naïveté and piquancy of expression, and melt you with the tenderness of their glances; with complexions of pure white and red—with full black eye, and profusion of glossy locks, and of majestic form, they are most attractive women.

The men are like all South American men (with few exceptions), well mannered, well dressed—gamblers and roués—no private and no social virtues. There is one very funny custom existing here; at a certain season of the year, the old men take to kite-flying, and no expense is spared in getting up the most elaborate styles, profusely ornamented, and at night lit up with numberless lanterns attached to them; to each kite is affixed a knife, and each kite-flyer does his utmost to cut his neighbor's kite-string. This is the Sunday afternoon amusement, and the old gentlemen are in great glee when they can cut loose their neighbor's property.

Leaving Valparaiso and many recently made friends, we steam steadily along the coast. Soon we are abreast of Coquimbo, the great copper depot of the country ; a miserable hole in itself, but of considerable commercial importance. We find some half-dozen ships anchored there. We next enter the port of Caldera, the terminus of the Copiapo railroad, an enterprise of incalculable importance to the mining interests of the country, and executed with great labor, by American engineers ; this road brings into market an immense amount of silver and copper ores, which would otherwise have remained in their native beds, on account of the great cost of transportation by mules. Caldera has rapidly increased in population within a few years, and is now one of the most convenient harbors on the coast, with its fine breakwaters and piers. Onward we go, and a day or two brings us into the harbor of Cobija, the only port of Bolivia, a pretty little place, of about fifteen hundred inhabitants, exporting large quantities of copper, as well as silver and tin.

We now are off the coast of Peru, and enter the port of Iquique, containing about 1,000 inhabitants, formed by an indentation of the coast. This is a wretched hole; not a drop of water fit for a human being to drink, nor indeed anything fit to eat. It exports large quantities of saltpetre.

The next place we make is the port of Arica, built on a commanding bluff some 500 feet above the level of the sea, and is a place of considerable importance, being the outlet of Southern Peru and the Port of Tacua, a considerable city in the interior. It has been several times destroyed by earthquakes, and has been the scene of several bloody revolutionary struggles. Large quantities of peruvian bark, copper ore, silver, and wool, are exported. A railroad to the interior has lately been constructed under the superintendence of our intelligent and able countryman, Mr. Walton Evans, and is now in successful operation.

More northerly still lies the port of Islay. On a barren rock are situated a collection of miserable houses which compose the town; not a sign of vegetation, and an infernal heat, and to add to its delights, a heavy surf continually breaks along its shores, rendering a landing dangerous and disagreeable; indeed, I myself came near being drowned once or twice in it. This is the seaport for the town of Arequipa, a principal city of the republic, and is consequently a place of some little importance.

Rich as Peru is in antiquities—intense as is the interest felt by the civilized world in the land of the Inca—brilliant as is the thread of romance woven into a beautiful fabric by the magic pen of Prescott—still it was reserved to her valuable deposits of guano to render the name of Peru a household word n the mouth of the farmer and of the merchant; a bone of contention among political factions, each party strives to get possession of the islands, for having control of them affords the ruling power every facility for feathering their own nests and taking care of their favorites. It is a well received fact, that the presence of gold mines is rather a curse than a blessing to a country, rendering it extravagant, and causing a neglect of her more staple resources. This is eminently the case with the guano, as regards the Peruvian government; the Chincha Islands affording a constant supply of ready cash, has begotten such systematic extravagance and laxity in the government administration, that the country is on the brink of ruin. National honor is unknown, and in spite of her wealth, Peru is and has been long a bankrupt, only paying the interest on her debts at the muzzles of French and British cannon.

Peering through the grey fog of a September morning, we see running along the beach a pretty rambling town, with here and there a picturesque-looking church, half hidden among olive and orange groves—and this is Pisco, a barrier of surf dashing its spray into the very portals of the houses. This Pisco is the port of Ica, a town far away in the interior; the market town, if it may be so called, of a fertile and rich valley bearing the same name, whose products are of great commercial importance. Its cotton, of strong and silky texture, is known from Oregon to Cape Horn, and its sugars are largely exported to the northern ports, as well as to Chili. Here the Italia grape is extensively cultivated, and is a magnificent fruit, white in color and rich in flavor; a delightful liquor is distilled from it, called Italia, which has a very pleasant aromatic flavor. This is the standard drink of the country, and the consumption is enormous. It is put up in long earthen jars with narrow necks, holding from two to three gallons, and is thus shipped about the coast. Don Domingo Elias, a man of unbounded wealth and great political power, is the principal landholder of this vicinity, and pays great attention to the cultivation of the vine and cane. His vineyards are most extensive, and besides his Italia distilleries, he has large wine vaults under the superintendence of experienced European vintners, who produce a very choice article of Madeira, Sherry, and Amontillado. This section abounds in delicious fruits, and the cheremoyas and oranges are here in perfection.

Looking seaward from Pisco, about eleven miles from shore, a thick yellow mist is seen to rise high into heaven, and through it the indistinct forms of three rocky islets, surrounded by a forest of masts. Puzzled at so uuusual an appearance, we ask what it means, and are told that those are the "Chinchas," the famous Guano islands. A few revolutions of our engine, and before we have half done ogling the pretty cholitas who came aboard at Pisco, we are abreast the group.—It was a curious sight.—A fleet of the world's finest merchantmen, the gems and pride of the mercantile marine, moored in tiers around three miserable rocks in mid-ocean, without the vestige of vegetation, or the sign (as far as we could see) of human habitation upon them. There, in a cloud of dust, they lay, besmeared with the yellow powder which nothing can escape, their hatches open, and ton after ton of earth and mud pouring into their holds. This is guano, to be carried to the worn-out fields of Europe, Asia, and North America, to be reproduced into food.

The north island is the principal of the group, and here the English and German vessels usually load. This island is under the superintendence of one Serate, whose reputation is world-wide among sea-faring men, as *a wily old diplomat*, and as smooth-spoken and corruptible an old fox as ever lived; and having the discretion of facilitating or retarding the loading of ships, he is always ready for a *proposal* on the part of an impatient captain.

The middle island is the rendezvous of the American ships; and a gay place it is, too, when there is a large assemblage of ships present (which is generally the case). The masters of the present day, having such elegant accommodations aboard their spacious clippers, often take their families with them, and I have seen, at a ball given on shipboard at the Chinchas, upwards of thirty American women. Each vessel, according to her charter, being obliged to lie there from two to three months, a greater part of which time they are doing nothing, of course every mode is resorted to for killing time, and balls, regattas, pic-nics, and boat excursions, are the order of the day, and one island vies with the other in fun, frolic, and the brilliancy of its entertainments.

The climate is most delicious—the atmosphere, always cloudless, is in the morning very still, without a breath—the sea calm and glassy; at noon the Paraca comes out strong from the southward, and blows half a gale till sunset—this gives elegant opportunities for boat-sailing, which are not thrown away.

One of the great features of this part of the world, is the indescribable number of birds which are continually flying about, almost obstructing the light of day. A hundred different species of the gull family, and pelicans *ad infinitum.* It is positively wonderful to watch them, as with military precision they form into line, and drawing up in crescent shape, they hover over a devoted shoal of fish frolicking on the surface of the water. At a given signal, every *mother's son* of them close their wings, and fall splash into the sea, like an avalanche of stones, and in a second out they come again, each with a quivering fish in his beak; this goes on eternally, and lines of clumsy old pelicans are seen stretching away, in single file, as far as the eye can reach. As soon as one platoon get their fill, they retire to the rocks, surfeited, to digest, and it is a comical sight to see those astute, long-billed pelicans perched on an eminence gravely surveying the world about them. Words can give no adequate idea of the numbers of this feathery kingdom —their name is Legion.

Another institution, peculiar to these islands, is the seals, who appear almost as numerous as the birds themselves ; you cannot look over the ship's side without seeing half a dozen of them frolicking about, and as you are pulling around in your boat, you may at any time see their devilish countenances grinning at you.

What with the birds and seals it is not so wonderful a thing, after all, the production of such immense amounts of guano ; for the excrement from seal and bird must be something enormous in one year alone, whereas these accumulations have been going on for thousands of years ; and not only that, but it is conceded that much of the guano is produced, not from their excrement, but from the decomposed carcasses of the seals themselves ; for it is said, that, by a wonderful instinct, this unwieldy, ponderous (if I may use the expression) animal seeks the shore to die. Certain it is that they travel a long way over barren rocks, and, by some method or other to me unknown, manage to scale great hills, with what object I cannot conceive, for it seems unnatural that these unwieldy leviathans should prefer a hot, sandy *climb* to a pleasant *swim* among the shady grottoes of their own caves.

The superficial extent of the three islands is about seven miles ; yet, says a good authority, ships may take annually 50,000 tons for more than a century without exhausting them. A late survey, made by practical men, give 6,000,000 tons, and estimate the yearly consumption at from 450,000 to

600,000 tons. Its color is of a reddish, or snuff-colored tint; indeed it looks more like Scotch snuff than anything that I know of, and is of the same consistency, When taken from the island, it has a large element of ammonia in it, so much so, that on going into a ship's hold laden with it, sneezing, coughing, and watery eyes are the penalty; indeed large lumps of ammonia are found running through it. The working of the guano is a most awful business, and is only performed by criminals, or by Chinamen imported for the purpose; these latter poor devils very soon get used up, as the quantities of dust taken into the lungs speedily produces phthisis. They are most inhumanly treated by their taskmasters, and, by way of revenge, commit suicide by throwing themselves off the cliff—a constant occurrence.

The guano is first loosened with the pick; then shovelled into wheelbarrows and wheeled to the brink of the cliff, and there dumped into a canvas tunnel which leads into the launches below, which are waiting to receive it and convey it to the ship. These tunnels are called mangueras or sleeves, and some of them are immensely large. Under these the large ships haul, the tunnels leading down into their hold, and their loading is thus completed in a day or two; nevertheless, they have to wait their turn, and are sometimes detained eighty or one hundred days before that turn comes, a pretty serious affair for a ship of 1,500 or 2,000 tons, whose expenses are not less than $200 per day.—Covered with dust, let us take a glass of Elias' excellent Italian sherry, and bid adieu to the Chincha Islands.

Following up the coast, half a dozen hours bring out "Cerro Azul," a quiet nook-landing place, and port for the lovely valley of Cañete. Loveliest and most fertile of all Peru, dear old Cañete, I will not soon forget the refreshing panoramic view that stretches away before the visitor, after he leaves the little village at the port, and winds around the hills and gallops over to Casa Blanca and La Quebrada—the waving cane, the rambling vineyards, the haciendas with their groups of buildings, sugar-works, negro-quarters, and tasty belfried chapels, while donkey trains and mounted pleasure-seekers, whirling over the plain, give life to an exquisitely rural scene.

In company with young Lord C——, I've galloped away over these green plantations, exhilarated and overflowing with spirits, until, arrested by the kind invitation of some hospitable hacendado, we have dismounted to do justice to his fare. Old Cerro Azul I will not soon forget your angry curling rollers.

One morning, coming to an anchor in the little harbor, C—— (who, by the way, was making a pleasure-trip with me in my steamer) proposed going ashore. Ordering my boat, we stepped into her, and pulled away to shore. The surf was running pretty strong, but I thought nothing of it, and had passed several rollers, when the thole-pin, confining my steering oar, gave suddenly away. In a moment the boat broached to; a sea shot her ten feet in the air, and left his lordship and myself struggling in the surf. We, however, got out without much difficulty, only at the expense of a wet jacket; but it might have been worse.

CHAPTER V.

LIMA.

Discovery of Peru—Thrillingly romantic Scenes enacted by Christian Knights and Yuca Warriors—Final subjection of the Incas—City of Lima—Its Aspect from the Bay—Its Cathedral—Its Plaza—Its many Elements of Population—Its Manners and Customs—Society—Insecurity from Robbery—Hotels—Her Majesty's *Plenipo* drubbed by an American Consul—Bull-fights—Patron Saint—Departure from Lima—Sail up the Coast—Paita—Entrance to Guaquil River—The City—The Peak of Chimborazo.

"Tumble up and take a look at Lima!" was sung out down the hatchway.

And is that really Lima?—then indeed is one of the fondest of my boyhood's dreams about being realized; to tread the streets of the "City of Kings."

On the eve of manhood, when the imagination was the most powerful, when the mind was craving excitement, and when the soul was all susceptibility, daguerreotyping each hour new and opposite impressions; at that period of my life my eye chanced to light upon a History of the Conquest of Peru: attracted by its title, I resolved upon reading it, and, glancing hurriedly over the first few pages, I began to grow interested, as, with thrilling eloquence of style, the unheard of energy and daring of the Christian knights was portrayed; as they went into battle, I accompanied them, and entered with all the ardor of youth into their unequal conflicts; with rapture I drank in the seductive descriptions of Inca wealth and luxury, and forgetting my admiration of the Spaniard, sympathized with the natives in their hour of trial when Pizarro treacherously made Atahaulpa a prisoner in his own domain; following them through the whole campaign—at one time glorying in the daring bravery of the handful of Spaniards in bearding vast hosts in their mountain fastnesses, and, at another, shedding tears of sympathy over the bitter lot of the "children of the sun," robbed, and forever, of their birthright; so enraptured did I become with everything connected with this romantic country, that I resolved before I died, if I could possibly effect it, to visit Peru, every foot of whose territory was classic ground, whose rivers as they flowed along chaunted a solemn requiem, and whose heaven-soaring peaks were splendid monuments of her ancient glory.

While yet my desire to visit South America was unrealized, I stumbled upon Prescott's Peru—that masterpiece of modern literature, that perfection of prose-poetry, if I may be allowed the expression—and never did an enthusiastic reader throw himself more completely under the influence of vivid description than did I, in devouring the contents of that peerless book; with him, too, I climbed the lofty Cordillera, and drank in his glorious sketches of mountain scenery; with him I luxuriated in the fairy magnificence of the palaces of the Incas, as "In secluded vales, refreshed by gushing fountains of running waters, with favorite wives about them, they dreamed away existence in the midst of gardens, whose flowers shed soft, intoxicating odors, lulling them to repose." Unimaginative indeed would be the youth who could follow the great historian through his captivating work, and not become deeply impressed with the individuality of each locality so faithfully described, and in each and all of the *dramatis personæ*, whose prowess was so spiritedly set forth. To the hot blood of youth, the reckless bravery of a Pizarro would kindle an irrepressible enthusiasm in his veins ; the quicker beating of the heart, the glowing cheek and kindling eye, would all indicate, while reading of his feats, the intensity of interest felt in his deeds : then how much more profound would be the emotion, when gazing upon a city, whose first stone was raised by his own hands, when distinguishing from the hundreds of steeples, standing out in sharp and well-defined outline against the lofty sierra, the towers of that ancient cathedral, 'neath whose dome repose the ashes of that mighty chieftain, where for more than two hundred years they have lain undisturbed.

Seven miles in the interior lay the city, with a gradual rise of five hundred feet from the sea ; the slope occupied by plantations of waving grass and grain, with here and there an orchard of banana or of orange to relieve its monotony, and fringed with the town of Callao, its buildings and its shipping, flanked by its far famed castle, the last rallying point of Spanish tyranny upon this coast.

With rapture I gazed upon the scene, gilded by the rising sunbeam, listening to the sweet bells summoning to mass, which, mingled with the low roar of the surf, softly stole through the quiet silence of a Sabbath morn ; for the harbor was resting from its weekly labors, and no sound arose to break the magic spell of dreamy revery. Two short hours found me kneeling, with some thousand others, listening to the strains of the organ as they pealed 'neath the dark arches of that grand old cathedral; before its altars of massive gold and silver, long processions of priests, arrayed in jewelled robes of fabulous value, preceded by acolytes with swinging censer, with measured tread and with many genuflexions, passed, slowly repeating with sonorous voice the holy petitions of their mass-books; the vast multitude, with bowed head and down-cast eye, apparently absorbed in the sublimity of the service; the brilliant blazes of a thousand tapers, their bright rays reflected from silver plate and glistening jewel, contrasted strangely with the awful gloom of this vast edifice, which, notwithstanding a morning's sun without, was shrouded in almost impenetrable darkness; spectral, indeed, appeared its vaulted arches and its long, dim aisles, with here and there an altar lit up by a few dim tapers, or a confessional before whose grated window a veiled penitent was whispering her shortcomings.

Beneath my feet was all that remains of the conquering Pizarro! and beside me the crouching form of the conquered! No longer worshipping the sun, but a slave in belief as well as corporeally, he now sends up his meaningless prayers before the same altar where worshipped the usurper! Long after the crowd had risen from their knees and had gone their ways, and the organ's trembling notes had ceased reverberating along the groined roof, I remained pacing the gloomy aisles, looking with awe upon the hideous representations of the Passion and the Descent from the Cross, painted by men whose only merit must have lain in their ability to impart a vivid idea of the horrible.

Groping about, I came upon the Sacristan, who offered to show me, if I *wished* to see them, the remains of Pizarro!

* * * * * *

And is that all that's left of the conqueror of Peru? Could those skeleton arms be those that had once wielded a battle-axe, before which no Christian knight could stand, no Inca-host could maintain itself? As he thundered forth his well-known battle-cry, "Saint Yago, to the rescue?" How humbling to human ambition the thought that the conqueror of half the world lay stretched before us a withered mummy!

Oppressed by the unwholesome damp of the cathedral vaults, I was glad to reach again the open air, and stepping forth into it found myself on the Grand Plaza of Lima; its centre is ornamented by a fountain with large reservoirs, the water flowing from the mouths of four lions, the lower basins resting upon a pedestal some ten feet high, the upper supported by a column, rising from which is a figure of Fame surmounted by a ball; this is quite a fine specimen of old Spanish art, and was executed some two hundred years ago, giving character to the square.

This is the rendezvous for half the water-carriers of Lima, who form an important element of the community; important, for every household in the city is supplied by them with every drop of water consumed, who, in their turn obtain it from the fountains. Each aguador or water-carrier (all of whom, with few exceptions, are negroes, and of the very worst class) owns his burro, a little jackass, on whose back is slung a frame-work, holding on either side a cask capable of containing five gallons of water, the negro himself sitting on the poor little animal's haunches behind his load, guiding him by striking him on either side of his head contrary to the direction which he wishes him to take, with a long pole which serves the double purpose of cudgel and as a support for the full cask, when its vis-à-vis is emptied. The fountain, as I said before, is the trysting place for a hundred or so of these negroes, and, of course, a perfect pandemonium when all are assembled. These Zambos, exuberant with their native wit, let no opportunity pass unimproved for a practical joke, which is the cause of constant and uproarious mirth, and oftentimes of bloody and fatal brawls; vociferating in the loud key peculiar to the African, their voices can be heard for a long distance, drowning every other sound. Fifty times a day have I gone to my window, during the period of a subsequent residence, thinking from the noise that a serious disturbance was taking place, but each time finding that there was nothing very serious the matter. I remember one day when riding across the plaza accompanied by a friend, being attracted by a row causing more than ordinary commotion; reining up our horses, we forced our way among the crowd. Struggling to maintain his turn at the spout to fill his casks, was a half-naked Chinaman, who had evidently only recently taken up the profession of aguador, and around him were some fifty blacks trying to thrust him from his position, he hanging on like grim death, his countenance perfectly distorted with rage, his eyes bloodshot, and foam running from his mouth, never did I look upon such a personification of passion as he struggled with his tormentors; still he clung to the spout with incredible tenacity, until at last suddenly relaxing his hold, freeing himself, and seizing an immense bamboo-pole, and bending himself backward to give force to the blow, he brought it down on the heads of his assailants with terrific violence, and so sudden had been this movement, and so actively were the blows followed up, that in a moment the ground was covered with the prostrate forms of half a dozen negroes. I can see him now, as with distended eyes and foaming lips, with hair standing on end, he rained the bamboo on their black skulls. Knives were soon drawn, and my companion, knowing the poor Coolie would be murdered if left to the tender mercies of the mob, seized him by his pig-tail, and, dashing his spurs into his horse's flanks, in a moment cleared the crowd, and was at the palace gate. Slinging the poor devil, crazy with fear and rage, into the portal, among the soldiers, we rode off. The next night he was assassinated!

On my right hand was the palace, occupying the whole of the east side of the Plaza—a long, low, rambling building, over which waved the Peruvian standard, and around whose gateways squads of dirty soldiers were lounging; a palace only by courtesy, it looked more like a huge stable. This was formerly the palace of the viceroys, and in a long hall were, until recently, hanging the portraits of their whole line, from Pizarro down, which have, however, been transferred to the national Museum. Some years after this, while living opposite to this building, I bore it a deadly spite; for each morning at day-break a réveillé of drums and bugles awoke all the echoes of the square, breaking the rest of the sleeping neighbors, loud enough, indeed, to awake the dead beneath the cathedral's dome; they tooted and tooted away to an extent incredible to any one unacquainted with the strength of lung vouchsafed to the Spanish bugler.

The other two sides of the square were formed by long rows of buildings, two stories high; the upper story projecting over the sidewalk, forming a colonade, along which are the shops of the dry-goods merchants, resplendent with all the wealth of French, Italian, and Indian stuffs, and so disposed as to make a brilliant display, and to attract the eye of the beautiful Limanian as she saunters under their cool arches. Between the pillars, busily pursuing their avocation, are embroiderers of gold and silver, with here and there an Indian flower-girl, with her bouquets tastily arranged for sale ; and outside are the ice-cream venders, extending along the two sides of the square, and whose benches are always occupied. The Limanians have a singular fondness for ices at all hours, but more particularly when they first get up in the morning ; and from daybreak until seven or eight o'clockit is almost impossible to get a vacant seat. Men, women, and children all congregate here ; and really it used to give me a cramp, to see a delicate woman gulping down the contents of an enormous glass, holding at least a pint of orange or lemon ice, on an empty stomach.

In the evening the whole surface of the Plaza is taken possession of by itinerant cooks, who, bringing their portable furnaces, provisions, chairs and tables, improvise at a stroke a kitchen and a dining-room, and at once set to work to compound national messes, such as the Peruvians delight in, the populace wandering around from table to table, stuffing themselves with ices and greases, which latter is the principal compound of all Peruvian dishes—of course the whole atmosphere is redolent of smoke and garlic.

The scene nightly presented from the balc[illegible] overhanging the square, was always entertaining—the indistinct forms of the cathedral and palace—the moving multitude gaily wandering around from booth to booth, and across the long shadows that shot from the shop-windows ; the little furnaces glowing red, and the hundred discordant cries of the hosts of pedlars vociferously praising their wares.

Suddenly the door of the cathedral is thrown open, a procession sallies forth, their low chant is heard, and with each a taper in his hand, they wind along the front of the cathedral, and a tinkling bell announces it to be the host being taken to the bedside of some dying man. At the first sound of the bell every man of this joyous, noisy multitude drops on his knees as if he were shot, every tongue is stilled, and a death-like silence ensues, unbroken, save by the doleful chant as they hurry on, on their gloomy errand. No sooner are they past, than Bedlam is again let loose, and the row is greater than before. To a foreign observer all this is extremely curious; the strange customs, the style of dress, the sudden and apparently deep devotion paid to religious forms, all strike the casual observer with great force.

On the northwest corner of the Plaza, occupying nearly half of the north side is Morin's "Hotel de los Baños," probably the best kept inn in South America, the great centering point for all foreigners, whatever their nation, but more particularly the Americans and English; having the best location in Lima, and looking out on the grand Plaza, and down the whole length of the Calle de Commercio, the principal street, and having a very good *table d'hôte*, and very fair sleeping-rooms, some indeed with parlors attached, and very handsomely fitted up, it offers great inducements to the traveller. The chambers and dining-rooms are in the altos or second story, while the ground floor is devoted to billiard and bath-rooms, and a handsome *café;* here at sunset the fashionables resort to sip their coffee and liquors, while some skillful players contest a game of billiards. The style of these buildings is very peculiar, for while the ground floor is built with great regard to strength, the alto or second story is constructed as slightly as possible, on account of earthquakes ; the long galleries running in every direction, along whose sides the apartments are arranged, being without a roof ; thus in going from one room to another one is obliged to go in the open air, no great drawback to one's comfort however, in a country where it never rains, and the thermometer rarely falls below 60° Fahrenheit.

One suit of rooms on the corner of the Calle de Commercio and the plaza were really quite elegant, fitted up by a French upholsterer in the last French style, with handsome mirrors, and lit by gas, and in them I was domiciliated on a subsequent occasion with my family, much to our comfort. Shortly before our occupancy quite an interesting scene was enacted in them. On board of one of the steamers coming down from Panama, happened to be passengers the English envoy to Peru and the American minister to Chili, and his wife ; on the arrival of the vessel at Callao, both diplomatists sent their servants up to Lima to Morin's Hotel to engage rooms, but neither of them speaking Spanish, the major-domo, by some mistake or other thought that they both represented one master (it being an unusual thing for two envoys-extraordinary to get aboard the same steamer in that part of the world), and consequently assigned them the *same* suite of rooms. In an hour or two, up drives the American and his wife, and he is bowed into his apartments. Well pleased at being so snugly quartered, he refreshes himself, makes his toilet, and goes out to call on the resident minister, leaving his wife to rest (in deshabille), from her fatigue. Scarcely has he left the house before up drives the English minister, and blusteringly demands to be led to his apartments, and the servant conducts him to the door of the room occupied by the American. Meanwhile the landlord smelling a rat, and instantly discovering his blunder, bowingly approaches H. M. minister, begs that monsieur will forgive the error, and that he shall have rooms a thousand times more comfortable, and all that sort of thing ; but it's no go ; the Englishman swears he will have the rooms, and commences knocking at the door. The American lady, throwing on a wrapper, opens the door, and on learning the cause of the disturbance, begs "his majesty" to desist until her husband returns when all will be arranged ; but his majesty is not to be appeased, insists upon the *woman's* leaving at once, and uses most insulting language—the lady seeking protection in another room. Meanwhile, the Yankee minister returns, and on learning the cause of the row, and that his wife has been insulted, seizes the unlucky Briton by the neck and gives him a most tremendous hiding, breaking his cane over his head ; he then walks to his writing-desk and pens a challenge which a friend bears; but his majesty is not a fighting man, and so the affair ends.

The Limanians have a most remarkable way of naming their streets, by what motive actuated I cannot conceive, unless it is to mystify strangers, for instead of calling a street running in a direct line by one name for its whole length, they call it by forty different ones at least, each square having a different appellation. This leads to endless confusion, and in order in some degree to modify it, they tell you, on inquiring for a person's residence, that he lives in such a street and such a number "in San Pedro or Santo Domingo," etc.—that is to say, that the street is in the immediate vicinity of one or the other of these churches, and there being some sixty of them in Lima, the place sought for is pretty certain to be in the neighborhood of some one or other of them. I had ample experience of the inconvenience attending this during a campaign of house-hunting, which extended over a space of some three weeks, during which time I believe I inspected some two or three hundred houses before I could get suited. Rents were most enormous—from $1,500 to $2,500 per annum for anything like a decent house, and they were invariably so excessively filthy and out of repair, that it would have required an equivalent to the first year's rent to put the house in habitable order.

One of the greatest nuisances incidental to a residence in Lima, is the difficulty of getting decent servants. In fact, there are none in the country; the negroes are insolent and robbers, and sometimes assassins besides, and the Indians, or Choles (half-breeds), are heavy, stupid, and lazy; yet for all that, wages are from $18 to $25 per month. No one can keep a servant unless he advances his wages, gives him a good chance to steal, and lends him a couple of dollars or so every month; otherwise they go off and leave you in the lurch whenever they feel inclined.

The washerwomen are the most independent persons of their class that I ever saw. One being recommended to me by the hotel-keeper, I made a bargain with her for $2 per dozen, besides buying soap and starch! and she was to wash and iron the clothes, and bring them to me in ten days. Ten days passed, and fifteen too, still no woman. Getting her direction, I set out to hunt her up, and after a walk of two hours or so, I spied her den; and there she sat, smoking and chatting with a priest, as comfortable as you please. She begged me to walk in and be seated; when, on my asking the reason why the clothes had not been sent home, she very coolly informed me that they were at the pawnbroker's, and that she hadn't money to get them out! There was no help for it—no use applying to the police, for in that case I would have lost my money and shirts too, so with a very bad grace I gave her the money to get them out, waiting another week for them to be washed.

The streets leading out of the Plaza are the most fashionable—the Calle de Commercio being the favorite promenade. Its sides, lined with beautiful shops, in whose windows every article of luxury devised by man is exposed for sale; judging by the "nouveautés Parisiennes" offered, one might imagine oneself in the Rue St. Honoré. These shops are invariably kept by Frenchmen, and tended by pretty young Frenchwomen, which is no disadvantage to their business. From the south side runs the Calle de Bodegones, in which are many of the wholesale establishments and offices of the heavy mercantile firms; indeed, they all centre in this vicinity. The streets running out of the square and back of the cathedral, are likewise appropriated to merchants' warehouses, and present, during business hours, an extremely animated appearance. Many of the houses in this section have a modern look, being two and three stories in height, with modern fronts. Proceeding in this direction, we come upon the San Pedro quarter, decidedly the most aristocratic portion of the city, and several of the houses, dating very far back, show fine specimens of carving. The old mansion of Torre Tagle is most elaborately and artistically ornamented in that way, and well worth examination. The church of San Pedro covers an enormous plot of ground, but has no architectural beauty, and is not at present very influential. It was formerly occupied by the Jesuits, and was the wealthiest church in Lima, but since their departure its glory has departed.

Further on, turning to the left, you come upon the Plaza de la Inquisicion, where many an "*auto-da-fé*" has been celebrated, sanctioned by the presence of the viceroys. On the abolition of the inquisitorial power, the maddened populace rushed into the palace and completely gutted it, liberating the unfortunate sufferers from confinement. The building is now occupied by the National Assembly. It is very extensive, and besides a chamber for the senators and deputies, there are also offices for the different departments of state. The chamber of deputies is a long room with hangings, with some good old pictures on the walls, and with elaborately carved seats. There are likewise galleries for lady visitors. The discussions are frequently very stormy, and if not conducted in a spirit to please the governmental ear, they are occasionally terminated by a corporal's guard appearing among them. In the year 1856, Ramon Castillo, the President, posted a park of artillery in the Alameda, and bearing upon the chamber of deputies, after which he strode into the hall, and intimated "that if certain obnoxious motions were not withdrawn, he would blow the whole party to —— !" A second Cromwell! although I very much doubt if the material of which the Peruvian Assembly was formed was such as was to be found in the praise God bare-bone Parliament.

The city is divided into two parts by the river Rimac, and one of the streets leading out of the square crosses it on a handsome stone bridge, 550 feet long, with six arches, and thirty-seven feet above the water. This bridge, built two hundred years ago, is a noble piece of engineering, having resisted the quaking of the earthquakes of two centuries, during one of which the town of Callao disappeared entirely, and half the city of Lima was buried in ruins.

Crossing this bridge, and turning off to the right, on the banks of the river is the grand Alameda, the most beautiful park perhaps, in the world—long avenues of shade trees, extending a mile or two, and whose branches, embracing each other, form a perfect bower or leafy arcade for near a league. Here all the fashion of Lima, in the evening, resort, either in coach or on horseback, consequently the whole cavalcade have to cross the bridge—and here the exquisites resort, where, seating themselves on the parapet, they quiz the senoritas as they pass by.

The view from this bridge is very fine. The walled sides of the river, from which quaint old buildings of the style of two centuries back arise, overhanging it—the beautiful Alaméda, with its rich luxuriance of green—the far-off mountains, and the stream itself, as like a silver thread it winds among the rocks and sand-banks forming the river's bed; turning round, one sees it still pursuing its course among verdant meadows, until it pours its waters into the sea, seven miles beyond.

A square or two off from the plaza, in another direction, is the post office, or the "*Administracion de Corréos*," as it is called, which deserves particular mention from the singularity of the method of carrying on its business. Necessarily, from the widely extended territory, the postal ramifications are very extensive, and it requires considerable talent to regulate them; still, upon entering the office, one would never imagine that there was any system observed whatever, everything being apparently intrusted to a few boys, while the letters and papers seem thrown together in inextricable confusion. This is not, however, the case; and I must acknowledge that one has about as good a chance of getting a letter addressed to him in Peru, as he would in North America. A most extraordinary mode is used to inform people who have letters, to that effect. There being no boxes, an alphabetical list is made out, consisting, perhaps of a couple of thousand names, which is hung in a conspicuous place, and which one can consult at his pleasure. If he finds his name, he observes the number corresponding, and on calling it out at the window, he gets his letter. This, of course, is a most laborious operation, but as it was the custom of their forefathers, they stick to it. On the occasion of my first visit, I was particularly struck with the dead-and-alive aspect of Lima, it seemed like all other Spanish towns, fast falling into decay; but subsequent visits showed a very sensible improvement. In every quarter of the town houses were being rebuilt and remodelled, and forgetting their dread of earthquakes, they were almost invariably two full stories in height, not with the jalousied alto, but in the out-and-out European style. One building, in particular, I remember, *el Hotel de Europa*, in the Calle de Commércio, was a splendid modern building, three stories high. Also the private dwelling-house of Candamo, the richest man in Lima, really a splendid affair in the Bodegonés. But, although when I last was in Lima it had been long since finished, still the owner (an exceedingly penurious man) only occupied one little room in it, furnished with an iron bed and washstand; the rest of the house he felt too poor to furnish. This Candamo is a Chilian of about fifty years old, who came young into Peru, and has amassed an immense fortune, so much so that it is a byword, "Rich as Candamo;" and, like all enormously rich men, *very near.* He owns the largest part of the railroad between Lima and Callao, which is extremely lucrative. The other proprietor is a wealthy Englishman. Each night the daily receipts are counted up, when Candamo's portion is sent up to his house, as is the Englishman's, reserving a certain percentage to pay incidental expenses. As a matter of course, Candamo is fawned upon by all who have need of him, but he is a man of uncommonly strong mind, and is not to be humbugged. Ambitious mothers with grown-up daughters are particularly sweet upon him, but thus far without making any impression upon his heart of gold. Indeed very recently, a foreign lady, the mother of some very beautiful daughters, angled for him and got a very fair nibble; and ill-natured people about Lima used to say that he had gone off with the bait, but we believe it was not so.

These buildings I mention from their prominence and elegance of style, but there are hundreds of others which have been improved within the last four or five years, and which would be an ornament to any city. The style of furniture now in vogue is precisely the latest Parisian style, and of the most elegant description; most of it being manufactured in the country by French artists. It is sold at the most exorbitant rates. The old style of Spanish chair and sofa is rapidly disappearing.

It would seem rather a dangerous experiment to build in the European style in this country, where the ground is so very unstable, especially as slight shocks are continually occurring, to remind one that, during the last three centuries, Lima has been twice almost totally destroyed by earthquakes. Indeed during one of my first visits, there was one of sufficient force to send the whole population, at the dead of night, bare-legged to the public square for security. They are, however, now of rare occurrence, and people begin to think that they are never to suffer again. As for myself, however, whenever I have been in Peru, I never could forget that there was an unpleasant possibility of being at any moment buried alive, and rarely did I awake at night, and cast my eyes upon the thick, jail-like walls of my bed-chamber, that I did not feel an uncomfortable sensation of dread, lest they should suddenly take it into their head to fall on top of me. It is highly amusing to be able to tell a lively story about being turned out of one's bed at midnight, and rushing in company with a few thousand other half-naked men and women into some open space for safety. But the reality is not so very amusing; that I can vouch for. One who has never experienced the sensation is apt to say, "What an absurd sight it must have been!" But I can assure any such person that on such an occasion, the sense of the ridiculous is swallowed up by emotions of a very different nature.

At the period of my arrival in Peru, there was no railroad between the port and the capital; consequently, one was obliged to go on horseback, which (the distance being only seven miles) would have been no great drawback to one's comfort had the road been moderately good; but it was execrable. During the time of the viceroys the road had been well paved and in good condition, but since the independence, I doubt if an hour's work had been expended upon it, and, consequently, it was in a terrible condition; the former pavement, lying broken and scattered about, only served to injure the poor animal's feet, while the dust arising was positively awful, as one can imagine would be the case upon a much-travelled road in a tropical country, where the soil is very light, and where it never rains. In addition to this, it was infested, in common with all other Peruvian roads, with bands of robbers, and not a day passed but some poor devil was relieved of his money and assassinated. Its very propinquity to Lima furnishing greater security to the banditti, the authorities never taking the slightest notice of their outrages. Gentlemen having business between the two towns always went well armed, and generally in companies; even then, oftentimes, being obliged to fight. A good old gentleman, a Mr. Pheifer, one of the oldest foreign residents in Lima, used to tell the following story.

He was riding along this road one night, and suddenly, when least expecting it, he was attacked by half a dozen robbers, some of whom, seizing his horse by the head, forced him to dismount, and, finding he had no money on his person, were about proceeding to extremities, when he exclaimed, "Gentlemen, I am Don Federico Pheifer, you doubtless all know me; now I promise, if you will unhand me and set me on my horse, that I will lead you to my house, where, after giving you a good supper, I will dismiss you with a golden ounce apiece, and say nothing of the affair." The robbers knew their man, and setting him on his horse, accompanied him home. Arriving at his house, he invited the gentlemen to dismount, and entering the house, begged them to be seated, telling his wife to order supper immediately; without at all understanding what it all meant, madam presided with great grace, and the repast being concluded, each guest receiving his ounce, took his departure ; of course Don Federico never divulged the names of these scamps, otherwise his life would have paid the forfeit. Poor old gentleman, his days are numbered now, and he has passed away; for years an active and influential citizen of Lima, he was respected by all who knew him, and by his wealth and influence, was enabled to lend great assistance to his needy countrymen. Having an affection of the chest, he found that he could not breathe freely at night in the city, and consequently, every evening would find him mounted on his tall, black horse, at the gate of our chacara, and right glad were we always to welcome him, for he was a genial companion, and one of the very few really *reliable* men on the coast of South America.

The banditti, who, by the way, are composed, generally speaking, of runaway slaves, who, after their work is done, sally forth in the evening, by way of recreation, to try their hand at highway robbery, do not confine themselves to robbing travellers, but often attack the country houses, pillaging them and murdering their inmates. A case in point occurred but a few years since, of rather a peculiar kind, upon the premises of an English surgeon, a Dr. Gallagher, who had a hospital at a place called Bella Vista, midway between Callao and Lima. The doctor and his wife, who were residing there at that time, had retired as usual, and fallen asleep, when they were awakened by a flash of light in their room, and on opening their eyes, to their dismay saw four or five men in their apartment, one of whom, ordering them to keep silence, under pain of death, held a huge knife in readiness to enforce his commands, the others proceeding to rummage the apartment. Of course the doctor and his good lady were struck dumb at first, but gradually recovering from their fear, commenced revolving in their minds what was to be done under the circumstances. The lady, suddenly remembering that she had an elegant diamond on her finger, had the presence of mind to let it slip under the bedclothes, without the movement being discovered. While the robbers were investigating the wardrobes, Mrs. G. noticed that they were appropriating a valuable moire-antique dress, which she valued very highly, so much so, that she resolved not to let it go without a struggle; addressing the robbers, she said: "Gentlemen, will you not do me the favor to leave me that dress, as it was a present, and I value it very highly?" Quite abashed at her assurance, they laid the dress down, begging the lady to *accept* it. After peering into every drawer and trunk in the room, they approached the bed, and ordered the occupants to show their hands, and at once relieved the doctor of a valuable ring, and were about taking one of plain gold from the hands of his wife, when she again demurred, on the plea that it was her wedding-ring, and they again acceded to her request; courteously bidding the worthy couple good night, they left them to finish their nap, with the intimation, that any attempt at alarm would be visited with certain death. Some twenty years ago, robberies were so very frequent, audacious and successful, that it became apparent there must be a regularly organized gang, and that its leader must necessarily be a man of great talent, and possessing universal knowledge of all that was transpiring in the mercantile circles; the evil became so great, that people were absolutely afraid to trust each other, each one looking with a species of distrust upon his neighbor, so patent was it that some one in whom all had confidence, was their betrayer.

About this time, a merchant, who had considerable money in his house, received an anonymous letter, informing him that on the next night, his house would be robbed, and advising him to call in his friends to assist him in defending it. The merchant at once called a secret meeting of the principal commercial men whom he knew he could trust, to devise the necessary steps, when it was universally determined by all present to volunteer to guard the house threatened, and the arrangements were about being made, when a Scotchman, who had previously said nothing, with a preliminary cough, arose and said, "Gentlemen, I don't look upon this communication in the light that you do; I believe it is a decoy, to concentrate our attention upon this one house, in order to give them an opportunity to rob some other establishment; therefore, I move that we all remain in our own houses, and prepare for their defence." By dint of argument, all became convinced that his was the proper view of the case, and a lucky thought it was for the Scotchman, for about midnight, his own house was attacked, and the assailants only driven off after a severe fight, during which, however, they were successful in capturing the notorious robber-chief, who proved to be neither more nor less than a young American, a cashier in one of the largest houses in the country, of whom no one had ever had the slightest suspicion, he having always acquitted himself to the satisfaction of his employers, and whose accounts and balances had always been a model of correctness; unknown to them, however, he had been a heavy gambler, and had formed the acquaintance of certain bad characters, who, in return for information given them, kept him supplied with funds, and in this way, for years, he had betrayed his friends. On being arrested, he was cast into jail, and notwithstanding the efforts of the American minister to prevent it (for his family's sake), he was formally executed.

During all my own travels in Peru, I never was molested but on one occasion. In returning from Lima to the port, in company with three others, late one night, a party of horsemen leaped the hedge some hundred yards in advance, and awaited our approach; simultaneously we drew our revolvers, and dashing spurs into our horses' sides, rushed past them and gave them a volley; never holding up till we reached Callao; a riderless horse galloped into Lima half an hour afterwards, and a dead Zambo was found on the benches of the Alameda. Who shot him, we did not know or care, but we kept our own counsel, otherwise we might have passed a year in jail.

If there was a confusion of tongues at Babel, there is a greater confusion of color and of race in Lima. Besides the hordes of French, English, Germans, Italians, Greeks, and Spaniards that throng the streets, there are at least twenty different half-castes, that maintain as marked a distinction from each other as do the natives of India. The Mulatto, the Mestizo, the Indian, the Chino, the Chino blanco, the Cholo, the Cuarteron, the Zambo, and an infinity of others, all possess a certain pride of caste upon which they plume themselves whenever the occasion presents itself. Thus, the Mulatto will taunt the Zambo with his blacker skin, though they may have been born of the same father; the Cholo will scornfully avoid the "Indio brúto," as he calls him, although to him he may bear the same affinity as does the Mulatto to the Zambo. Individuals of either caste are frequently thus designated instead of being called by name, thus in calling your half-breed Indian servant you would say: "come here, Cholo," or addressing a beautiful woman in whom by long experience in the art, you can detect the half-caste, you would say without giving offence, "good evening, lovely Mestiza." The Cholos, a cross between the white man and the Indian, perform as a general thing, the duties of house servants, and are a lazy, inoffensive race; the women, some of them very beautiful, occupy no very high position in the social scale, being generally the mistresses of the middle classes. The Mulattoes are a very numerous class, and are generally occupied in shop-keeping—the females are also extremely beautiful, and *extremely* frail. The full-blooded Indians I always looked upon with a sympathetic eye, for although so many years have elapsed since their subjugation, they still seem the rightful owners of the soil. Rather below the medium height, they are exceedingly stout and athletic, with the heavy, sullen look, characteristic of all the American aborigines; they seldom occupy any menial position for any length of time; soon tiring, they disappear, escaping to their homes in the mountains. The ranks of the army are almost entirely supplied from them, and they make capital soldiers, being possessed of great natural bravery, but unfortunately, their officers being deficient in that article, they are not often led to the deadly breach—poor devils! they seldom enlist of their own accord, but are barbarously pressed into the service, torn away from their families and sent down to the sea-coast, where they pine and languish from home-sickness, and the enervating effects of the climate. The press-gang is here to be seen in all its horror; the poor Indian, little suspecting the cruel fate awaiting him, is seized in his hut, or in his corn-field, and with his hands tied behind him, is set upon a horse and driven off, perhaps forever, from wife, family, home, and all he holds dear!

What wonder, then, that his brow is dark and lowering, that he wears an aspect of sullen misery and despair?

There are large numbers of women-followers accompanying the army, who appear to possess superhuman powers of endurance; marching in the van, with their own wardrobes as well as their husbands', their cooking utensils, and perhaps, a baby or two, they unweariedly plod along, and reaching the halting-place, without resting, build their fires and prepare their husbands' food; thus day after day, week after week, they toil over burning plains, mountain passes and frozen snows, always the same patient enduring, and faithful beings.

The people of Lima are to be seen to the greatest advantage when assembled to witness a bull-fight, in the spacious arena, situated midway on the Alameda, perhaps the finest affair in the world of its kind, and capable of containing ten thousand spectators.

The performances usually take place on Sunday afternoon, and for an hour or two previously, the streets leading to it are thronged with a motley crowd pouring thither, composed of all ranks and conditions, some on foot, and others rolling along in elegant equipages.

The scene presented within is a most brilliant one, magnificently attired ladies, with brilliant jewels, seated in their luxurious boxes, thousands of the lower orders, in their bright and picturesque costumes, together with the gorgeous uniforms of the president and his suite, while a fine band of music gives an additional zest to the affair.

Suddenly the hum of ten thousand voices is stilled, a gate

opens, and half a dozen fantastically dressed men, each with a small red flag in his hand, rush in, and bow before the President's box; following them, come mounted horsemen, armed with long spears, and pennons flying, who after curvetting about the ring, draw up in line, and then in rushes the bull, with a maddened, infuriated look, head down and tail in air ; suddenly he pauses, and raising his head, gives a savage roar, and then makes for the men in the ring; they disperse in all directions. He then dashes at the horses, whose riders with great dexterity avoid his attacks, irritating him, however, still more by pricking him with their lances; sometimes, however, the bull is successful in putting in a blow with his horns, when he gores the horse, and capsizing him, rolls him and his rider in the dust. The footmen then approach and divert his attention, and adroitly avoid his attacks by waving flags, which they hold in their hands before his eyes, and as he makes at the flag, they jump on one side, and escape collision. This goes on for some time, the men showing great address in evading his attacks.

The bull by this time becomes frantic, and his impotent rage is fearful to witness, as with glaring and blood-shot eyeballs, and foaming nostrils, he stands at bay, quivering in every joint, and sending forth bellowings of anger and defiance. Armed with small reeds, tipped with steel and filled with combustibles, and ornamented with little flags, his persecutors now approach him, and at every opportunity hurl at him one of these little missiles, which piercing his flesh, explode with the concussion, and produce painful, smarting wounds, which increase his frenzy, to an incredible degree. In vain he endeavors to annihilate his opponents; rushing at one, he is pursued by others, until paralyzed by rage, with lowering brows, he warily watches his tormentors, and only attacks at intervals. A flourish of trumpets, and in comes the matador, attired in black velvet, after the style of Philip II.; bowing to the president and the audience, he is received with thundering acclamations ; his esquire then hands him a long Damascus blade. Examining it with critical care, he satisfies himself of its temper, apparently perfectly unconcerned at the propinquity of the bull, who presents a most threatening aspect ; in the meanwhile, the others withdraw and leave to the matador the field. Taking his position, he unsheathes his weapon and awaits the charge. There is something majestic in the cool indifference with which a single man, with a frail blade, awaits the onset of an infuriated demon. Pawing the ground, and sending forth roars of rage and agony, the bull measures the distance between himself and his antagonist, and charging, the earth fairly trembles with his violence. The matador cooly poises his weapon, and with scarce an effort, it descends with unerring certainty into the spinal marrow of the brute, who, with an agonizing groan, sinks on his knees, the life blood spirting from his mouth and nostrils, when after a few ineffectual efforts, he rolls over, and his glazed eyeballs, announce his death. Thousands of vivas hail the successful matador, and purses lined with gold, and boquets, fall in showers at his feet. Another blast of trumpets, and four magnificently caparisoned horses are driven furiously around the ring ; suddenly they halt before the carcass of the dead animal, and hooking fast to it, draw it rapidly out of sight.

This scene is enacted over and over again, until half a dozen bulls are slain ; most cruel sport, and the sympathies of Europeans generally go with the bull. I, on several occasions, both in Mexico, Manila, and in Peru, have seen men and horses killed by the infuriated animal, and I must say that I never felt much commiseration for them. One must admire the cool bravery and skill of the matador, and the address and daring of the picadores, but when he sees the agonized eye of the bull in vain looking for sympathy, and hears his heart-rending groans of despair, he finds his feelings enlisted on behalf of the persecuted animal.

It is a gay scene to witness the exodus of the thousands from the amphitheatre, including every class, from the president to the lowest peon who grovels in the streets. Diamonds and rags, delicate female lovliness and coarse flaunting courtesans pour forth together : vehicles of all sorts await their fortunate possessors, while battalions of elegant horses impatiently curvetting, await their masters. Pouring out from the gates, the masses disperse themselves along the magnificent arcades of the Alameda, some sauntering along enjoying the exciting scene, others resting upon the benches beside the river, watch the gay cortége of horsemen and carriages filled with beauty and elegance, rolling along the drive.

The grand gala day of Lima is the celebration of the birthday of Santa Rosa, its patron saint. She was born in 1586, of poor parents, and while yet young, displayed uncommon holiness, and did voluntary penance at the age of six years, when she consecrated herself to God, and took oath of perpetual celibacy. At fifteen she was examined by theologians and entered holy orders ; her life was most exemplary, and filled with examples of devotion to the cause of Christ. She died in the year 1617, and her obsequies were celebrated with great pomp ; the archbishop and viceroy assisting. She was canonized in 1671, and the 26th day of August was fixed upon as her festival, and it is celebrated in Lima by a grand procession ; in the church of St. Domingo there is a fine marble statue of her reclining alongside the altar. The whole town is in a state of excitement—troops being marshalled—societies being assembled—males and females hurrying to the cathedral, where high mass is celebrated before an immense assemblage, among whom are the president and high officers of church and state. The interior of the cathedral is magnificently decorated—altars covered with gold and silver and diamonds—the walls adorned with the richest drapery, with fringe and spangles of gold : innumerable and variously colored wax tapers glow from massive chandeliers. Priests clothed in their richest sacerdotal robes, move slowly backward and forward to the lovely cadence of the grand old organ, whose tones are softened by a flood of liquid female voices. On an elegant pedestal, hung with garlands, is the heavenly figure of the saint, crowned with a tiara of diamonds of fabulous value, robed in satin, sprinkled with costliest jewels, holding in her hand a brilliant, sparkling rose, composed entirely of diamonds.

Mass is then said, after which the procession is formed amid the crash of artillery and the din of pealing bells, the order of the procession being as follows :

Soldiers, bare-headed ;
Acolytes in surplices and red breeches ;
Novice, bearing a silver cross ;
Officers of colleges and students, robed in crimson ;
National deputies ;
Lawyers and magistrates ;

The President, with his staff;
Banner of the cross, borne by priests, followed by Acolytes, singing;
Choiristers and musicians;
Twenty virgins, dressed in white;
Image of the Saint, surrounded by priests and bare-headed friars, accompanied by a body of soldiers;
The Archbishop, under a silken canopy, borne by six priests, each holding a silver staff.

Following these come the persons composing the different professions and trades, and bodies of troops with bands of music, bringing up the rear guard: the houses in the streets through which they pass, being decorated with elegant hangings, and festoons of gay flowers; the whole atmosphere ringing with artillery and redolent of gunpowder, while the population follow "en masse."

The young ladies on a day like this appear "en grande tenue," and beaux, got up within an inch of their lives, promenade the streets, taking advantage of the opportunity so seldom offered for ogling the beauties.

I LEAVE LIMA.

Gliding along the barren coasts of Peru, dreamily gazing at the interminable chains of lofty mountains rising one above the other—suddenly from out the clouds stands forth grim old Chimborazo, his hoary head covered with the snows of centuries; twenty thousand feet in air, yet so distant from us as scarce to o'ertop the surrounding peaks of half his height.

Moving rapidly though noiselessly through the water, we soon come up with the river Guayaquil, a noble stream, dividing the republics of Equador and Peru—at its mouth eight miles in width, and bearing down a swollen current, discoloring the sea for miles. Entering it, we breast the swift current, and, puffing away, leave behind us the island of Puna, and, after six hours' steaming, find ourselves abreast the city of Guayaquil, a town of considerable size and commercial importance. It presents a very pretty appearance as it runs straggling along the river's banks, faced by a fine stone quay extending for a couple of miles, where each morning myriads of canoes, laden with luscious fruits and other products of the country, resort to dispose of their little cargoes ; thus giving it an exceedingly lively and animated appearance.

The fruits of this province are superb; the orange and banana here attain their highest perfection, while the Guayaquil pine-apple is incomparable ; no fruit of the kind on earth can equal it either in size or perfection of flavor.

The hat so widely known as the Panama hat, costing from $2 to $150, is here manufactured. They differ from other straw hats in being made of a single piece, and of great lightness and flexibility. The plant from which they are made is the jipi-jape, and looks like a palm ; the leaves are gathered before they unfold, all the ribs and coarser veins being removed, and the rest, without being separated from the stalk, is reduced to thread. After exposure to the sun for a day or two, the straw is tied into a knot, and immersed in boiling water until it becomes white; this is then hung in a shady place, and bleached for several days; the straw is then ready for use, and made into cigar and card-cases, and put to innumerable other uses. Hats are made on blocks placed between the knees, requiring to be constantly pressed to the breast; the plaiting is exceedingly troublesome, commencing at the crown and ending at the brim, requiring of course more or less time, according to their fineness. These hats are universally worn on the coast and in the West India islands; those generally used by the higher classes costing from forty to sixty dollars.

CHAPTER VI.

PANAMA.

Panama—Its magnificent Bay, studded with bright Islets—Ancient Appearance of the City—Sufferings of Emigrants from Fever, Cholera, and Want—We retire to Flamingo Island, and there luxuriate on luscious Fruits—Take on board a horde of Passengers—A Description of them—Continuous Sickness of the Passengers—Steamboat converted into a gambling Hell—Burying a Man under Difficulties—Acapulco.

The voyage from Guayaquil to Panama is extremely uninteresting; losing the trade wind, the heat becomes excessive, accompanied by frequent and violent rain-squalls. Of whales there are generally an abundance, of the sperm species, rolling lazily along, spouting occasionally, and baring their grey old sides to view. With this exception, there is no sign of life; not a gull, nor a porpoise, nor yet a flying-fish, and no sail ventures into this windless region.

Swinging in our hammocks, and dreamily watching our cigar smoke upward curling, we loll away the dreary day, wishing for our arrival at Panama.

On the morning of the —— day of September, as the sun arose, the island of Taboga, at the entrance of the harbor of Panama, appeared in view; and, on nearing it, the sun's oblique rays, falling upon its wooded sides, enamelling its rich verdure, portrayed as vivid a picture of high tropical beauty as ever the eye rested upon. Rapidly coming up with it, and threading our way through smaller, though not less beautiful islets, we shortly opened the city of Panama. Letting go our anchor within a couple of miles of the town, as the ship swung her head to wind, we sat ourselves down and feasted our eyes upon the lovely view spread before us.

With a lofty hill for a background, clothed with an eternal verdure, fresh and luxuriant, crowned with palms whose feathery branches gracefully and sadly waved against the sky, lay the picturesque old city of Panama; a long line of rampart —a graceful sea gate—a projecting bastion, tumbling in ruins—towers of graceful, though odd construction, feathery with tropic verdure springing through every insterstice, and glistening with the ornamental pearl-shells with which they were tiled —irregularly built houses, dazzlingly white, and native huts with high conical thatches, looking like immense wicker-baskets —all these grouped among and peeping forth from a very forest of banana and palm, formed an enchanting whole, and delighted our eyes, which had been accustomed to the stiff architecture and sparce vegetation of a temperate clime.

On our right hand was the beautiful little archipelago formed by the islands of Perico, Flamingo, Otoque, Taboguilla, and Taboga, from the centre of which latter rises a hill of one thousand feet, cultivated nearly to its summit, sending down streams to the valleys, where, amidst the cocoanut, palm, and tamarind trees, the native huts lie nestling.

The island of Flamingo is also lofty, conical in formation, covered likewise with the generous luxuriance of the tropics. The other islands are lower, but perfect gems of beauty, between which are lovely, secluded little bays, whose wavelets ripple on their snow-white beaches, casting up shells most unique in form and beautiful in color. To our left stretched away in the dim distance ranges of hills half hidden by cloud and vapor, along whose crests incessant lightnings played—connecting links of the great mountain ranges of the Cordillera of the northern hemisphere and the Andes of the southern.

Ours was the only ship in port, and the vast bay lay motionless before us without a ripple, the long reef, stretching out a mile and a half beyond the town, being marked by the line of surf which lazily broke upon it, its low musical roar relieving the unnatural stillness of the hour. As the sun rose higher and higher the heat became intense, but towards one o'clock, the clouds which had been gathering on the hill-tops suddenly grew dense and black, and burst upon us with terrific violence. The crashes and din of the thunder were awful, and the vividness of the forked lightning as it played along the crests of the hills, over the turrets and fortifications, almost blinding; but the scene was sublime and impressive. In about an hour's time the grand pyrotechnic display was concluded, when the clouds suddenly dispersed and the sun burst forth with seemingly unwonted brilliancy. At sunset we went ashore to take a look at the old place and hear the news from the United States, for we had been some eleven months without letters.

The pull on shore was a very pleasant one ; a light westerly breeze, cooled by the afternoon shower, filled our sail and sent us merrily over the water, and as we glided along we momentarily discovered new beauties in the landscape. The rays of the setting sun bathed the whole scene in her golden hue, which was in fine contrast with the rich green of the vegetation, glossy and dripping with the rain. As our keel grated on the beach we jumped ashore, and passing through tne rampart by the "Monk's Gate," we found ourselves in the principal street of the town. Tall, balconied houses, whose blackened, dilapidated appearance gave ample testimony of their age; fine old ruins, whose peculiar architecture showed them to have belonged to a remote period, and evidently to have originally been intended for ecclesiastical purposes. Huge churches, monasteries and convents, obstructed our view on every side, making us feel that we were indeed, not only in a foreign land, but walking among the relics of the past; but although in a strange land, we were evidently not among strangers. Hundreds of desperate looking men, armed with knife and revolver, were thronging the streets, whose "vernacular" announced them indubitably as Yankees. Over the doorway of almost every house were signs in good old English, descriptive of the wares for sale within, while through the open portals of many might be seen the showy bar-room of our own country, fitted up with all the tinsel of painting, mirror, and gilt with which they are wont to decorate the rum-palaces of Yankee-land, while almost every available apartment was filled with monté, roulette, and faro tables, around which were crowds of betters, whose oaths, exultant or otherwise, according to their luck, grated harshly upon the ear.

The hotels and dwelling-houses were full to overflowing, and every tenement was occupied. The hotels, if such they could be called, were huge, old native houses, utterly unadapted for the purpose; the barn-like rooms, damp, windowless, and overrun with vermin, looked more like prison vaults than sleeping apartments, and instead of the weary traveller—half dead from exposure and jaded with his long mule-ride across the isthmus—

being assigned an apartment where he could retire to rest from the fatigues of his journey, he was ushered into one of those tomb-like rooms, and told to choose his bed from among some fifty cots ranged along its walls, and in tiers throughout its length—his dressing-room and toilet appointments being an open corridor furnished with a gross of tin basins, any quantity of filthy, brown soap, a huge sheet (for a towel), suspended on a roller, and a cracked looking-glass. The feeding arrangements as may be supposed, were utterly disgusting ; the *table d'hôte* served on long pine tables stained with grease, without covering, on which were plates and dishes of every variety of form and shade, and utterly uncleanly. The viands were of the coarsest description, and served up in the filthiest style. After some difficulty I made out to get a cot at the American Hotel, situated in the principal street, and decidedly "the place." As we entered, the supper-bell rang. After being nauseated by a senna-like compound, the waiter called tea, and having almost choked myself with a hard-boiled egg, the only cleanly thing available, I drew my chair out on the balcony and, lighting my cigar, gave myself up to revery.

My mind wandered back to the days of the Pizarros and of Almagro, when Spain was in the zenith of her glory—when Panama, the key to the Indies, was a bright jewel in her diadem—when her officers, high in rank, presided in the councils of that grey old town—when her tried veterans garrisoned her towers, and mailed knights—the flower of European chivalry—held gay tourney on her plains ; proud of her fame and exultant in her untold wealth, Spain would then ill have brooked a stranger on her soil.

Alas, alas, for human foresight !—howdifferent now ; where

crouch those mouldering ruins, blackened and dank, by the eternal rains and damps, and seething evaporations of this decay-bearing climate, then proudly stood the embattled turret, from whose height waved the rich and dreaded banner, of Castile—along those tumbling arches, proud churchmen with swinging censer led brilliant processions, amid the thunders of artillery, to do honor to some favored saint; within those mouldering walls, whose grated windows cause an instinctive shudder, mayhap many a writhing victim has abjured his heretical belief; on those over-hanging balconies, where in days of yore many a lovely damsel has paced at vesper hour, exchanging smiles with the gay cavaliers, as they on their chargers pranced gracefully thro' the street, beneath—now throng drunken Californians, whose foul oaths and obscenities poison the surrounding atmosphere. Within that stately temple, rich in lovely chefs-d'œuvre of Moorish and Gothic art, beneath whose roof many a swelling anthem of exquisite harmony has pealed—now are tethered mules and cattle, and the very churches themselves, only approached with reverential attitude by the natives, now resound to the coarse laugh of the emigrant, as he lazily lounges through their dark and solemn aisles, sneeringly deriding the kneeling devotee.

Saddened by such reflections, and disgusted with the uproar in the street below, I sought out my cot, and from sheer fatigue was soon snoring in concert with my fifty room-mates, and after a wretched night I arose at day-break and sallied forth. Panama, before the discovery of gold, was a lazy old Spanish town, with no commerce, and only awakened from her lethargy by the periodical visits of the British steamer bringing treasure from the south coast, and by an occasional passenger who in haste to get to Europe, braved the dangers of the Isthmus transit. Now all was life and animation ; the population of the town was more than doubled by some thousands of Yankees, awaiting conveyance to California ; having bought through-tickets for California in the United States, in good faith, and supposing that they would be at once forwarded on their arrival here, they now, to their dismay, found that they had been misled, and that they would be obliged to wait months before they could get a passage. The situation of these people was deplorable, many without means, in a deadly climate, and unable to speak the language, with families of women and little children dependent upon them ; exposure and unhealthy diet soon produced their natural consequences, and the fatality among them was awful—the cholera and native fevers vying with each other in their ravages. As I walked the streets that morning, my heart sickened within me ; fathers on their knees besought me to use my influence with the agent, to get them a passage for their families, and mothers held up their emaciated children, with the seal of death upon their sallow faces, in dumb but eloquent appeal—but alas ; I could not help them.

Finding that our steamer would be detained some fifteen or twenty days, I at once went on board, glad to escape from the horrors of that very charnel-house, polluted alike by deadly miasmas and by human vice. Lifting our anchor, we sought a more secure harbor under the lee of Flamingo, in one of those secluded little nooks which abound in that locality.

On the southern extremity of the island of Flamingo, some two hundred feet above the sea, stands a stone cottage of tropic build, whose balconies overhang the bay, and through whose halls the air gently circulates, forming a most cool and delightful retreat ; this, with the exception of a couple of native huts, is the only house on the island, and being at that time unoccupied we took formal possession ; sending off the necessary supplies, with a few grass hammocks we proceeded to make ourselves comfortable.

Our life, as may be supposed, was not a very active one ; a sea-bath on awakening, a cup of coffee and cigar, with a stroll on the beach, or, spy-glass in hand, a climb up the hill for a scan sea-ward, a loll in our hammock, with the late periodicals within our grasp, a breakfast of fruit, in which the banana and green cocoanut figured conspicuously, served by a troupe of yellow damsels who acted as our caterers and femmes-de-chambre ; after breakfast a long siesta, then a shower-bath, the water, dipped from a cool fountain, thrown over our heads from calabashes in the hands of the aforesaid damsels ; then a change of raiment and a pull off to the steamer for dinner ; then a stretch shore-ward before the sea-breeze, from whence, after hearing the gossip, we enjoyed a cool sail off to our castle before the gentle land-wind ; this, with an occasional trip to Taboga or the Pearl Islands, made up the history of our sojourn. Occasionally we spent a day ashore with some newly-arrived friend from the "States," or in examining the "lions" of the place ; but its unhealthiness and its infernal climate, effectually deterred us from a longer stay.

Among the ruins of this dilipidated city, those of the Jesuit College are the most interesting ; commenced in the year 1739, it progressed but slowly until 1779, when the Jesuits were expelled the country, and of course nothing further was done to it, but it was allowed to fall into decay ; in the whole western world there is probably no building so chaste and beautiful in design, but, alas! its courts are now occupied as garden spots and parade grounds, while multitudinous creepers and broad banana leaves conceal many a lovely relic of art; over an arched gateway, blackened by the rains of a century, can be descried the famous motto of the order: "In nomine Jesu omne Genu flectatur." Could those grey old fathers rise from their graves, and see these aisles desecrated by cock-fights and circus riders, methinks their smooth faces, in spite of their habitual calmness, would show signs of horror.

The crumbling walls and ruined arches of the Merced, St. Augustine, and San Juan de Dios convents, straggling irregularly through the town, give it a most romantic and interesting, though sad appearance. Stumbling among some old rubbish within a four-walled inclosure, filled up with banana, orange, pomegranate and cocoanut trees, digging with pointed sticks, searching for hidden architectural treasures, and occasionally striking them against some splendid old bells hanging just clear of the ground, when, on raising our eyes, we discovered, to our astonishment, something which seemed to us scarcely less wonderful than that architectural anomaly, "the leaning tower of Pisa;" it was a *flat arch*, with an almost imperceptible curve of a span of *forty feet!* The construction was most peculiar, but the whole affair, though probably built a hundred years back, was as firm as if of yesterday. There probably is not at present living that *architect* who could make its equal.

The vegetable world here flourishes in the richest and rankest luxuriance; the constant moisture and the fierce rays of the sun, bring forward to maturity each seed and plant with wonderful celerity; the products of the forest are absolutely monstrous, as one may well conceive when he looks upon a native canoe, *of twelve tons burden*, carved from a single tree.

Of flowers, the woods and swamps are filled with them, of form most delicate and hue most gaudy ; each parasite, as it winds its loving embrace round some tall tree, wreathes it with tendrils rich in loveliest blossoms, while springing from the interstices of every ruined wall, shoot forth the "holy passion flower," or the exquisite "flower of the Holy Ghost." This most lovely and wonderful product of the floral kingdom, resembles closely the opening bud of the tube-rose, with its waxen petal and polished green leaf ; pluck it—when, lo ! within that opening bud is a perfect representation of a dove, with wings extended, just ready to take its flight, its graceful head perfect in form, with eye and bill. A more complete "lusus naturæ" never was looked upon. The cedron tree here flourishes, which has a world-wide celebrity, from its possessing certain properties which cure the bites of serpents ; the natives greatly esteem it, always carrying with them a piece of its seed ; when any one is bitten, a little mixed with water is applied ; or a few grains in brandy are often taken internally with great success.

At this time the gold fever was at its height, and people were absolutely mad to get to California, and tickets for steamers expected to leave at an early date were sold at an enormous premium ; there was as much excitement manifested as at the New York Stock Exchange, and at noon the corners and drinking shops were thronged to excess, and speculators frantic. Shrewd Yankees, who held tickets for the first vessel bound up, *calculating* that a month would not make much difference, sold out at an advance of a cool thousand or so, and pocketing the money, quietly bided their time. The excitement became so intense, that many did nothing but buy and sell tickets on commission.

Fresh arrivals came pouring in, and each afternoon long trains of the most wretched-looking people, bespattered and bedrabbled, their hats slouched over their faces, and the steam rising off their dank garments, mounted on mules hobbling and stumbling, scarce able to drag themselves along, might be seen entering the gateway over the drawbridge into the city. Poor mortals! how I pitied them! Jaded and worn, half dead from exposure and fatigue, and with the seeds of cholera and fever germinating within them, they were, many of them, literally entering their tomb; the flush of excitement which passed over their livid faces as they dismounted amid the excitement of the gathered throng, was only a last effort of nature; many, yes, many never descended those steps alive, which now, under the vigor of excitement, they so manfully ascended; cholera and fever swept them off, unmourned and unrecognized. Many a mother yet deplores an absent son; many a wife, a missing husband, whose unconscious remains, putrifying with fever, were unceremoniously hurried forth at midnight and pitched in some slimy pit, or into the swelling tide. Judge not, ye wives—murmur not, ye mothers—who think yourselves abandoned; mayhap the dying words of that long-lost husband or son may have been an agonizing petition to Heaven for your protection.

While we were lounging at the island and initiating ourselves into the lazy habits peculiar to the climate, our agent was ashore doing everything he could to expedite our departure, and had succeeded in engaging some three hundred passengers (more in truth than the vessel could at all accommodate, but people bound to California were in nowise particular as to their accommodations), and had made all the necessary arrangements for the resumption of our voyage, when, after a month's sojourn, we were informed that on the morrow we would be once more on the move.

Next day, we unmoored our steamer, and leaving our quiet little nook, hauled up from our anchorage, abreast the town and proceeded to embark our passengers. Such a motley looking set never before were seen, all western men and principally gamblers, the roughest, most uncouth lot of desperadoes that ever climbed over a ship's side. Our steerage passengers numbering about 150 belonged to that delectable class of men called "Hoosiers," filthy and villainous-looking to a man, with a fair sprinkling of women and children—pleasant prospect for the remainder of the voyage.

As may be imagined, three hundred passengers and their luggage, and sufficient to feed them for twenty-five days, with as much fuel as it was prudent to put on board, our steamer was pretty well down in the water, so much so indeed that when I embarked the last batch of passengers from my boat, I stepped from her gunwale to the vessel's deck without the least effort; and as I did it I made up my mind that in case of a gale it would go hard with us.

The scene that presented itself on the next morning, as I roused out of my bunk, beggars description, there were of course not berths for more than half the passengers, and every available space was occupied by miserable looking devils, many of whom were in the agonies of sea-sickness, and who, rolled up in their blankets, were retching and blaspheming in the most horrible manner, while others were tossing and burning under the first symptoms of Panama fever, then beginning to make itself manifest; poor little children were rolling around indiscriminately among loose carpet-bags and bedding, while their mothers lay groaning beside them. Outside the saloon, the gangways were filled up with luggage, stores, and fuel, and the wind, blowing a gale, had raised a sea which, occasionally breaking aboard, kept everything afloat; the long dining-saloon on the promenade deck was likewise appropriated by the sick and sleeping, the floor and tables presenting apparently inanimate masses wrapped up in that everlasting accompaniment of the western traveller—the blue blanket. Fore and aft the ship, everything looked woe-be-gone and uncomfortable, while seaward the prospect was quite as unpromising: the sky looked black and angry, the rain drove by in violent squalls and the gale evidently increasing, God help us I thought, as I looked to windward! Anything like regularity in serving meals to such a crowd, or in such weather was impossible; in fact, oftentimes the whole cabin dinner as it left the galley was seized *in transitu*, and carried off in triumph by the steerage passengers. The scenes enacted at table were brutal beyond description, and fights and brawls were generally the accompaniments of every dinner, but I having a friend at court in the shape of the head-steward, managed to fare pretty well. By dint of confining myself to my room and through the aid of some interesting books I managed to pass the time.

The weather for the first ten days was terrible, it blew a constant gale, the sea-sickness was universal, while the Isthmus fever was making sad havoc among our number; day after day some poor fellow gave up the ghost, and was unceremoniously hurried over the side, oftentimes without even the formality of a prayer.

Well I remember, one afternoon during the height of the gale, as our bell tolled forth its mournful summons to bury the dead, picking my way through the prostrate forms of many poor wretches, and in company with a dozen others, finding myself on the forward deck to assist in the ceremony; the corpse, sewed in a hammock, was just ready to launch overboard, while we, uncovered (in the blinding storm), were listening to the beautiful service of the English ritual, when suddenly a tremendous sea struck the ship and in an instant, every soul of us went sprawling down to leeward. Half-stunned with the fall we lay struggling with each other, with the corpse in our midst, until we could recover ourselves. That was the last of the burial-service. As we got into better weather and smoother seas, our delectable fellow passengers emerged from their lairs and then commenced such a saturnalia as is not often enacted on the ocean.

Drinking and gambling became the order of the day, and from early morning, till late at night, nothing was to be heard but the fierce oaths of the gambler, or the ravings of the drunkard. Our long dining-tables during the intervals of serving the meals were occupied by roulette tables, faro banks, and by parties gambling in every known game; fights of course were frequent, but fortunately none terminated fatally.

CHAPTER VII.

CALIFORNIA.

We arrive at San Francisco—First Impressions—Dreadful Winter—Fires—Murders and Gambling—Leave for the Diggings—Are overtaken by a Flood at Sacramento—Funny Scenes—Leave for the Upper Country—Scare the Landlord of Nocola's Rancho—Tramp into the Interior—Remarks about that Section of Country—Go to the Southern Mines—Get Sick—Leave for Home—Take passage in the Steamer Tennessee—Pleasant Companions—Panama again—Delight of Trip across the Isthmus in the Rainy Season—Arrive in New York—Leave New York in a little Brig bound round Cape Horn—Some remarks touching the Intellectual Improvement of our Merchant Marine, mainly due to Lieut. Maury—Arrive in Mexico after a Seven Months' Voyage..

THE twelfth day brought us into Acapulco, where we remained some fourteen hours, taking in coal and fresh provisions. It would be more than a "twice-told tale" to recount the outrages committed by the passengers, while on shore, upon each other or upon the natives; sufficient to say, that at midnight following the day of our arrival, we again got under weigh, heading up for San Francisco, off which port we arrived on the —th day of October, without further incident worth recording, after a voyage of upwards of two hundred and fifty days! As we steamed in through the open portals of the "Golden Gate," my own impressions, and probably those of every man aboard that ship, were of the same indescribable nature. They must have been somewhat akin to those experienced by Cortez and his followers, as the rich and beautiful panorama of the valley of Mexico and her capital, dazzling in all the splendor and magnificence of Aztec wealth, burst upon their astonished vision; in it they saw the realization of all their ambitious dreams. Our dreams, too, were in process of realization. The bourne for which we had so long been struggling was gained at last, and the land for which we had all sacrificed so much—for which for months we had panted—was now spread before our eyes. This, however, was no time for analyzing our feelings, and we soon became engrossed in what was passing around us.

Skirting the barren sand-hills on the southern side of the bay, we rapidly shot in among the shipping, which, to the number of hundreds, lay moored off the city; and coming-to within a few lengths of the shore, we let go an anchor where were then three or four fathoms of water, but where is now the very business centre of San Francisco. We were immediately boarded by hundreds of people who had lined the shore, to see us come in. Indeed it was a sight worth seeing, to witness the entry of an American river steamer into the harbor of San Francisco after a voyage of eighteen thousand miles! and proudly suggestive of the invincible energy of American enterprise. Many were the congratulations which we received from friends who had given up all hopes of ever seeing us again, and many the cordial shake of the hand from strangers, in admiration of what they were pleased to term our pluck, in trusting ourselves on *such a voyage in such a machine.*

Our first inquiries were, of course, as to the state of affairs in California; whether gold was plenty? if people were making their fortunes as rapidly as ever? etc., etc., etc., to all of which questions we received answers most favorable; and most marvellous stories were bandied from mouth to mouth, which to us, seemed more exaggerated than fiction itself, but which were, generally speaking, true! The excitement which every one whom we saw appeared to be under, rapidly communicated itself to ourselves, and appeared not only to possess animate, but inanimate things also. Houses appeared in the very act of rising without visible human agency, and sides of hills, presenting only a few hours before a bare and barren look, now were white with tents, hastily erected by some recently disembarked company. Another notable feature was the manifest desire of all respectable people to present as ruffianly an appearance as possible; and although the weather, on landing, was intensely hot, yet every one whom we met was enveloped in red flannel, high boots and monkey-jackets, while the lower classes seemed to think filthiness in personal appearance a requisite of respectability. The very demon of gambling seemed to have been let loose; every house, every available apartment was appropriated by these desperadoes, and everybody appeared frantic for a chance to be swindled. The Parker House, the general rendezvous, and where every fresh arrival went to meet their friends, was the grand rallying point of the gamblers, and their tables, piled up with gold, invited their victims, and here many a youthful adventurer, fresh from the pure and chaste atmosphere of home, in quest of friendly faces, innocently has entered, bewildered by the glare reflected back from many mirrors, discovering to his astonished gaze gaudy paintings of vilest obscenity, abandoned women decked off in tawdry tinsel, whose debauched countenances caused involuntary shudders of loathing to creep over him ; his ears saluted by instrumental music which crashed through the din of wrangling oaths and the chink of coin, his every breath inhaling a dense atmosphere laden with the fumes of liquor and tobacco, till becoming stupified with its novelty, and familiarized with what was passing around him, he has gradually succumbed to the seductive influence of the game.

It would be a work of supererogation to attempt a description of the state of things in California during the fall of the year 1849, or the winter of 1850. So many thousands of letters, books, and paragraphs, have already appeared on the subject, that the stirring scenes of those days are daguerreotyped on the mind of every intelligent reader.

I remained at San Francisco during that terrible winter, and suffered, and, like Mark Tapley, was jolly amid the desolation caused by fire, flood, and disease. I saw the embryo city swept off by the never-to-be-forgotten conflagration of December, 1849; I saw sickness and death from pure want in the midst of that golden city; I saw men bleeding and gasping fresh from the assassin's knife, and highwaymen and murderers hanged by an indignant populace. During my stay, too, the members for the first California legislature were elected, and I saw them start off for the seat of government at San José, in the little steamboat "Mint" (scarcely larger than a wash-tub), and watched her from the heights as she battled with a furious gale, making such bad weather of it, that for a long while it seemed doubtful whether or not she would not founder with all her *precious freight.*

After a dreary, stormy winter, such as had never before been known, in the month of March the rains ceased, and the dark clouds which for weeks and weeks had hung over us like a pall, suddenly dispersed, and, like a curtain drawn, discovered the beautiful azure sky of California.

With the bright sunbeam came renewed hope, and thousands who had been eking out a dead-and-alive existence, with loss of energy, and careless of the future, felt its genial influence, and cheerily buckled on their armor for the fight.

During the winter I visited the city of Sacramento. My journey was undertaken during the period of the heaviest rains, and I arrived there only on the evening previous to the disastrous flood, which will never be forgotten by the early settlers. The waters, which had been very high previously, at this time gave indications of overflowing the river banks, and as the streets of the town were, as a general thing, much lower than the natural levee, it became apparent to all that a farther rise would be most calamitous, and attended by the most fatal consequences, if immediate precautions were not taken to secure life and property. At the moment of my landing all was bustle and confusion. The female portion of the population were being transferred to the vessels lining the river's banks, and the men were following suit, or betaking themselves to the upper stories of their houses (when they had any). A number of men, women, and children, however, preferred taking refuge in the church, a little wooden building which had lately been erected, trusting for safety to the sanctuary.

By this time the torrent had burst its natural barrier, and rushed through the streets with great fury, the whole country, as far as the eye could reach, being under water. Being informed that there were several families who had deferred seeking safety until the height of the water had rendered it impossible for them to do so unaided, I, in company with some four or five others, jumped into a whale-boat and started to the rescue. Pulling up through Jay street, we found it required all our strength to make any headway, so strong was the current in the streets. In turning a corner we would frequently be swept back a long distance in spite of our utmost efforts; we succeeded, however, in rescuing all who required our aid.

Still the water continued rising, and the howling storm and rushing flood, and the black night without, caused an involuntary shudder as the thought suggested itself of the possibility of some of our friends being exposed to its pitiless fury. With these thoughts uppermost in our minds, a party of us sat in the snug cabin of a vessel moored to the bank, anxiously speculating as to the result of the affair. Thus the night wore on, none caring to retire amid this uncertain state of things. A little after midnight we were startled from our reverie by the tolling of a bell. There was but *one bell* in Sacramento, and that hung in the belfry of the church where the women and children had taken refuge. In a moment fifty stout arms were pulling away for dear life through the blinding storm and pitchy darkness. Reaching the church, we found that it had floated from its foundation, and was in imminent danger of capsizing, or of being carried off into deep water. Filling our boats with frightened women and children, we paddled back to the ships, stiff with cold and half perished with exposure.

For days the whole city was under water, and business of course suspended; even after the flood had in a measure subsided, it was a long time before the streets were clear of water, and for weeks scows were used at the crossings, and for transporting goods. The lower stories of the greater part of the buildings being submerged, the upper ones were occupied, and the only mode of egress was of course through the upper windows. It was a comical sight to see housekeepers and storekeepers kicking their heels out of their second story windows, or hailing a scow to take them to dinner (all at that time dining at hotels). I remember one day visiting a friend in his sky-parlor, and while gracefully occupied in swinging my legs out of his window, commenting upon the state of affairs generally, we espied a scow floating leisurely along, propelled by an individual whose countenance was somewhat familiar. This person occupied a boat of the very smallest dimensions, in which was placed apparently all his earthly goods, viz., a chest, a pair of blankets, and several old boots. He himself, being a man of no small proportions, together with his plunder (as the trappers have it), completely filled the little shallop, making it appear a part of himself. As he neared us we recognized a Philadelphia acquaintance, "Dick E." by name. The last time we had seen him was in the guise of an exquisite, promenading Chestnut street. Shouting to him to heave-to, we hailed him as to whence from and whither bound, begging to know his longitude; but poor Richard was inconsolable. He had been drowned out of house and home, and was, with his available assets, on his way to the San Francisco steamboat.

Being anxious to visit the northern mines, I started off one fine morning, in company with a friend, in the little "Lawrence," a stern-wheel boat of the smallest imaginable dimensions, bound to Marysville, and scarcely larger than a ship's longboat; she was crowded to excess with passengers and freight. Indeed there was scarcely standing room for us. The day was lovely, but although the rains had ceased, the floods had not subsided ; as far as the blue mountains bounding the horizon, the whole country was submerged, presenting in appearance one vast lake ; a few trees here and there marking the river's course. Onward we went, puffing and paddling, our only amusement an occasional shot into a flock of duck or geese, who ventured too close, for, like the dove from the ark, they were in search of where to rest their feet; and being evidently unacquainted with the genus steamboat, mistook it for *terra firma*, but soon found that they were jumping out of the water into the frying-pan. As darkness set in, we held up, and made fast to a tree, at a place called Nicholas' Ranch, an original farmhouse, situated on a high bluff above the flood. The building, a huge Dutch farmhouse, with an immense kitchen and a yawning fireplace, filled with blazing logs, large enough to roast an ox entire.

Rushing in without ceremony, we spied, by the flickering light of the fire, a long table loaded down with smoking joints of elk and bear meat, with the other et-ceteras accessory to a western table. At once the attack commenced, and was vigorously sustained, till, wearied and surfeited, one after another fell over upon his blankets next the fireplace and instantaneously began to snore. Picking out a soft spot, I followed their example, and drawing my blankets closely around me, I was quickly snoring an accompaniment. Soon after midnight, from the effects of my hearty repast, I was seized with a severe indigestion, which brought on a nightmare, and I commenced shouting murder at the top of my voice. In an instant, a hundred men were on their feet, with knife unsheathed and pistol drawn, all staring wildly and inquiring the cause of the riot. Scarcely had the sounds passed my lips before I was aware of what had occurred, but I prudently kept my own counsel and joined in with the rest in anxious inquiries as to the origin of the disturbance; and to this day those sleepy miners have no idea of what waked them. Old Nicholas, the Dutch landlord swore it was "der tuyvel."

This rancho is situated near the junction of the Sacramento with the Feather River. At their confluence, leaving the former, we went puffing away up the latter, cheered with the prospect of reaching Marysville in the afternoon. This river's banks were lined with trees, from the feathery appearance of whose leaves it derives its name. The effect against the clear blue sky was very beautiful and graceful, the light waving foliage having precisely the effect of expanded plumage.

Had it not been for the trees, we would not have been able to have determined the channel of the river; for, for leagues on every side, stretched away the water.

A very funny incident occurred in reference to this. The pilot of a small steamboat, drawing but little water, and bound to one of the up-country settlements, finding that he could shorten his trip some sixty or a hundred miles by taking advantage of the flood, abandoning the river and cutting across the country, resolved to make the trial. For the first sixty miles he succeeded admirably; but an accident happening to the machinery, a delay of twenty-four hours was unavoidable, but "*miserabile dictu*," when the repairs were completed, the waters had receded, and the economical pilot found himself, with his steamboat, in the interior of a wild country, from thirty to forty miles from any water!

Arriving at Marysville, we found a city consisting of a dozen or so tents, and Nye's rancho house, a long adôbe building, which had been erected several years before. The site of the town was on a high bluff, sufficiently elevated to be out of the reach of inundations, and said to be one of the healthiest places in California. At the time of my visit, the idea of locating a town had only recently suggested itself, and the originators were most desirous to induce settlers, and to interest all travellers in the undertaking. To us it seemed absurd, the idea of valuing lots in that mud-hole at from one hundred to a thousand dollars. Many inducements were held out to me to take an interest here ; the most liberal terms being offered me by one of the principal proprietors, a New York lawyer, which, had I accepted, would have given me an independent fortune ; but my lucky star was not in the ascendant.

Rolling up our blankets, after a not very comfortable night spent in Marysville, in a muddy tent, we strapped them on our shoulders, and started off on a tramp through the mining districts.

We proposed making our first halt at a station ten miles distant, and there to remain that night. Right manfully we buckled to our work ; over hill and swamp we went, enjoying the elasticity of the air, and the beauty of the natural scenery; the wild flowers blooming in the early spring, sent up a delicious perfume, and the undulating country, carpeted with softest turf and besprinkled with the California oak, recalled the parks I had wandered over only a few years before in Staffordshire and Devonshire ; while across our path would occasionally bound a deer, as if to keep up the illusion. Little heeding time or fatigue, onward we plodded, admiring all we saw, until suddenly meeting a horseman, and inquiring our way, we were informed that we had pursued a wrong direction, being at least twenty miles distant from our destination. By way of parenthesis, it might be well here to observe that this was my first experience in pedestrianism, while my companion was celebrated for his walking feats.

As may be imagined, the horseman's information was not agreeable to me, at least; for, although I had not previously felt any fatigue, the very mention of a twenty-mile walk produced a fainting sensation. Tired and hungry, it seemed impossible that I could walk half the distance. There was no help for it, however; my companion would not listen to my proposal of throwing myself under the first tree, and starting again in the morning. He was inexorable. So, at it we went, my blankets, weighing only ten pounds, seemed a ton upon my shoulders, and my shoes chafed and blistered my feet, as, mile after mile, I dragged myself along—nothing but the bracing, invigorating air of California carried me through it. Late at night we came upon our station; when, pitching my blankets under a wide-spreading tree and throwing myself upon them, in a moment I was unconscious, fatigue having deadened even my craving for food.

Next day, stiff and sore, I refused to move, much to the disgust of my companion, who was provokingly fresh, but who, by way of keeping his hand in, walked off some dozens of miles, and brought back a saddle of venison for our supper.

On the following day, however, shouldering my traps, I jogged on beside my companion for some twenty miles, and halted in the evening at Rose's bar, with scarcely a sensation of fatigue, so rapidly does one become accustomed to this sort of thing. At the first set-out the fatigue is seriously distressing, but after a few days one falls into a regular gait, which can be kept up for many hours without tiring. Many a man in California could step off his thirty miles, day in and day out, while there *were* men who could walk their forty miles without making much of it, but they were possessed of extraordinary powers.

Visiting all the principal diggings in the northern mines, and penetrating almost to the Sierra Nevada, I retraced my footsteps, and, late in May, found myself again in San Francisco.

Arranging my business, I proceeded to Stockton, and from thence into the southern mines, where, establishing myself in a store made of four upright posts and covered with boughs, I, in company with a cousin, proceeded to retail dry goods and groceries to needy miners.

Our residence was at the city of Columbia, then containing two or three thousand inhabitants; but one fine morning better diggings were found, and before night there were not ten people left in the place. So perforce we pulled up stakes and went off too.

Attacked by a nervous affection, brought on by anxiety and irregular mode of life, late in the summer of 1850, I left the southern mines, and going down to San Francisco, embarked in the steamer Tennessee for New York.

Depressed in spirits, I hardly took the trouble to notice who were to be my fellow passengers; indeed I scarcely left my room until we had been several days at sea. On emerging, however, from my cabin, I found that there was a crowd of people on board, including several ladies on their way to the East.

Among the passengers were Commodore Jones and suite,

beside several other navy officers, who were going home on leave. Having previously known these gentlemen, and becoming acquainted with the ladies, we formed a merry party, and fifteen days consumed in the voyage to Panama glided quickly away. My health gradually improved under these social influences, and before our journey was half completed, my spirits were as light as those of any one of that gay coterie.

We found old Panama just as picturesque, just as hot, and just as filthy, as we had left it one year before. There were more niggers, to be sure, and fewer swaggering Yankees, but with that exception, I saw no particular change.

It had not forgotten to rain, that was very certain ; indeed our arrival was celebrated with a deluge which, had it continued forty hours, would have floated old Panama off its foundations, and I am afraid that there would have been among all its inhabitants no good Noah to have built an ark— in fact, I should rather have been excused from being a passenger, if male and female of every different species that exist on the isthmus must necessarily have become my *compagnons du voyage.*

Our anticipations of being obliged to imitate that very respectable old gentleman, Mr. Noah, were suddenly cut short by a cessation of the celestial fire-works, and a moderation in the fall of water, and presently a very elegant rainbow made its appearance, reproachfully gazing upon us and dispelling our fears.

We did not anticipate a very comfortable passage across the isthmus, but little did we imagine the annoyances, delays and dangers to which we were to be subjected in the transit.

After a detention of a week in Panama in making the necessary arrangements for mules for the coveyance of ourselves and luggage, we at last got under weigh, our train consisting of some seventy animals, mounted on thirty of whose backs were male and female passengers—and a picturesque looking group we formed.

In anticipation of heavy rains, we were enveloped in the most grotesque looking india-rubber garments; the ladies coming out particularly strong in the variety of their dreadnaught costumes.

No sooner were we fairly started than the heavens opened, and its very flood-gates seemed to have broken loose; for hours, soaked and bespattered with mud, we toiled over broken roads, until at last reaching the borders of a mountain torrent, which in ordinary times a mere brook, was now a swollen river; we were told by our guides that we must halt, as a passage for that day, at least, would be not only unsafe, but impossible.

From sympathy with the deplorable situation of the ladies, we proposed going back to Panama, not knowing how long we might be detained here in this wretched swamp, without the vestige of a habitation; but to our dismay we were informed that the streams in our rear were likewise too much swollen to admit of a retreat. This was a pretty predicament; not a sign of a human habitation—a furious deluging rain, and a party of forty people without provisions; for the male portion of the party it was bad enough, but for the delicate women it was embarrassing and distressing.

After a long search we succeeded in finding a shed—a roof upon poles—and taking formal-possession, we proceeded by means of our luggage to inclose it in a measure, so as to keep out the storm, and some of the party having hammocks, we swung them for the ladies, thus keeping them from off the damp earth ; reconnoitering the vicinity, we discovered some native huts, and at once pressed their occupants into our service as foragers, and by dint of threats and dollars, succeeded in getting a good supply of provisions ; the ladies suffered extremely, neither did the gentlemen particularly enjoy this picnicking, but there was no remedy. Three mortal days did we exist in this wretched hovel, but on the fourth the rains ceased, when dragging ourselves out of our mud-hole, cold and stiff, we mounted our animals once more, and slowly stumbled through muddy sloughs, deep ravines, and over broken rocks, the only variety of the road being from bad to worse.

The sufferings of the ladies may be imagined, as one moment saturated with a pouring rain, and the next suffocated with a burning sun, they clambered up the precipitous mountain side, or urged their mules through miles of liquid mud and swamp. I had one young lady under my charge, who in spite of all her womanly courage, several times fairly gave out ; once the poor thing was thrown head-long into a stream, by the stubbornness of her animal ; at another, having stuck fast in a mud-hole, she had to be lifted, and carried bodily, a distance of twenty yards, to terra firma.

On the fifth day from Panama, we arrived at Cruces ; a filthy, wretched negro village, at the head of canoe navigation, on the Chagres River, and were informed for our consolation, that the steamer for New York had already left Chagres, and that there would be no opportunity again in ten days. What to do we did not know, a week's residence in a negro settlement, which at this season was half under water, and whose habitations of straw and bamboo, looked like immense bee-hives, was not very inviting—the alternative, a ten days' sojourn in Chagres, whose climate was absolutely deadly, and whose population, outlaws to all decency, was made up of thieves, robbers and assassins, with a sprinkling of Jamaica, and Carthagenian niggers!

We determined to remain where we were. For seven days it poured without intermission, so of course we could not stir outside of our wicker baskets. Inside, we had recourse to all imaginable modes of killing time, but with small success. The atmosphere, heavy and dank, weighed upon our spirits, and gave us all a terrible fit of the "blues;" one great incentive to exertion, was the desire of keeping clear of the centipedes tics, and piqués which abounded in these huts; by one species or other of these insects, some one of us was constantly attacked, when all the rest would assist in relieving him.

On the eighth day of our suffering, having chartered canoes for the purpose, we embarked on the swollen Chagres for the port.

The morning was lovely, the rains having apparently subsided for our benefit, and in high spirits we stepped aboard of our "original" conveyances, with the hopes of reaching our destination that night.

Our vessel was an immense dug-out, thirty feet in length, by six in breadth, the whole affair surmounted by an arched roof, made of bamboo, and thatched with palm leaves, thus forming beneath it a sort of cabin, through which a pleasant breeze circulated. Having stowed our provisions to our liking, and lighting our cigars, we proceeded to ensconce ourselves aboard the ark.

Our crew consisted of five strapping Carthagenian niggers,

all but one of whom, having a sovereign contempt for dress, were stark naked, while the fifth, the patron or captain, was arrayed in a broad-brimmed straw hat, in the possession of which he considered himself dressed; his part of the performance was to steer the bungo, and it was a most comical sight to see him perched up upon the high stern smoking in solemn gravity ; the other niggers were rowers, but there was no call for oars during our voyage, as the swollen stream carried us along as quickly as we dared go.

The voyage down the river was one splendid monotony ; its banks heavily curtained with verdure, lined with gigantic trees, interlaced with parasitical plants entwining themselves from trunk to trunk, and from branch to branch, until forming an impenetrable jungle, beautiful in its coloring and shade, and mysterious in its intricacy.

Clouds of parrots of the richest plumage shot screaming among its leafy bowers, monkeys leaped from branch to branch of the tall palm trees, and alligators splashed heavily from the green banks into the muddy stream.

Drifting quickly down with the strong current amid alternate sunshine and shower, we gazed with pleasurable awe upon the mighty effort of nature in her wanton display—the effect of the sunshine bursting from behind the great inky clouds, and casting its bright glance on the dripping foliage and peeping into the deepest recesses of the morass, was fine indeed.

Occasionally shooting around an angular point, we would suddenly come upon a little village peeping from the wilderness ; scarcely distinguishable, however, were the bamboo huts, from their similarity to the surrounding foliage. These houses are usually built upon long poles sunk in the ground, the first floor being at least ten feet from the earth, and the only mode of obtaining access to the domicil by means of a notched pole, which serves as a ladder. The motive in building these houses so high from the ground, is to keep them free from the humidity of the earth, and out of reach of the thousands of venomous reptiles which abound in the jungle.

As night approaches the air becomes illuminated with enormous fire-flies, and the deathlike stillness now and then broken by the dismal roar of wild beasts.

Before midnight we reached our destination, thus making the distance from Cruces to Chagres—about ninety miles—in fifteen hours, where only a few months before I was eight days in ascending the same distance!

Chagres was certainly the most villainous place that I ever did see, and proverbially the unhealthiest place in the world, and nobly has it sustained its reputation, for I verily believe that two out of three, at the least calculation, who visited it were taken ill with the local epidemic, and once attacked with it, it was very apt to prove fatal.

Chagres is an old Spanish port, with a huge fortress splendidly located on the brow of a lofty promontory. This fortress was considered impregnable in the time of the Spaniard, but since the revolution, has fallen into decay, and is now rarely ever garrisoned—the only testimony of its former glory being some elegant, old brass guns of ancient date. The promontory overhangs the mouth of the river, and on a little plateau at its feet, lies the old town, a mere collection of bamboo huts; its inhabitants a mongrel breed between the African and Indian. On the opposite side of the stream is situated the American town, consisting of a couple of dozen or so of white wooden houses, all of which are either hotels or drinking houses. The hotels were curiosities in their way, the accommodations consisting of one huge dining-hall, ornamented with greasy tables, on whose bare pine planks were served the coarsest of fares in the filthiest of styles.

Of sleeping apartments there were none, the nearest approach to them being an immense room or dormitory, fitted up with bunks or berths in lieu of bedsteads, and here every one, whether gentle or simple, must of necessity ensconce himself. The denizens of this delightful city were in keeping with it—made up of the very lowest and vilest wretches from the purlieus of New York and New Orleans, of Jamaica and Carthagenian negroes, and of a sprinkling of desperadoes from the different West Indian islands; these gentry maintained themselves, some by boating the thousands of passengers that weekly came ashore from the different steamers up the river, others by gambling, and the rest by robbing and murdering all who fell in their power. There was no law, no restraint, and all decent people felt that their only safety lay in the pistol and knife in their belt—murder and robberies were of not daily but hourly occurrence.

The ladies of our party were quartered in the private room of the landlord, while the gentlemen occupied the grand dormitory, in common with a hundred cut-throats and assassins.

One night I was awakened by the rattling of metal, and on looking from my bunk, saw, in the moonlight, a couple of fellows breaking open a trunk; in a moment a pistol was drawn, and several shots were fired in quick succession within a few feet of us—then all was quiet, but constantly, during the night, I could hear people crawling on all fours about the floor.

The inhabitants of the two sides of the river were hostile to each other, and rows were of frequent occurrence ; just as we left, there was a grand battle, which lasted all day; the negroes gaining possession of the fortress, brought one of the guns to bear on the American side, and were about firing, when an old Kentuckian, covering himself behind a ruined wall, drew up his rifle, and in an instant the gunner fell dead ; his place was quickly supplied by others, but the moment they showed themselves, crack went the rifle, and down fell a negro ; in this way, it is estimated that the Kentuckian brought down at least twenty men in one day, effectually silencing the gun.

The climate of Chagres is, as I have said before, deadly, and its inhabitants looked like ghosts, pale, wan and emaciated, with glassy eyes ; they seemed to be unconsciously on the brink of the grave. The constant alternation of heavy rain and powerful sun upon the rank vegetation and decayed matter brought down the river by the rapid current, produced a seething and miasmatic evaporation, which it was positively sickening to breathe, and glad were we to escape from it ; embarking once more in canoes, and passing a dangerous surf, rolling on the bar, we were delighted to find ourselves aboard the good steamer " Crescent City."

A voyage of ten days quickly passed, unvaried save by twenty-four hours' sojourn at the island of Jamaica, for the purpose of coaling. On the 20th day of August, 1850, I found myself again in New York, after an absence of a year and a half. Once passed the pleasure of saying how d'ye do to my friends, I again began to crave the excitements of the life that I had been leading, and in thirty days from the day of my arrival, I was again sailing out past Sandy Hook, in a little schooner-brig of 120 tons, bound on a voyage of 20,000 miles to Guaymas, a port on the western coast of Mexico.

Our vessel, an hermaphrodite brig, of but little over a hundred tons, was but a small craft to undertake such a voyage, and being pretty heavily laden with machinery, seemed scarcely higher out of water than a ship's quarter-boat; she was certainly no beauty either, but she was well built, which, after all, was the great desideratum.

We were four of us in the cabin—a cousin of mine, one Bob N., who was off for a lark; a young Mexican, who had been educated in the United States; and a Scotchman, who was going out to try his fortune. In view of the long voyage before us, after the first few days, we all settled down in a quiet methodical way, as if anticipating a life-long residence aboard the little craft. Each one gave his energies as his inclination led him, and followed its bent during the day; but in the evening, by one accord, we always met around the cabin table, as regularly as the sun went below the horizon, and played whist until ten o'clock. Nothing interfered with our game; blow high or blow low, we were always at our post, though occasionally we would be unavoidably interrupted by reefing or taking in sail. Every spare hour of the day was given to my studies, of which navigation, Spanish, and French were the principal; and having been previously well-grounded in each, as may be imagined, during a voyage of eight months, I got to be tolerably proficient in all three.

Few can understand the inestimable benefit conferred upon sea-faring men, and upon the ship-owning community generally, by Lieutenant Maury in his new system of wind and current charts,—based upon the extract of the rich experience of a thousand voyages, as found in their journals, and so classifying them as to point out to the young mariner the probable strength of wind and current, and the indications of fair weather or of foul, which he may meet in any particular latitude, at any season of the year. Armed with these invaluable epitomes of information, the young ship-master steers boldly into unknown seas with as much confidence as if he had spent his life upon them, and with as fair a chance of a successful voyage. In exchange for all this valuable aid, Lieutenant M. merely asks the shipmaster to be a co-laborer with him in the field of nautical science; and in the outset of his voyage, hands him a blank book, in which, each day, he is to note his position, the temperature of air and water, and the direction and strength of winds, and any other natural phenomena which may present themselves to him. At the expiration of his voyage, this log is to be forwarded to Lieutenant M., who adds it to his store of accumulated information, and in turn draws from *it* for the benefit of others. It is most astonishing the electric effect that this presenting an object—*a something to ponder and reflect upon*—has had upon ship-captains, and the zeal with which men who previously never aspired to anything further than the ability to take an altitude of a planet, have evinced in carrying out Lieutenant M.'s wishes. Men who, for years, had dreamed life away amid nature's most startling phenomena, now awoke to the pleasant assurance that even their humble efforts might be made valuable to science; and with all the impetuosity of a sailor's nature, they eagerly seized upon the idea, and nobly have they sustained the opinion formed of them by their distinguished coadjutor.

It is interesting to note the change that this has wrought in the character of many of our American navigators. Men who never thought a gale worth their notice, when once they had escaped its fury ; who snapped their fingers at a current, so long as they had a good breeze with them ; who cared not a fig for thermometrical or barometrical observations, so long as the weather was fair ; and who would not deign a glance at fish or fowl, so long as they were out of reach of harpoon or fowling-piece, may now be seen anxiously pondering upon the centre-circles of a cyclone, and endeavoring to compute its strength and velocity. No current ripples the sea that they do not note it, and endeavor, by comparison with observations, to calculate its force.

At mid-day and mid-night, they carefully scan the mercury in barometer and thermometer, instituting strict comparison between atmospheric changes and the actual state of the weather. No fowl soars above their head, but they watch its flight and jot it down in their log, and no fish shaves the cutwater, but they anxiously note his species and class, and log it too. In a word, the animated pieces of mechanism who formerly directed merchant ships across the boundless wastes of ocean, who pooh-poohed anything like scientific acquirements as unseamanlike, have been converted into rational, thinking men, whose energetic and impetuous natures once enlisted, have put their shoulders to the wheel, only requiring the direction of their accomplished leader, Maury, to compass great results.

Set ignorant men once to thinking, and give them a taste for study, and you at once remove the great barrier which exists between them and their intellectual superiors, and by arousing an *esprit de corps* (which Maury has eminently succeeded in, in this case) you at once smooth the asperities and roughness of ignorance, and give character to men, who, hitherto, having no respect for themselves beyond the vulgar self-esteem, inseparable from ignorance, had no incentive for bettering their position of life.

The ship-owner, sitting in his easy chair at home, taking up a newspaper, and glancing over the marine news, chuckles over a splendid run which his new clipper has just made to San Francisco, and naturally concludes that his skipper is a paragon of smartness. But no thanks does he award to Maury, who by years of patient investigation, in overhauling musty, mildewed log-books, accumulated for a century back, has elicited such stores of information, as has enabled him to point out to the smart captain, the very route which he has pursued, much to the satisfaction of himself and owners.

Maury tells him, that bound for Cape Horn, there is no necessity of first standing over to the coast of Africa, and from thence to the Cape, thus making two legs of a triangle, instead of sailing straight along its base, and thus traversing a space of nearly two thousand miles more than there was any necessity for, as used invariably to be the custom. He tells him, when once around the Cape, to cross the equator in about 110° west longitude, instead of standing over to the Sandwich Islands, and thus going hundreds of miles out of his course ; and in fact, as previously stated, he gives him the cream of the accumulated experience of a thousand navigators, which, sifted by a thoroughly educated and analytical mind, cannot be otherwise than inestimably valuable to all who follow the sea.

No one who has not practically experienced the isolated loneliness of a shipmaster's position on a long voyage, without passengers, wearied out with monotony and ennui, can thoroughly appreciate the benefit conferred upon his class by Lieut. Maury; indeed, even looking upon the system, as an entertaining way of killing time, I will venture to say, that no sea-faring man, who has his sympathies fully enlisted in this cause, will ever complain of too much leisure aboard ship, the constant changes incident to the life, affording abundant food for thought, in connection with the great scientific results of which he feels himself an humble promoter. I myself became deeply interested in these researches, and must acknowledge many delightful hours spent in ruminating upon the theories suggested by Lieut. Maury, and have from that time henceforward, always endeavored to carry out his views in every respect, by keeping a "log," and forwarding it to him as opportunity offered.

CHAPTER VIII.

SONORA.

Guaymas—Its snug Harbor—My Uncle—Appearance of his Residence—Salute his Family in Mexican style—Am installed in my new Home—Go to Work—Mode of doing Business not in strict accordance with the Revenue Laws—Government badly administered—Proclivity of Mexicans to Revolution—Social System—Pretty Girls—Native Grace—English Men-of-war—Balls on board—I get sick—Go to a Watering-place to recuperate—Appearance of Captain Ellis in the Schooner Alice—Fillibustering—Count Rooaset's Expedition, his Campaign, his Defeat and Execution—General Walker—I buy a Vessel and cruize about in her.

After a long but not unpleasant voyage, on the 13th of April, the breaking day revealed to us Cape Haro, near the entrance to the harbor of Guaymas ; rapidly coming up with it and descrying "las tétas de Cábra," or "Kids-teats," a well known land-mark indicating the true entrance, we headed in among the islands which form the harbor ; passing San Vicente and the Isla de Pajaros, we jibbed ship, and shooting through the Almagros, came to an anchor abreast the Punta Arenas, at a distance of only a few hundred yards from the town. The excitement of coming to anchor being over, we had time to look about us, and examine the place of which we had heard so much and so much longed to see.

The bay, one of the most secluded little nooks one could

imagine, so completely land-locked that the entrance is scarcely distinguishable, is a perfect little basin, surrounded by lofty mountains, whose bare sides, destitute of a sign of vegetation, reflect a heat which cannot be exceeded at midsummer at any other point on the globe. The town itself, situated at the base of a lofty hill, and built in the old Spanish American style, with flat roof, and of adobes or mud-brick, is lost to the eye of the casual observer, among the immense hills which overtop it, and give it a background of the same color with the houses themselves; it is only when informed of its whereabouts, that the stranger awakes to the fact that the town is spread directly before him, and he at once detects the individuality of the houses.

Our arrival was on a Sunday, about mid-day, just the hour of siesta, when every one had retired from the intense brightness and heat of the sun; the place seemed deserted, for, except a few solitary, half-naked Indians, not a soul was to be seen; indeed the national ensign which flaunted in the strong sea-breeze seemed to be the only thing possessed of motive power. The arrival of a foreign vessel, however, was too important an event in this dull old town not to create some excitement; and in a few moments the male population came streaming down towards the mole, and the custom-house officials came pulling off in their gay gig, and but a short time elapsed before an old uncle whom we had not seen in twenty years, came aboard to welcome us. I would have singled him out of a thousand, for although a residence of thirty years under that burning sun had browned his cheek, still he stood preëminent among the dark-visaged throng about him, as his white hair floated in the wind, and his bright, intelligent eye and animated features testified to the pleasure he felt, in welcoming us to his house. Bidding us jump into his boat, we were quickly on shore, when leading us up to his almacén, or place of business (spacious storehouse fitted up with sales-rooms and offices, such as would do credit to any commercial town in the world), and handing us our letters, which had been long awaiting us, he proposed our accompanying him to his dwelling, and being introduced to our aunt and cousins, none of whom we had ever seen. Inasmuch as not one of uncle's whole family spoke a word of English, and *we* spoke scarcely a word of Spanish,* and, furthermore, taking into consideration that of some eight or nine cousins, nearly all were young ladies, we looked forward to our presentation as rather an awkward ordeal; nevertheless, it had to be done, therefore, buckling up our courage to the sticking point, we begged to be *led on* to the charge. Arriving at our future residence, we found it to be a long, rambling building fronting on the sea, with immense corridors or piazzas, so deep as always to be shaded from the sun; entering a wide doorway called the *sauan*, we found ourselves in a large courtyard blooming with the most beautiful and fresh looking flowers and plants, appearing to our eyes, so long strangers to anything like it, and dazzled by the intense heat and glare reflected from the bare sand and shell without, a very paradise. Without stopping to admire, we were ushered into a long saloon, paved with tesselated marble, furnished after the European style, with great taste; my heart sank within me, as a glass door opened, and a whole bevy of demure young girls came forward to receive us; my aunt headed the procession, and not waiting for the ceremony of an intro-

* I was the only one who spoke it at all!

duction, threw her arms around us, embracing us with great unction in Mexican fashion. I was completely dumb-founded, and all the pretty little Spanish phrases which I had conjured up for the occasion flew to the winds; however, putting a bold face on the matter, I took my cue from my aunt, and commenced an indiscriminate hug, which the demure misses aforesaid enjoyed, I know, by the twinkling of their bright little eyes; a social meal and an impromptu dance, soon dissipated all feelings of awkwardness and restraint. A description of my new home may not be here inappropriate.

The house, situated directly on the bay, at a distance of not more than twenty yards from the water, is constructed of adobe, one story high, with a front of one hundred and fifty feet, and a deep piazza running its whole length; entering a wide hall, to the left is the dining-saloon, with grated windows from floor to ceiling, looking out on the bay, and to the right a suit of sleeping-rooms, ventilated in a similar way. The hall leads into a large courtyard, with raised flower-beds, filled with flowers of the richest perfume and of the brightest hue, besides a variety of orange, lemon, pomegranate and fig trees; here is to be found the only verdure that exists within several miles of the town, and which is kept up at great expense, the earth being brought from a long distance, and which has constantly to be renewed, while the water used for irrigation has likewise to be brought a distance of a mile or more in casks. To the right of the garden, and elevated some six feet above it, is a covered corridor, of fifty feet in length, by twelve broad, into which open the doors of the parlors and bed-chambers; the first room entered is the parlor, very spacious, the ceiling carried up to the roof, and instead of being plastered, the rafters, highly ornamented, are exposed to view ; its furniture of rich French pattern, the walls hung with paintings, while a magnificent piano by Collard and Callaro, and a mammoth harp by a French celebrity, indicate the taste of its occupants. Through a pair of glass doors, you enter into a large bed-room ; prominent stands an immense gilt bedstead, of elaborate workmanship, such indeed as is only manufactured for the Mexican market, highly ornamented and massive ; the curtains of rich lace, and coverlid a chef d'œuvre of Chinese art ; this elegant piece of furniture never cost less than $1,000 ; Japan divans and lacquered wardrobes are placed in appropriate positions, while the washing and other utensils are of pure silver ; passing through another glass door you enter the sala-grande or large parlor, a room measuring 60 feet in length by about 20 in breadth, with a tesselated marble pavement, and hung with chandeliers—this hall is reserved for festive occasions, although a delightful lounge in hot weather ; from hence you pass into and through several chambers, and thence into the pantries and bath-rooms. Stepping again into the corridor, at the extreme end and crossing to the other side of the garden, you enter the kitchen ; the Mexican kitchen is a very different place from the cuisine of Yankee land ; merely used for cooking purposes, it contains no furniture, its unwashed walls blackened with smoke, and its unpaved floor, give it a dirty and gloomy appearance. Moreover, there is no range or cooking-stove, the apparatus used in preparing food being made in this wise : a solid earthen or brick platform is carried along the wall, three feet in height ; at intervals of a foot, little walls of brick, some eighteen inches high are raised dividing the whole affair into pigeon holes ; in these apertures fires are built, while over the top of each, small bars of iron are laid, on which the meat is placed for roasting or broiling, or earthenware pots are set for boiling or stewing. The most primitive utensils are used, made usually of earth, and it is astonishing how, with such simple appliances, such excellent success attends their culinary efforts. Leaving the kitchen on the left and pushing through another large door and under an arch, you enter the court-yard, containing the stables, poultry-yards, etc.

The large corridor, during the hot season, which lasts from March until November, is used as a-bed chamber, and each night the cots belonging to every member of the family are brought out and extended ; the excessive heat prohibiting the use of bedding, a sheet laid over the sacking-bottom of a cot, and a hair pillow, is all that is requisite. During the months of July, August or September, it is impossible to sleep under cover, and during that time the cots are placed in the open courts or on the roof. Speaking of the excessive heat, I would observe that during the above mentioned months, the thermometer shows an average during 24 hours of 90° Fahrenheit, the maximum at 2 P. M., being at about 100°—while the minimum at 2 A. M., would not be less than 85°. From the month of November, however, until March, there are times when the mercury falls as low as 50°, and a fair average of that period would probably be in the vicinity of 70°. The heat during the summer is most oppressive, and the winds as they sweep down from the hills become so charged with caloric as to be absolutely unbearable when exposed to them, making it necessary during the warmer part of the day, to close the doors to *exclude* the breeze ; during this period the place is subject to what are called *los vientos calientes* or hot winds, when the wind comes from a certain quarter, passing over a mountainous district entirely destitute of verdure, whose rocky surface continually exposed to the fierce rays of the sun becomes heated to an incredible degree ; these winds rushing over them and becoming charged with their heat, reach the town, and bring with them a temperature so high, that exposure to their blasts would be absolutely painful to one ; during their continuance everything contracts and withers, and furniture is often rent asunder with great violence, they last generally three or four hours, leaving the atmosphere, however, much clearer than before their approach.

One singular thing connected with them is, that the water usually luke-warm and undrinkable, after the passage of one of these winds, becomes icy cold and most refreshing, caused by the excessive evaporation.

On the occasion of one blowing, I noted the mercury at its approach to stand at 95°, at sundown ; at 9 P. M. two hours after, it showed 107°, and at its cessation it again fell to 89°. On entering a room which had been closed throughout the day during their prevalence, one experiences a cold shiver, although the mercury should indicate 90°, inside—the change of temperature being so great from without.

There being an absence of all dew and rain during a greater part of the year, there is no humidity whatever in the temperature, which is very disagreeable, parching the skin, and not inducing perspiration, which is so necessary to the comfort in these latitudes. The temperature is so uniform day and night that it is almost an impossibility to sleep with comfort, and one wakes languid and enervated, notwithstanding all his precautions of having his bed placed on the housetop, or even in the street—an expedient frequently resorted to. The poorer classes, not having the advantage of spacious court-yards during the "heated term," use the street as a bed-room, and before each door there may be seen a family circle quietly snoring away; some funny scenes often result from this. I remember one moonlight night, returning home quite late with some companions, and, espying a street full of sleepers, one, less sober than the others, resolved on playing them a trick: routing up a herd of jackasses quietly snoozing, and giving a series of diabolical yells, he sent them full tilt through the dormitory. Such a hubbub never was heard or seen, every cot overturned, women half dressed rushing about crying "Indians! Indians!" and the poor children lay sprawling and screeching in the road, while men, seizing their arms, let fly into the unfortunate donkeys, who, bewildered with the uproar and smarting from their wounds, returned full tilt to the charge. The chagrin of the sleepers may be imagined, on discovering that they had been fighting their own asses.

My initiation into business was immediate, the details of my uncle's affairs having gone behind for some eighteen months, on account of his clerks having left for California. I found myself plunged into a mass of intricate accounts, which seemed at first utterly beyond my powers of unraveling, more particularly so from the fact of their being kept in a foreign language; however, at it I went, day and night, for six months, the morning's sun often shining in upon my labors, protracted through the long night-vigils until after dawn of day. Hard work it was, indeed, but the unceasing application necessary to accomplish it made me more thoroughly conversant with the business transactions of the country, and its *commercial dialect*, than years of ordinary routine would have done. The heat I found a very great drawback in pursuing my avocation, enervating and debilitating, and at times almost forcing me to abandon it; sitting at my desk, with no clothing but a linen shirt and pantaloons, the perspiration brought out by the effort of writing would drop from off me on my papers, so as almost to obliterate my work; it likewise induced a feeling of intense sleepiness, which, at night, it seemed almost impossible to overcome. My preparations for night-work were as follows: on a table beside my desk, a basin of water, a coffee machine, with a *spirit* lamp and a bundle of cigars; as soon as I felt that I was losing myself, I would plunge my head into the water, then take a cup of strong coffee, then smoke a cigar; in this way I was enabled to get through a wonderful number of nights. My work commenced in April, lasting with but little intermission till July, when my final balance was made; and, as may be supposed, I fell ill, and was on my back for weeks with a severe nervous affection.

The mode of conducting business operations on the coast of Mexico is peculiar to that country, and is worth describing; we will take the port of Guaymas for an example. The only port of entry for the state of Sonora, all foreign goods consumed by its inhabitants, besides a large amount sold annually to the state of Chihuahua, go through its custom house, and are from thence transported on mule-back hundreds of miles into the interior to the different towns and trading posts; upwards of two millions and a half of dollars worth of goods being annually disposed of in this way. Now, the Mexican tariff of duties, it is well known, is so high in its rates, that it amounts almost to a prohibition; and, naturally, if importers could not evade the payment of these duties, a total suspension of business would be the result. But, of course, such a thing would be absurd. Nor, indeed, could a people long accustomed to European articles of luxury, be induced to forego their use. The mode in which goods are passed through the custom house, is in this wise. A merchant, who is in expectation of a foreign cargo, stations a boat outside of the harbor, to communicate with his ship before entering: upon heaving in sight, she is boarded by the person from the boat before mentioned, to whom the master of the ship hands over a manifest of her cargo; this is immediately smuggled ashore to the merchant, the vessel meanwhile cruising off the harbor out of sight. The merchant, putting his manifest in his pocket, walks over to the custom house, and, calling the collector aside, says to him, "I am expecting a ship on the coast, and this (producing the manifest) is an account of her cargo. Now, I want to know on what terms you will enter her, provided she comes here; for, if you do not make a liberal offer, I will send her to some other port." After a great deal of haggling and conferring with his officers, a bargain is struck, allowing the ship to come in at a reduction of say from twenty to thirty per cent. upon the tariff rates; the collector receiving as a bribe from ten to fifteen thousand dollars. In the meanwhile the merchant has, perhaps, two or three hundred bales on board, which he *has no idea of paying any duty whatever on;* so he charters some snug little craft to steal out of port—go alongside the vessel outside—take the said bales out of her, and land them at some uninhabited place, where he has his mule-trains awaiting to transport them into the interior; the muleteers being furnished with the necessary forged papers to enable them to pass the internal custom house, the officers of which, probably, have received a large bribe, not to look too closely into the affair. In consequence of this last transaction, of course a new manifest must be made out; for the collector knows nothing of this affair. The new papers are consequently drawn, *the signatures* of the *European officers* affixed, together with *their seals of office; a duplicate of which every merchant is furnished with by his correspondents!* Affairs being concluded with the custom house, the ship enters, and the cargo is discharged into the warehouse of the merchant under custom-house seal. The vista (an officer of the custom house) is then ordered to take an account of the goods in store, in order that they may be compared with the manifest; but he, in turn, is willing to make a little money: so at night he comes, breaks his seal, allows the merchant to take out certain contraband goods which he has among the cargo, and then reseals the door, and on the morrow makes the most *rigid examination.* Thus the goods are entered for, say fifty per cent. less than the tariff rate of duties; and, assuming the actual duties to amount to, say

$100,000—50 per cent., would be	. . . . .	$50,000
	Bribe to collector, ...	10,000
	" " vista, ...	2,500
	" " guards, etc., ...	2,500
$65,000		$65,000

$35,000—Amount saved by the merchant; exclusive of duties on goods smuggled outside the port, showing a saving of $35,000. By means of the false manifests the government is only credited with $50,000, and out of this amount rarely receives a dollar, as it is *accounted* for by the collector, in his returns, as expended in salaries, coast-guard expenses, etc. etc.

The above is no exception to the general rule, but is the usual and only way of getting a cargo into the country. Should a collector prove contumacious, and not be willing to accept a fair offer, the ship is kept off the port until he comes to terms, which he almost always does, or if not, she is sent off to some other port. Should a collector have conscientious scruples, which once in a very great while is the case, every effort is resorted to, to get rid of him by way of bribe and menace, and almost invariably one or the other is successful; if not, then he is forcibly ejected from the town, taken on board some vessel in the night, and sent off a long distance, with a gentle hint that his life will pay the forfeit in case of his return. I remember an instance of a gentleman by the name of Malo, one of the few honest Mexican officials who have held this office; he was collector of Mazatlan; in vain offers were made for entry; for a month or more he held out, and during this time, on one occasion, he was offered $30,000 to go to his country-seat and remain two days, but he was really too honest, and rather than lend his connivance to these affairs he resigned. To show the utter want of principle in these men, it is a fact that when the English bond-holders agreed to take the receipts of the Mexican custom houses in payment for their dues, they appointed *their own* officials from the best recommendations in the country, *and not one man turned out true to his trust*, although paid *liberal salaries.* As I before observed, the collectors, in hopes of getting a larger bribe, or from some equally worthy motive, sometimes refuse to allow a vessel to enter on any terms less than the legal requirements. In this case, the ship goes to some other port; but it occasionally happens that, on account of the state of the market, she must enter at this one port; in which case she cruises outside until the collector comes to terms: and I knew of one vessel being outside the port of Mazatlan *six months;* so that together with her five months' voyage from England, her crew were eleven months on board ship *without going ashore.* The export duties on money, make it necessary to smuggle it all off aboard ship; the gold dust and uncoined silver is contraband, and coined gold and silver pays a heavy duty. Large quantities are smuggled off in this wise: a man-of-war comes in harbor, and makes it known privately to the merchants that she will take a specie freight. Every night two or three boats are sent ashore, and their crews, with their smuggling jackets inside their shirts, are ordered up to the different counting-rooms. Each man is laden with sufficient, so as not to cause suspicion; and then they are accompanied down to the boats by an officer, the guards of course not daring to interfere with them. Officers, also, enter into the business, and receive pay for all they carry off; so that on every occasion of coming on shore, they load themselves down. Generally, several balls are given on board, and occasion is taken to hide a bag of dust in each lady's dress previous to embarking, the gentlemen likewise taking their proportion; and in this way large quantities are smuggled. The bar silver, however, gives more trouble, and seizures are frequently made. On many occasions I myself have been obliged to get large sums off on board ship; and I remember once, within a few days, taking off over one hundred thousand in hard dollars, six hundred at a time, which was really very hard work, as the money, fitted in a canvas jacket, has to be put on under the shirt; and, consequently, one is obliged every trip to dress and undress himself. This does not seem a very creditable business for the men-of-war of a friendly nation to engage in; but the English men-of-war have been in the habit of doing it for years, and from the port of Guaymas alone, take perhaps three million dollars annually; the freight on specie is about one per cent., one-half per cent. going to the Admiralty, one-quarter per cent. to the Greenwich Hospital, and one-quarter per cent. to the captain. This is an immense perquisite, and, of course, is a great inducement for the captains of vessels to use their utmost endeavors to secure the freights, little caring how it is got on board. The English men-of-war's men are not very nice in their idea of international courtesy, as may be imagined from the following incident:

During the year 1849, the frigate Meander made her appearance in Mazatlan; during her presence, a foreign merchantman came into port, and her owners made an arrangement with the captain of the man-of-war to assist in smuggling a certain amount of goods ashore, to be landed on a beach directly in front of the town; an understanding was had with the police not to interfere, and at midnight, two cutters, filled with armed men from the Meander, took two heavily-laden barges in tow, and succeeded in landing the goods high and dry on the beach. The soldiers getting wind of the affair, rushed down and fired into the boats, and several volleys were exchanged, but I don't think any one was killed; a pretty piece of business for one of her majesty's crack frigates to be engaged in! Business on the coast is conducted on the credit system, eight months' time being usually given; when a ship comes in, notice is given throughout the state, and buyers flock to the port to make their purchases, which they usually do very expeditiously, and oftentimes in less than a month the greater part of the saleable goods of a heavy cargo are disposed of at prices not by any means exorbitant. The goods mostly in request are linens, cambrics, cotton goods, calicos, French and German silks of the richest description, French fancy manufactures, with every variety of fine hardware, chinaware, groceries, wines, etc.

After disposing of the goods, it is an immense job to pack them, for, as everything is carried on mules, the weight of all the packages has to be very nicely adjusted; besides this, they must all be reëntered in the internal custom house, the process of the entry being extremely intricate and tedious, and here comes another piece of smuggling into play. Certain goods paying much higher duties than others, substitutions must be made, representing the article to be of the kind paying the lesser duty; for instance, say that one hundred casks of Madeira wine are to be forwarded into the interior—now Madeira pays more duty than Muscatel, therefore, on the entry, two hundred casks Muscatel is written, and the duty computed accordingly, all, of course, under the approval of the custom-house officer; these formalities and details are extremely laborious, and involve an immense expenditure of time and patience.

The currency is most diversified, and is another element of confusion in conducting business. The bar silver, weighing some eighty pounds to the bar, is composed of pure silver, or sometimes with an admixture of gold; on the back of it is branded its weight, and if mixed with gold, the weight of the gold in it. These marks are government brands, and pass current in all transactions, the value of the metal being estimated by varying rates. Plata fuego is silver in lumps, extracted from the ore by fire, and Plata piña is also lump silver, extracted by quicksilver. Gold appears also in small bars of from $1,500 to $2,000, and also in dust in large quantities, as well as in lumps, likewise extracted by fire and quicksilver. Spanish and Mexican coin is also largely in use, as well as North American money, which is becoming common; as may be imagined, with all these different values, the cash-keeper has his hands full in keeping his cash accounts straight and making his remittances.

Notwithstanding the immense amount of labor entailed by the absurd requirements of Mexican law at the hands of the merchant, still every occasion is taken advantage of for a holiday or an excursion of some sort or other, and the community all harmonizing, it needs only a suggestion from one party, seconded by another, to set the little world in motion for a grand pic-nic to one of the many delightfully appropriate localities for such an affair. No sooner thought upon than put into execution; a committee is organized, subscriptions solicited (always forthcoming), provisions are furnished, the little flotilla of boats got ready, men sent off to the scene of action to pitch tents and clear off a spot for dancing, and the next morning the whole population is off—merry girls and young men, papas and grand-papas, mammas and grand-mammas—all set off, and after a day spent in feasting and dancing, midnight sees them returning, fatigued but delighted, and ready to go to work with renewed vigor.

Taste in dress is inherent to the Spanish women, and really

one would be astonished to observe the effect produced by them when arrayed for a ball. They are the most desperate flirts, and I pity any poor fellow who falls in love with a Guaymanian before he is ready to marry—if he be of a jealous disposition, he will never survive it. One of the nicest girls in Guaymas, at the time of my arrival, was one Margarita, a blonde among brunettes, with the most prodigious flow of animal spirits, but tempered by a good sense, which made her a charming companion ; she was a delightful partner in a ball-room, and most interesting in her own snug house ; she was the sister of the priest, and having had access to his library, was rather more conversable than her companions ; many an hour has melted away in her society, but she too, poor girl, melted away like the pleasant hours, and although she fought the grim old knight, Consumption, hard, he was at length her conqueror, and as I saw her pass to her long home, her opened coffin strewn with flowers, my heart turned sick within me—pobrecita !

But the jolliest, merriest, most roguish little "*sprite*" of all the town was a certain little Carmelita, in form most diminutive, but graceful as an houri, her eyes like dancing water, and her face beaming with intelligence ; of marvellously quick perception, she would unravel, in an instant, any "pretty speeches" obscurely rendered in bad Spanish, and, rapping my knuckles with her fan, would, with serio-comicality, correct my blunders. I could not do otherwise than quickly learn the language under the tuition of so lovely a professor, and I must say my progress surprised myself. Every evening the setting sun found me before her window opening on the sea ; and many a well-remembered hour have I passed with her there. Standing looking at the red-faced moon as she peeped over the eastern hills, she would say, "Ah, Don Tomas, what would you not give to see your Doña Isabel, who is probably also looking at that lovely moon?" Then I would say, "Ah, Querída Carmelita, what would you not give to be *tête-à-tête* with your Don Joaquin, who is at this moment blessing that moon, because she looks on thee?" Then the little witch would blush most suspiciously, I never dreaming, however, that all this time her troth was plighted to that same Joaquin. She carried too many guns for me! As a standing rule, she always gave me the first polka in all assemblies, parties, or pic-nics. Indeed it was useless for any one else to apply, not even the redoubtable Don Joaquin himself; she, the very smallest of females, and I, rather a tall specimen of humanity, would go twirling around, till, from very dizziness, we would be obliged to seek refuge in a corner to *recuperate.* Half the time during the dance her feet would never touch the floor at all; nevertheless, she was never out of time or lost step, for all that.

One great drawback to the comfort of a residence in Mexico is the constant dread one stands in of the numerous vermin and poisonous reptiles and insects which infest the country, the bite of which latter is sometimes fatal, but always attended with the most unpleasant consequences. The most to be dreaded of these reptiles is the scorpion, or alacrán,—not longer than the first joint of your finger. He finds a secure hiding-place in the toe of one's boot, or in the sleeves of the coat, where he ensconces himself in ambush, when, woe to the unfortunate who attempts putting on the *inhabited* article; for, enraged at being disturbed, he inflicts a series of stings—until he is removed from the person—any one of which is oftentimes sufficient to throw one into spasms. The sting to an infant is *always* fatal; rarely to an adult, but generally attended with great pain and temporary paralysis of the part affected, nervous people being thrown into convulsions. These little torments abound in old houses, delighting in dark corners, and hiding themselves in the crevices of walls. They salley forth at night, and drop upon one when least expected. They are often found beneath one's pillow, or between the sheets, causing a shudder when discovered. For months after my arrival in the country, I was scrupulously careful in examining every article of clothing before putting it on, shaking out my boots, and turning sleeves and stockings inside out; yet, notwithstanding my precautions, was several times bitten, and, at last, gave it up in disgust, resolving to run my chance. The alacrán, though usually small, sometimes grows quite large, and I have seen them as large and as thick as my thumb, a most hideous object to behold; but, fortunately, the largest are least to be dreaded, for as they increase in size, they become less venomous; they look more like a crab than anything else that I can compare them to, having, however, a long tail, which they carry in an arc over their back, the extreme end armed with a horn-like substance, sharp as a cambric needle, and hooked; and this is their weapon; and, on being molested, they wield it with unparalleled activity and spite. The young ones, on being given birth to, immediately climb upon the mother's back, and attacking her, gradually eat her up, leaving only the shell, and, by that time, are sufficiently strong to go off into the world, literally on their own *hook*. The alacrán of Durango is the most venomous, and hundreds of children are yearly killed by them in that province. So great is the dread of them, that the mayor pays a standing reward of sixpence for every one captured, and boys armed with stilettos wage constant war upon them.

The *centipede* is another loathsome reptile, which is more dreaded than the alacrán itself. Several inches long, of a dark brown color, and covered with a repulsive-looking hair and slime, and walking upon its thousand legs, the very sight produces a sensation of sickness and disgust. In order to bite, he must make great preparation, and get himself into a particular position. This manœuvering makes his presence known to grown people, who shake him off, but helpless children rarely escape, and his sting is almost always mortal.

Of spiders, of the most venomous description, there are innumerable species, the most noted among which is the well-known tarantula, which grows here to an enormous size, and is revolting to look upon. Of snakes, there are every variety, and of the most poisonous nature, the rattle-snake abounding. This horrible reptile frequently finds his way into human habitations. On several different occasions they were killed in our own house—once rolled up in a lady's stocking—again ensconced in her bath-tub—and again by the side of my bed. A young girl, a cousin, coming in to call us in the morning, while sitting by our bedside, seeing something glistening on the floor, stooped to pick it up, supposing it to be a ribbon or sash which we had carried off as a trophy from the ball of the night previous, when she was horrified by seeing it curling itself, ready to spring, and sounding its rattle. We did not take long to wake *that* morning, and his snakeship was dispatched by an article of bed-room furniture which is not commonly used for that purpose. One of the greatest drawbacks to sleeping in the open air is the exposure to a certain kind of bat which abounds here, and while flying about, drops a fluid, which, in falling upon the skin, acts as a powerful caustic, raising a severe blister. If it falls into the eye, it blinds it. They are excessively annoying, and one rarely escapes being victimized for more than a week at a time. A sheet drawn over one is no protection, as their fluid has blistered my skin, having passed through a sheet and a pair of linen drawers.

The principal town in the state of Sonora is the city of Hermosillo, some forty leagues inland from Guaymas, a place of from ten to fifteen thousand inhabitants, with nothing, however, remarkable about it, excepting that, for an inland town, it is an unusually active and stirring place; for here, the goods that are purchased in large quantities at the port, are retailed to the minor traders of the adjoining country, creating a good deal of life and animation, and rendering it, as it were, the market-town of the whole northern part of the state. In the vicinity there are numbers of rich plantations, on which are raised large quantities of wheat, which is ground and sent by mules to the port, and from there shipped in sufficient quantities to supply the whole Mexican coast.

The country in this vicinity, and for a long distance inland, is extremely fertile, and in many instances well watered, but these poor devils of Mexicans dare not occupy the land, from a dread of the Indians, who infest the entire northern part of the state, and when the poor farmer is least thinking of them they bear down in overwhelming numbers upon him, and massacring him and all his family, carry off his stock, leaving his plantation a mass of ruin. The Appachees, knowing the cowardice of the Mexicans, venture oftentimes within sight of their largest towns to commit their depredations, and on several occasions have been seen by the people of Hermosillo from their house-tops, burning the farm-houses not a league distant. The central government every once in a while makes a great flourish of trumpets about sending troops to put them down ; a military commandant is appointed to lead them, and a regiment or two of soldiers are assembled at some agreeable town in the interior. Here the commandant establishes his headquarters, never dreaming of troubling himself about the active part of the campaign, but sends off his officers in quest of the savages ; they march off to the frontier, and by means of scouts, get a pretty good idea of the whereabouts of the Indians ; acting upon which information, they march in a *contrary* direction, thus entirely avoiding any collision. After remaining out a month or so, they march back to headquarters, with flaming accounts of bloodless victories, gained beneath the banners of the Mexican eagles. Dios y libertad ! and all of that ! accounts of which go the round of all Mexican newspapers, and the Secretary of War forwards, by a special aid-de-camp, a package of medals for the *veterans*, and legions of honor for the officers.

Ures, the capital of the state, is situated very near the frontier, and is unimportant, excepting as being the seat of government. Alamos is the second city in size in the state, and is a place of a great deal of wealth, there being extensive silver mines in its immediate vicinity. It can boast of some beauty, too, being half buried in orange groves, and presents a delightful appearance to the wearied traveller whose eyes, accustomed to the hot and mud-baked towns of the coast, feast themselves upon the fresh luxuriance of its vegetation. The good folks of Alamos are a very stay-at-home sort of people, who, instead of going abroad to look for wives, have found sweethearts among the beauties of their own town (indeed, they are said to be the prettiest women in the whole republic), and have been in the habit of doing this so long that they have all become nearly related to each other ; in fact, the whole ten thousand are cousins-german, and the result is (as is always the case where near relatives marry and have issue), that there is an incredible amount of deformity, blindness, and deafness, existing to an alarming extent, while insanity and physical deformity are met with at every step.

They are most desperate gamblers, but as they play among themselves, and fairly, luck deserting at one time favors them at another, so that they are not often ruined. A very wealthy man was sitting one afternoon in front of his house, taking the air, when he observed a pedlar, whom he knew very well, looking intently at his premises ; hailing him, he asked him what he was about, and what new peculiarity he had discovered in his mansion. "Oh !" said the man, "I was only thinking that possibly some day this establishment may belong to me ; especially as we Alamanians are very fond of cards, and luck often favors the poor man." Tickled with the man's effrontery, and delighted to get some one to gamble with, he offered to lend him ten dollars, if he would sit down and take a hand ; a proposition no Mexican was ever known to refuse. At it they went—they became very much excited—the pedlar won, won, won, and wanted to leave off, but his opponent would not hear of it, but insisted on doubling the stakes ; at it they kept until daylight. The next morning the pedlar rose from the table a winner of every cent the other possessed in the world—houses, land, stock, everything.

The Indian ravages in this vicinity, likewise, are frightful; to illustrate which, I would remark, that an aunt of mine who resided there, lost twenty near relatives by Indian assassination! brothers, cousins, sisters, aunts and uncles!

The northern portion of the state is particularly rich in minerals, the gold and silver mines being exceedingly productive; there are also surface diggings which yield largely; but, unfortunately, the most valuable mining districts are in the hands of the savages, who ruthlessly murder any white man who ventures to approach them. The famous silver mine of Arizona, called "planchas de Plata," which may be rendered "surfaces of silver," from its incredible wealth, is left unworked for fear of them.

A journey in the interior is an affair of great importance. The old family coach, more like an ark than a vehicle, is rolled out and furnished with all the requisites of pots and pans for cooking, and bedding for sleeping; for there are no inns on the road. A troop of horses are driven in from the "labor" or farm, and the family servants, some five or six in number, are mustered and drilled in musket exercise. At the appointed time, off they start; the coach with three wheel horses and two on the lead, all galloping and kicking to the extent of their ability, the servants following on horseback, with carbines slung, and their long spears with gay pennons fluttering; while all the dogs in the neighborhood swell the cavalcade, apparently with a bold resolve to accompany the expedition.

The instability of the government is proverbial; but no one

who has not resided in that delectable republic can form any idea of the mode of its administration, or of the constant changes to which it is subject. No state governor ever serves out his term of office; indeed, as a general thing, during the term for which he is elected some four or five incumbents usually fill the gubernatorial chair. A change of state government is always accompanied by a local civil war. The aspirants for the governorship being, generally speaking, military men who have strong influence in the state, they do not hesitate to back their pretensions by an appeal to arms, which is as promptly responded to by the opposite faction, and a bloodless war ensues; marching and counter-marching, and flourishes of trumpets being the order of the day, while the whole country is in a state of anarchy, from there being no established head to execute the laws. The mode of procedure in getting up a revolution is as follows: the rival chief incites all friendly to him to revolt, and offers large bribes to the subordinates of the opposite party; when he thinks himself sufficiently strong, he raises his standard, puts himself at the head of his "mob," marches to the custom house or public treasury, and takes possession of the public funds. He then stations his men about the town, and, proclaiming martial law, forbids any one leaving their houses. Then proceeding to the public square, he causes to be read, amid the cheers of his adherents, the ringing of bells, etc., his pronunciamento or apology for assuming the reins of government. He is then hailed as a liberator and deliverer from bondage, and by this time, the other party becoming infected, flock to his standard. This is the *modus operandi* of all revolutionists—the "grand coup" being the seizure of the treasure; this done, the success is sure to be complete, for the Mexicans can smell money as far as a *rat can cheese.* These little affairs are almost constantly occurring.

The administration of government in detail is most defective in every branch, but in none more so than in the tribunals of justice, venality being here a prominent attribute of the "blind goddess." Indeed, the halls of justice are nothing more or less than auction marts where favorable judgments are sold to the highest bidder, and the judges, receiving their appointments through influence or bribery, and without regard to their legal attainments, unblushingly make their *price* known in all cases appearing before them. An example in point. At the port of Mazatlan a cargo arrived from Europe, and insured there. The vessel discharged, and everything turned out in first-rate order; but the merchant to whom it was consigned, not content with an enormous profit, took it into his head to defraud the underwriters, which he managed in this wise. He went to the judge of the first instance (who, in absence of a consul) certifies all foreign documents, and said to him: "I want your signature to a protest, what will you charge for it?" "$3,000!" "Done—sign this, and here's the money." The paper was a protest that damage to the amount of $30,000 had been done to the cargo, and claiming damages to that amount. The claim was allowed; the underwriters mulcted to the tune of $30,000, the merchant putting it into his pocket.

Judging from their attention to outward forms, one would imagine the Mexicans, as a nation, to be the most devout in the world, for there is not an hour of the day, or scarcely of the night, when one is not reminded, either ocularly or auricularly, of the celebration of some one of the services peculiar to the Catholic Church. Awakened out of his soundest sleep by the deafening din of bells ringing for early mass at two o'clock in the morning, one writhes uneasily, until his ears becoming accustomed to the clamor, he again falls asleep, only to be awakened by a repetition at sunrise, which continues for an hour or so, accompanied by the explosion of some dozens of rockets, which are sent up by way, I suppose, of boosting up their prayers on their way to heaven. At twelve o'clock another attack on the bells is commenced, which lasts for half an hour, the heavier metal being swung on their axes, while the lighter bells are beaten with stones or clubs. At six o'clock the assault is again made, as a call to evening prayer, and during its continuance one must off hat and kneel, the horseman must dismount, and go on his marrow-bones, while the coachman must pull up at the sidewalk. At nine P.M., the ringers make one final effort, which is called the Queda, warning all honest folks to bed, like the old English curfew. Of all nuisances in Mexico, this is one of the greatest. I myself lived for two years within a few yards of five cracked bells, which were performed upon by half a dozen Indian imps, who were my utterest abomination. And it gives me sincere delight to remember that no opportunity ever escaped me of wreaking my vengeance upon them when I caught them without the precincts of the church. During the interval of the bell-ringing, processions are continually passing, which, *nolens volens*, one must kneel to, upon the pain of being stoned. In Guaymas the respect paid to religion was not so extreme, probably from the fact that there was only one priest, and he a very young man, whose all-engrossing idea was to get money. No one was ever married without bleeding pretty freely. Indeed I remember one instance, where a bridal party were assembled and waiting for the priest, but he would not officiate, as the fee (an unheard of one) was not all paid up, and consequently, the party had to disperse, and the bride doff her wedding attire.

The church itself was not half built, only sufficiently finished to allow mass to be celebrated within its walls, notwithstanding that a gentleman told me, who had charge of the church funds, that there had been money enough subscribed to build half a dozen churches, but that the priest had pocketed it all. The little miscreant was one of the most oily-tongued rascals that ever was seen ; butter wouldn't melt in his mouth ; it used to be our delight to get him boosy—he would drop in at dinner time. Ah Señor Cura (Mr. Priest) glad to see you, sit down, take a bite with us. You really must excuse me—just dined. Ah now, do. Cannot indeed. Nevertheless he always did, and then such trencher performances never were seen. A glass of wine, Señor Cura ? Excuse me, never drink any but sacramental wine without spirits. But this has no strength. Well, if you will have it, here goes. And although the strongest of port, glass after glass disappears, gradually he becomes confidential, offers to marry or *bury* us all for nothing ; says he wouldn't object to us for a brother-in-law ; and finally, tells us of his amours which we are dying to know ; next day he cuts us all. His masses were amusing, the music being *done* by a band consisting of a trombone, bugle, clarionet and drum, played upon by Indians; any air, it was all the same, polkas, Yankee doodle, God save the queen, etc, being the ordinary accompaniments of the chanted Psalter.

Marriages of foreigners with natives are a source of great profit to the priest, who always makes the most of them.

According to the ecclesiastical law of the country, no foreigner can marry without first abjuring his faith (should he be a Protestant), taking the sacrament of the Catholic Church, and going through a long and tedious formula, which can be interminably lengthened out, or cut short, according to the caprice of the priest or amount of the bribe paid him, which must be in proportion to the wealth of the groom; several instances occurred during my residence there. On one occasion a young doctor, an American (a great scamp, by the way, as almost all Yankees styling themselves doctors in that country are), became engaged to a very interesting and respectable young lady; his suit did not progress very favorably, to be sure, but perseverance on his part, and strong natural affection on hers, gave him the victory, and the parents becoming reconciled, they gave a reluctant assent. The wedding preliminaries were gone through with, the doctor abjured the Protestant belief, took the sacrament and confessed his sins, the curate exacting the most minute proofs of his conversion, such as walking in procession with the host, learning catechism. etc., on account of a grudge he had against him for not marrying his own sister. The day was fixed upon and the guests assembled, but lo! the priest did not make his appearance; two hours passed by, and the guests were on the point of taking leave of the unfortunate bride who was fainting with chagrin, when in walked his reverence and the ceremony was hurried through with. It appears that the doctor was a few dollars short in his fee or bribe, and the priest refused positively to stir a peg until the whole amount was made up.

Feast days are innumerable; it would be useless to attempt to chronicle them; never a week passes without the cessation of business, for at least one day; foreigners, however, braving public opinion, only observed the principal ones. The holy-week is celebrated in Sonora with great pomp and merits description.

On Holy-Thursday the ball opens, all business *must* be suspended, no vehicles are allowed in the streets, fastings *must* be observed, no animal food being permitted in the markets. The whole community clothe themselves in black, in grief for the approaching death of Christ; the churches are open night and day, and masses and prayers without intermission are celebrated; constant processions, headed by priests and followed by the whole community bare-headed, perambulate the towns, chanting hymns, halting every few steps and going down on their knees while the host is elevated before them. On Thursday night, torch-light processions again take place. Friday morning opens with awful solemnity; the ships in the harbor half-mast their flags, cock-bill their yards (nautical type of mourning), while the church bells are silenced, being supplanted by an instrument called a tric-trac, making a noise corresponding to its name, and which is shaken about the town as a signal that church services are about to commence. All must dress in deepest mourning; at mid-day our Saviour is formally crucified before the assembled multitude, none of the revolting features of the real sacrifice being omitted. Prayers interminable are followed by a sermon, only remarkable for its absurdity, and impiety. Somewhat in this wise was one that I heard. After a long, and as the priest no doubt thought, a very eloquent peroration relating to the passion of our Saviour, he wound up with the following adjuration:

"My brethren, in spite of my having depicted to you in the

most vivid colors the sufferings of our dear Lord, you show no sign of sorrow ! not a moistened eye, or a stifled groan ! Had a pet *dog* so suffered, would you not have wept ? Still, here your Lord and Saviour is lacerated and torn, and you exhibit no signs of sympathy. Ungrateful wretches ! what *will* become of you ?" This was enough ; the whole multitude sent up the most outrageous wail, groanings and tearing of hair were the order of things for an hour or more. After endless services, the evening and night of Good Friday is devoted to torch-light processions, in which the penitents take a prominent part. These are people, who, having been sinning the whole year hope for expiation through self-torture. Some bind huge wooden crosses to their backs, and drag them around for hours, in the line of procession. Others bind crowns of thorns upon their heads, every step they take blood exuding from their pierced brows ; others are bound with huge chains, while others, naked, are followed by scourgers, their backs a mass of blood and gore. I have seen delicate women fainting by the wayside under the cruel pressure of the cross, and stalwart men fall apparently lifeless, under the hand of their scourgers—so blind is faith ! Saturday morning opens with like solemnity, and until noon the mournful services continue ; then the Lord is raised from the tomb in which he has been deposited, and all is joy again. The bells ring forth joyful acclamations ; the ships in the harbor right their colors, and booming guns show their participation in the general joy, and all the world goes on to sin again. The gambler and the harlot dry up their penitential wounds and busily resume their avocations.

People living in Europe or America, on changing their residence from the populous city to the rural districts, make it a great desideratum in locating, that there should be a good physician somewhere in the vicinity. Accustomed to these civilized prejudices, I was very much astonished to learn that in Guaymas there was neither physician nor apothecary, nor indeed had there ever been one permanently located there, if we except a few quacks who had honored the place with their presence, where, after having killed rather more than their quota, they usually fled to parts unknown to escape the summary vengeance of the populace. I was very much surprised at the *sang-froid* of my uncle in view of the breaking out of the cholera which took place shortly after my arrival, as it was only fair to surmise that in its violence, some one of the many members of his family would be liable to an attack. Cholera at any time carries a feeling of horror with it, but more especially in small communities where every victim is known; but in this instance, from its extreme fatality, was more particularly to be dreaded. The heat—which was most intense—from an absence of electricity with which the atmosphere is generally filled at this season of the year, produced a feeling of lassitude which was particularly favorable to the spread of the contagion, and spread it did in a manner most terrific. No hour of the day or night passed but what some one of the rapidly diminishing population was prostrated in the dust. No one could be found who would voluntarily bury the dead, so great was the fear of infection! the ordinary grave-diggers recoiling from a task which might make them the next victim; consequently, persons passing along the street were, unceremoniously, and to their great horror, pressed into the service at the point of the bayonet. Coffins there were none—the mode of procedure being: immediately a person breathed his last or was *supposed* to be dead, his two hands were tied together at the wrists, and his legs at the ankles; a pole was then thrust through the *nooses* so formed, and two men shouldering the pole, then bore him off to the *Campo-Santo* and pitched him into a sort of ditch formed for the purpose. I remember at the height of the epidemic, lying ill on my cot of a fever which was raging at the same time—it was at mid-day—the sun was glaring its fiercest, when two Indians came along bearing a corpse on their shoulders. Arriving in front of our house, and peering about the deserted street to see that no one was observing them, they coolly deposited the putrefying body on the balcony in front of my window, and were in the act of marching off, when a shout and the sight of a rifle (unloaded by the way), quickly checked their progress. Sullenly returning, they again hoisted the dead man upon their shoulders and trotted off towards the burying-ground, cursing their luck, probably wishing in their hearts that the Scripture command, "let the dead bury their dead," might be carried into practical effect.

The fever with which I was lying ill appeared simultaneously with the cholera, and not a *creature* escaped it. Ours was a deserted village indeed; for hours one could look up and down the streets, and not see a living soul. All business was at a stand still; not a shop was open, and many a poor devil died from sheer want of a drop of water to drink; all the water-carriers being down, there was no means of getting it by the poor. In our own immediate family, some fifteen were down at once. No food was cooked for a fortnight, our only nourishment being a little gruel and tamarind-water. As I lay with a burning fever in that furnace-like atmosphere, with no other sound, day or night, than the solemn tread of the corpse-bearers, as they hurried past with their ghastly burdens, my thoughts wandered to the cool shades and sympathetic faces of home and friends, and a shudder would pass over me as I thought of the possibility of adding one to the putrefying denizens of that awful grave-ditch yawning in the distance. The atmosphere was dull and heavy during all this time, to an extreme never before known, and it was confidently surmised that a thunder-storm would quickly dispel the poison—the electricity purifying the air. Every little fleecy cloud was hailed as the precursor of a squall; and at last it came, but not before a thousand bodies, nearly the half of our population, were laid beneath the hot sand of the Campo-Santo. A severe storm arose, accompanied by the most terrific lightning, and with the first flash was a reprieve, and at its conclusion not a vestige of the destroyer remained. A singular fact, interesting to science, connected with this :—a large horse-shoe magnet, of great power, hung in the counting-room of one of our largest merchants; at the breaking out of the epidemic, the magnet ceased to attract, and the steel bar fell to the ground. During its whole continuance, its power was neutralized; but immediately on its dying out, the magnet again regained its wonted powers, and the steel clung with its former tenacity.

Guaymas was, after all, as jolly a little place as I know of anywhere. There is an uncommon unanimity existing in all appertaining to fun or frolic, in the way of balls, pic-nics, and parties, scarcely a week passing without something of the kind occurring, every one entering *con amore* into the spirit of these affairs, where, although there is nothing very elaborate in their getting up, still they answer very well for all purposes of diversion. Sunday, of course, as in all Spanish countries, is devoted to gaiety. Mass being concluded, the young ladies open their saloons, the beaux visiting around from house to house; a guitar or a piano is sure to be standing open, and two or three meeting together, a dance is at once improvised.

English men-of-war make periodical visits to the harbor three or four times a year, and during their presence conviviality reigns supreme. Their officers, relieved from the monotony of the sea, are ripe for enjoyment, and liberal in their scale of entertainment. General invitations to come on board each afternoon, and more formal ones for dinners and balls, are frequently issued. Balls on shipboard are very different from the so-styled affairs ashore, and are particularly esteemed by the young lady portion of the community. The idea of shining before foreign beaux, and making conquests of a gringo, would in itself be delightful, not to mention the frolic of embarkation in small-boats, where all are huddled together so unceremoniously, quite in contravention to the strict laws of Spanish etiquette. Indeed, it was a strange sight to see the demure-looking damsels of yesterday, to-day escaped from duenna thraldom, and crowded promiscuously into the stern-sheets of a frigate's cutter, a fluttering mass of dark eyes, glossy tresses, and flashing silks, relieved by the gold lace and flaxen locks of their naval admirers, who, nothing loth on the score of propinquity, were availing themselves of the opportunity never suffered to pass *unimproved* by those gentry, of making fierce love to every young lady in their immediate vicinity.

A frigate's deck, canopied with the flags of every nation, lighted up by a hundred battle-lanterns, whose uncertain rays flickering in the breeze, revealing but indistinctly the dusky forms of the long black guns, also exposing the cloud-like drapery of the young girls gracefully reclining against them, offers no mean substitute for a ball-room. All conventionalities are at once thrown aside, gaily and merrily the moments fly—what though the music be performed by sailor amateurs—what matter if the holy-stoned decks be a little sandy, the very zest of the thing is its novelty, and daylight generally looks in upon an affair which is always a success. Then comes the return home in the chill morning air; the light drapery of the girls is covered by the rough boat-cloaks of the officers, all crowding together in the different boats, and during the pull shoreward, many a sly squeeze of the hand is given and returned, and many a vow exchanged. If my own memory does not deceive, I can recall more than one instance where a light and lovable form shared my rough capote, the beating of whose heart, and the flashing of whose eyes, told me that many such *voyages* would be mutually dangerous to our peace of mind. Of course the civilities of shipboard are returned, and with interest, ashore; and thus, during the stay of the vessel, the town is in a constant state of excitement.

It was a matter of astonishment to me, here at the very fag-end of creation, to find the young girls so exceedingly lady-like, displaying such good taste in dress, and so completely *au fait* in the accomplishments of the day; no late European dance but what they were familiar with, and the generality of them played the piano and harp with exceeding taste. The mode of dress with them is European, modified to suit the exigencies of the hot climate; the only nationality in dress, is the reboza, a long shawl, which is worn by every Mexican woman over her shoulders, the end gracefully falling over an arm when in the house, and over the head and face, exposing oftentimes only the eye, when in the street.

Their education is extremely defective, but their inexhaustible spirits, their quick perception of the ridiculous, their love of quizzing, and their gentle, affectionate manner, make them agreeable companions for any one.

After having been some six months in the country, from an intensity of application, and an inordinate use of stimulants to keep me up, under the depressing influence of the heat, I was attacked with a severe malady, which completely prostrated me, confining me to my bed for months, during which time, however, I was nursed with the tenderest care by my relatives; the recollection of whose unwearied kindness causes sentiments of the deepest gratitude to arise within me. In our household, no word of English was spoken, and therefore it was impossible *not* to have acquired the language, and although it seemed strange at first, on returning to consciousness after a severe attack, to hear my nurse soothing me in a foreign tongue, yet, in a short time it became so familiar to me, that my thoughts would inadvertently clothe themselves in the Spanish idiom.

My illness was a protracted and painful one, but as soon as I could with safety be moved, I was taken to a place called Cochori, a perfect little paradise, an oasis in the desert. Directly open to the sea, with a strong surf breaking upon a fine sand beach, it was the summer resort of one or two families, who had built residences there, for the purpose of enjoying the fine fruit and bathing. Being offered the use of one of these summer palaces, we forthwith ensconced ourselves; the whole place was one vast fruit orchard ; long avenues of fig trees, whose fruit was bursting in luscious maturity, immense graperies, whose white and purple clusters, hung in graceful festoons, while delicious guavas, mellow and golden, sent forth their almost overpowering incense, at the feet of the huge, oriental-looking date trees, whose feathery branches slowly waved against the deep blue sky.

My diet was to be strictly a vegetable one, and for weeks I kept it up, and at the end of that time was a new man. An old Indian major domo, awakened us at early dawn, when springing out of bed, we jumped into the surf ; exhilarated, we entered our garden, where a rustic table was spread out with clusters of blushing grapes, with the dew glistening upon them ; figs, whose distended skins were bursting with very plumpness, with an infinite variety of smaller fruit, and large basins of rich milk. Our hunger, sharpened by our bath, being appeased, we sought our hammocks, so hung as to catch the sea breeze, and thus, partly reading and partly dozing, we passed the heat of the day.

At sunset we sallied forth, and sauntered through the gardens, inhaling the rich perfumes, oftentimes most overpowering, and listening to the vesper songs of the bright plumaged-birds.

After an evening meal, we would stroll down to the beach, and for hours beneath the moon's soft rays, and soothed by the surf's musical roar, our thoughts would wander homeward among the haunts of boyhood, till rendered melancholy, we would summon one of our little Indian household, to strike up on the rude banjo some lively strain of the country.

Previous to the discovery of gold in California, the state of Sonora was unknown to all the world outside of the Mexican

Republic ; and even that government never recognized its existence, save when wanting to provide a lucrative berth for some importunate politician, or wanted to get rid of somewhat too popular a soldier, it appointed the one Collector for the Port of Guaymas, or the other Commander-General of that state.

During the rule of the Spaniard, agriculturists, attracted by the richness of its soil (capable of returning five hundred fold the labor expended upon it), protected by government troops, penetrated the Indian wilds, each step opening to them a very terrestrial paradise. Secure in the protection of government, the land was tilled, towns built up, and a chain of outposts established, such as kept the savage in check. Since the throwing off of the Spanish yoke, the central government, consumed by feuds, and administered with the most bare-faced corruption, has totally neglected the more remote states, and only acknowledges them when wishing to make levies upon their treasuries. The settlers, unprotected, constantly harassed by hostile tribes, who carried off their cattle, fired their dwellings, and committed the most horrible atrocities upon their families, at last gave way before them, and in a few years the Apaches and Comanches had overrun the most beautiful and most productive portion of northern Mexico.

Troops were occasionally sent, and some turbulent general put in command, with orders to pursue and exterminate the Indians ; but the Apache was more than a match for the Mexican soldier, and the general, knowing this, never engaged them ; but, instead of endeavoring to protect the suffering people against their incursions, usually assuming the supreme power, laid the very people whom he was sent to relieve under contribution.

It was enough to make one's blood boil, to see those beautiful plains a vast solitude—extensive ranchos abandoned and uninhabited, and villages in ruins. Travelling for a hundred miles in the very heart of this natural paradise, one may not meet a human being, though on every side he may see fine habitations lying waste ; indeed, for a space of eight superficial degrees in North Sonora, there is not an inhabitant. Droves of horses and wild cattle, remnants of the beautiful herds of the last generation—ruined dwellings—ruined forts—ruined churches—and, hovering upon the borders of this desert, ruined men who tremble, and ruined women who mourn—tell the tale of a corrupt and impotent government.

No sooner had the intense excitement in the search of gold subsided in California, than the turbulent spirits of that country began to turn their attention thither ; and many projects were formed for organizing companies, obtaining grants from Mexico, and taking possession of this abandoned country.

In the year 1851–2, a Frenchman by the name of Pindray formed an association of four hundred of his countrymen, for the purpose of exploring and colonizing the frontier, and proceeded to Guaymas, and from thence into the interior ; but its members becoming disaffected, a dissolution took place, and many of the adventurers returned to California, while others remained in the country, following their different callings. About this time, a young French nobleman, belonging to one of the oldest families of the *ancienne noblesse*, and an officer of some distinction in one of the African regiments, came to California to seek his fortune, which had been impaired by the overthrow of the Orleans family. After several months spent in severe labor to gain his bread, this young officer conceived the idea of a military expedition into northern Sonora, to be conducted with the connivance of the Mexican government, for the purpose of founding a French colony, and, by expelling the savages, to regain possession of that valuable domain. Making known his views to the French consul, M. Dillon, he found them warmly seconded by that official, who furnished him with passports and letters to the French minister in the city of Mexico.

Arriving there, he was warmly received by Mr. Levasseur, the French minister, who entered with enthusiasm into all his plans, and induced the kindly interference of the Mexican president, Arista.

Through the mediation of the minister, the wealthy house of Yecker, Torre & Co. became interested; and a company was formed under the title of the "Restauradora," of which Yecker, Torre & Co., of Mexico, Aguilar, governor, and Cubillas, provisional governor of Sonora, and Jose Calvo, French consul at Guaymas, were the principal directors; the agreements being regularly drawn up and signed by Manuel Arista, President of the Mexican Republic. Armed with this instrument, Count Raousset de Boulbon made the best of his way back to California, enlisted two hundred and seventy Frenchmen, and embarked them for Guaymas, where they arrived in June, 1852.

In the interim, it becoming known that the valuable mines of Arizona had been ceded to Count Raousset and his associates, on his fulfilling certain conditions: a strong feeling of jealousy sprang up in the capital at his success, and intrigues were soon set on foot to mar his enterprise, in order that others might enjoy its benefits. The house of Barron, Forbes & Co., one of the largest concerns in Mexico, formed a league, at the head of which was General Blanco, who, through political influence, was at at once appointed commander-in-chief of the state of Sonora, whither he at once repaired with his troops, with directions from the *new league* to throw every impediment in the way of Count Raousset and of his company.

Finding that this new company possessed more means and influence than the *Restauradora*, the two governors of Sonora, Aguilar and Cubillas, and the French consul at Guaymas, Calvo, joined the new company (styled the Barron Company), thus deserting the old one ; of this, of course, all but themselves were ignorant. A most iniquitous breach of faith ! but such things are thought to be matters of course in Mexico.

The count, to his surprise (being in utter ignorance of the machinations of his supposed friends), found, on his arrival, that every impediment was thrown in the way of his marching into the interior. Meanwhile, General Blanco having arrived, openly forbid the count from moving towards the frontier. Raousset, ignorant of General Blanco's interested motives in thus attempting to thwart him, and secure in the assurances of support from the president and from the Sonorian authorities, and tired of being humbugged by the intriguing general, pushed forward his men and gained the frontier. Contrary to his well-founded expectations, instead of being supported by the authorities, every obstacle was thrown in his way, and being encamped on the frontier, instead of receiving the promised rations for the support of his troops, they were obliged to forage for themselves, and to appropriate, *vi et armis*, the necessaries of life. Meanwhile General Blanco, nettled at the pertinacity of the Frenchmen, threw off all disguise, and commenced such a series of persecutions that the hot blood of the Algerine soldier, revolting at their continued insults and bad faith, resolved upon taking the field, and openly defying the whole Mexican force. This was a daring step, with a force of 270 men to brave a thousand regulars, and a whole host of Indians and volunteers ; but nothing daunted, the count, ordering his men to fall in, at once commenced his march on Hermosillo, the capital of the state, and the head-quarters of General Blanco.

Arriving before the capital, a deputation under a white flag waited upon him, composed of several of the principal men of the city, bearing proposals from the Mexican general, which were insulting to French pride and French understanding.

Listening coldly to their arguments, the count pulled out his watch—it was 8 o'clock. In two hours, he replied in a loud voice, I shall enter Hermosillo, and at eleven o'clock precisely I shall be master of the city !

True to his word, in two hours his little force were fighting desperately in the streets, each man seemingly possessed of the spirit of ten other men combined. In spite of volley upon volley of musketry from housetops and from behind old walls, loop-holed for the purpose, in spite of a tremendous cannonade which raked the streets at every angle, the gallant count led his brave handful step by step to the centre of the town ; he seemingly, bore a charmed life, for, mounted on his gallant white charger, he rode undisturbedly through a shower of balls, which, riddling his hat and clothes, left his person unscathed.

Like sheep he drove the Indians and volunteers before him, and the regulars, under Blanco, soon gave way, and in the incredibly short space of one hour from the time of their entrance, that heroic little band had subjugated a city of 15,000 inhabitants, garrisoned by 1,000 regulars and hordes of savages. The French suffered severely in their officers, and lost in all 17 men killed and 25 wounded.

Unfortunately, and fatally I may say for the interest of his company, the count was attacked by a violent illness which for months incapacitated him for command. Meanwhile, deprived of their master spirit, the company accepted of a proposition from the Mexican general for an armistice, and ultimately a treaty was entered into, whereby the French were guaranteed a safe conduct to the port, a gratuity of $40,000, and a free passage to San Francisco. This ended the first act.

Raousset becoming convalescent during the voyage, arrived in San Francisco in good health, and was there received as a hero, fêted and lauded on every hand.

Internal troubles now convulsed Mexico. Arista, the president, was deposed, and Santa Anna recalled.

Hopes were now held out to the count that the new administration would do him justice, and reinstate him in his claims. Hastening thither with all speed, he met with the most flattering reception from Santa Anna, and was the lion of the capital—the hero of Hermosillo. The count had several interviews with the president, who promised him everything—but never performed—and at length, disgusted with delays, he sought a final interview, and bluntly demanded his rights. After backing and filling for some time, the president, at last, told him that public opinion was strong against any renewal of the grant, and that he did not care to oppose himself to it, but that he would be too happy if Monsieur Le Compte would serve under him, insinuating that, in that case, he would receive a staff appointment. The count, disgusted with his duplicity, refused to serve under him, and abruptly left the capital and returned to California. Exasperated, he entered into correspondence with some parties in Mexico, which correspondence handled the executive without gloves, and the documents falling into the hands of government, the count was declared an outlaw, and was forbidden to set foot again on Mexican soil.

Meanwhile, the opposition, or Barron company, were in the ascendency, and orders were given to the Mexican consul in San Francisco to enlist 2,000 French, as military colonists in Sonora, their expenses to be paid by the Mexican government. 800 men were enlisted and embarked aboard the American ship "Challenge," for Guaymas.

Although the directors of this company were inimical to the count, and watched his movements with suspicion, nevertheless he had a secret understanding with the principal officers of the expedition, and it was arranged that he was to join them after their arrival in Sonora. This was, of course, entirely unknown to the Mexicans. Some ten days after the sailing of the "Challenge," the count, escaping surveillance, embarked in a little schooner and arrived safely off Guaymas.

The new expedition having arrived at their destination were quartered ashore, and for a few days all went on pleasantly. Soon the Mexicans began to show their cloven-foot; they were exposed to no end of petty annoyances ; their rations were kept back, and at last the Mexican general insisted upon their relinquishing their nationality, and enlisting under the Mexican standard. The French, disgusted with this treatment, became turbulent, and brawls ensued between themselves and the townspeople.

Things gradually grew worse until at last the Mexican general presented his ultimatum in shape of instant enlistment under Mexican colors, or forcible expulsion from the territory.

At this juncture the count appeared on the tapis, and was hailed as a deliverer ; he made his countrymen a short speech, showing them the duplicity of the Mexicans, and wound up thus :

"My friends," he said in an electrifying voice, "I do not come here to influence any one—you are free to choose ; but understand me, it is necessary to side one way or the other. Will you become Mexican soldiers, ruled by its military code, submissive to its rod, without future or without hope?—If so, say the word and ground your arms. If, on the contrary, you wish to remain worthy of the name of Frenchmen—to resist unjust oppression—to vindicate your rights—maintain your violated nationality, signify your wishes by shouldering arms! Which shall it be?" "March on!" they cry. "Think well of it—you are isolated in a far-off land, in drawing your sword you become outlaws, there is neither grace nor pardon left. In this case you *must* be conquerers, there will be no alternative! What will you do in case of defeat?" "Die! die!" they cried. "Well! well! my friends—March on—and 'Vive la France.'"

Insane applause followed this order, and the troops insisted upon his assuming the chief command. "No, no," replied the count, "you have your officers, obey them implicitly, I come among you only as a volunteer, my only ambition being to be in the first rank, at the point of danger!"

The battalion marched out of their barracks, and fire opened simultaneously from both sides ; the Mexicans were posted on the housetops, and the streets were swept by their artillery. The commander of the French, not a man of much military talent, lost his presence of mind ; disorder soon ensued. The count tried to re-form the men while a few rifle-men decimated the Mexican artillery, but in vain—all was confusion—and officers and men all fought on their own responsibility ; thus a guerilla warfare was maintained for two hours, the count being unsuccessful in concentrating more than twenty men at any one time, and then too late, he saw his error in refusing the commandership-in-chief.

From some mistake the Mexican guns were silenced, and the count essayed a last effort. "Give them the bayonet," he cried, and rushed forward, several men following him. Springing on top of a wall exposed to the whole fury of the enemy's fire, he cried for the last time, "Forward ;" his hat was riddled, and he received two thrusts of a bayonet.

With fifty men he would have gained the day, but unsupported he had to yield.

A retreat was effected to the French consulate—and the vice-consul offered all who would lay down their arms the protection of the French flag.

"Will you guarantee the life of Count Raousset ? without that assurance we will not surrender." Mr. Calvo stretched forth his hand and in a clear loud voice exclaimed, "Monsieur Raousset aussi aura la vie sauvée." Thus terminated the Battle of Guaymas.

After an interval of ten days—during which time the French were in daily expectation of being shipped off—contrary to the promise of the vice-consul, the Count Raousset was arraigned before a Mexican council of war—tried—and condemned to be executed.

His countrymen were aghast ; and even the Mexicans shuddered at such a palpable breach of faith. Every effort was made to induce the vice-consul, Mr. Calvo, to insist upon the prisoner being taken to the capital, and there being tried—if trial he must have—but of no avail. Calvo, a Mexican by birth, and a partner of Cuvillas and related to Aguilar, the governor and vice-governor of the state, and, together with them, a director in the "Barron Company," had no sympathy, or dared not show any, with the poor friendless Frenchman, and did not exert the official influence he was possessed of to endeavor to get a commutation of his punishment. And alas! on the 12th of August, in presence of the whole populace, and of several regiments of the Mexican army, he was led to the place of execution. His sentence being read, placing his hat upon the ground, and addressing the Mexican soldiers, he cried in a firm, cheerful voice: "Allons, mes braves! Do your duty; fire true—aim at the heart." He folded his arms upon his chest, made one step forward, and awaited his fate. A volley rattled past him, and he fell on his face—dead!

Thus perished, in the prime of life, a young man of high promise, a victim of Mexican intrigue. His judges were low, vulgar men, who could have no sympathy with the high-bred gentleman of the *ancien régime*—Colonel Campuzano, a villainous and notoriously cowardly half-breed, who, for the last quarter of a century, has left no opportunity unimproved for plundering the citizens; Isidro Campos, a stupid old Indian, who, always drunk, boasted of his exploits beneath the Mexican banner. Not a man, probably, assisted at his execution but who, politically and morally, better deserved death than the poor Raousset.

During the interval of the first and last expedition of Count

Raousset, one William Walker, a native of Tennessee, and for some years previously a resident of San Francisco, and the editor of the *Herald* newspaper, being fired with military ardor, and with a desire to appropriate some of the rich but neglected districts of Mexico, resolved upon organizing a force sufficient for the accomplishment of so laudable a design, and with characteristic energy, exerted himself so successfully, that in an incredibly short space of time he obtained the necessary means for taking the initiatory steps. Having formed his plans, he, in company with a gentleman who became interested with him financially, took passage for, and arrived in due course of time at Guaymas, and applied at the American consulate for the necessary documents to enable himself and suite to pass into the interior, for the purpose of "spying out the land." Unfortunately for Mr. Walker, his scheme had been divined by the shrewd consul of Mexico at San Francisco, and he, by a previous vessel, had advised the authorities at Guaymas not to permit Mr. Walker upon any pretext to visit the interior, as he purposed doing so with treasonable designs. Of all this the American consul was in the most happy ignorance, and, of course, as in duty bound, he espoused Mr. W.'s cause, as he could see no reason why an American gentleman should not be permitted to penetrate as far into the state as he chose to do. A voluminous correspondence ensued between the authorities and the consul, very decided on both sides, and consuming much valuable time, but all to no purpose; and Mr. Walker becoming disgusted, reëmbarked for San Francisco.

During the brief visit of this afterwards-noted filibuster, the writer had an opportunity of seeing a good deal of him, and became greatly impressed with his astuteness and determined character; for although sanguine in temperament, and insanely confident of success, still he evinced such an extreme degree of caution as almost to disarm the suspicions of the Mexicans themselves before leaving them.

To have looked at William Walker, one could scarcely have credited him to be the originator and prime mover of so desperate an enterprise as the invasion of the state of Sonora.

His appearance was that of anything else than a military chieftain. Below the medium height, and very slim, I should hardly imagine him to weigh over a hundred pounds. His hair light and towy, while his almost white eyebrows and lashes concealed a seemingly pupilless, grey, cold eye, and his face was a mass of yellow freckles, the whole expression very heavy. His dress was scarcely less remarkable than his person. His head was surmounted by a huge white fur hat, whose long knap waved with the breeze, which, together with a very ill-made short-waisted blue coat, with gilt buttons, and a pair of grey, strapless pantaloons, made up the ensemble of as unprepossessing-looking a person as one would meet in a day's walk. I will leave you to imagine the figure he cut in Guaymas with the thermometer at 100°, when every one else was arrayed in white. Indeed half the dread which the Mexicans had of filibusters vanished when they saw this their Grand Sachem, —such an insignificant-looking specimen. But any one who estimated Mr. Walker by his personal appearance, made a great mistake. Extremely taciturn, he would sit for an hour in company without opening his lips; but once interested, he arrested your attention with the first word he uttered, and as he proceeded, you felt convinced that he was no ordinary person. To a few confidential friends he was most enthusiastic upon the subject of his darling project, but outside of those immediately interested, he never mentioned the topic.

Returning from Mexico to California and nettled at the opposition he there met with, he at once hoisted his filibustering banner, and the work of enlistment went on very rapidly; every ruined gambler, outlaw, and used-up person in California flocking to his standard.

Meanwhile the Mexican consul in San Francisco was on the *qui vive*, and took all measures in his power to thwart the accomplishment of the filibuster's design, but all to no purpose, for public opinion was decidedly in favor of the scheme.

A brig was purchased, and laden with provisions, and all needful for the undertaking, and was about being dispatched, when through representations of the Mexican consul she was seized by government; but after considerable litigation was again released, and immediately dispatched by her agents, lest a second time she should fall into the hands of the Philistines.

Having succeeded in getting off the supplies for the army, the general was at a loss to know how he was to convey his troops to their destination, for the Mexican consul, now thoroughly awakened, had insisted upon the authorities taking the most stringent measures, and consequently the general was non-plused as to how he was to embark a number of men with all their arms and equipage without being discovered.

In his quandary, he made a proposal to the captain of the "Caroline," a Mexican bark, belonging to the son of the American consul at Guaymas, that he should receive on board, his two hundred men, without arms or munitions of war, merely as passengers, and conveying them to a small port on the edge of the Mexican boundary line, there disembark them, and then proceed on his voyage, thus violating no law. The captain, seeing no prospect of a freight and anxious to make a good thing, accepted Walker's proposal, and in order to save annoyance from the authorities, agreed to receive the men at midnight, and having a tug alongside immediately to go to sea.

There is but little doubt that the captain of the vessel knew perfectly well the object of the expedition, but he could see no violation of Mexican or American law, in receiving 200 passengers for a port outside of Mexican territory. At midnight however of the day appointed for sailing, he saw his error, for instead of two hundred peaceful passengers, two hundred organized men, in squads of twenty, came down aboard the vessel armed to the teeth, and without ado forthwith took possession, and at once commenced taking aboard large quantities of guns and ammunition. When all was arranged, under cover of night, the vessel was cast off and the tug coming alongside ran her out of the harbor under the very bows of a revenue vessel appointed to watch her. To make a long story short, these desperadoes took possession of the ship, and arriving in the gulf of California, took her into La Paz, and disembarking their men and "materiel," left her in charge of the mate and one or two men, as a refuge in case of defeat. The mate not liking the new régime, at the risk of his life, with the assistance of the two men left behind, got the vessel under way in the night, and leaving the filibusters to their fate, stretched across the Gulf to Guaymas, to deliver her up to the owners.

Immediately on his arrival, the Mexican authorities, instead of thanking him for thus cutting off the retreat of the filibusters, threw him into prison, and confiscated the ship, and ordered the consul forthwith to leave the town!—rather a high-handed measure, considering he was absolutely innocent of even a knowledge of the schemes of the filibusters, and moreover was personally unpopular with them for not being willing to countenance their original schemes.

Meanwhile, such representations were made to the American minister at the capital regarding his complicity, that the consul was at once removed from an office which he had filled for thirty years, and for which services he had never received a single penny—on the contrary, spending at least five hundred dollars yearly in giving aid to distressed Americans. Thus the American government pays her faithful servants!

But to return to Walker—his campaign is now a matter of history; his troops, made up of the worst material of Californians, were neither soldiers nor brave men, and consequently, in contending with the large odds brought against them, were invariably beaten, and at last, ignominiously driven out of the country. Walker himself showed a thorough contempt for danger, and great energy, but no generalship; some of his officers and troops were high-toned gentlemen and brave men, but thrown in among such a set as formed the greater part of the expedition, they could not redeem its character; and thus ended Walker's first grand filibustering expedition.

Anxiously as the eyes of the Americans are directed to that portion of Mexican territory lying between the twenty-fourth and twenty-eighth degree of north latitude, and more particularly that section comprising the states of Lower California and Sonora, it might not be inappropriate here to give some facts respecting their resources.

Sonora is the richest of these provinces, for although its surface is extremely mountainous, still, intersecting these ranges, are broad and fertile valleys, well watered with never-failing springs, and wooded with superb forests.

Here, growing side by side, may be found the productions of the torrid and temperate zones—fields of wheat and sugar-cane, and the vine and the orange tree may be seen blossoming at the same moment, with the cotton plant, which is indigenous to the bottoms along the rivers Gila and San Pedro. Every metal precious and useful have been thrown pell-mell from the burning furnace of the Sierra. Silver as well as gold is found in its virgin state, and in masses; the very marble is veined with gold, and the stones themselves sweat with quicksilver.

With a seaboard of 500 miles on the Gulf of California, its ports are those through which must necessarily pass all its own imports and exports, and those of that immense tract of country, comprising the states of Durango and of Chihuahua.

When we take into consideration these vast tracts of country of unheard of fertility, abounding in mineral wealth, the extent of which we dare not dream, utterly devastated and given over to wandering tribes of savages, does not the certainty suggest itself to our mind, that before many years the American people, proverbially ambitious and restless as they are, will spread themselves over this hidden paradise, and, driving out the Indians, will, in defiance of Mexico, and whether or not protected by our own government, establish themselves so firmly (as they did in days gone by in Texas), that the United States will, by force of circumstances, be necessitated to annex and countenance them. When this takes place, as it most assuredly soon will, who can estimate the importance that will be attached to the outlets of a country more rich and fertile than the valley of the Mississippi itself. Guaymas, from its central position and its wonderfully safe and commodious harbor, will of course be as it is at present, the principal seaport town; and there are men living, who may see the now miserable town of Guaymas as flourishing a city as is San Francisco at the present day, more particularly should it be chosen as the terminus for the Pacific railroad as has been suggested. Even now, we hear of heavy American ships, in search of freight, leaving San Francisco, bound to Guaymas, in order to load guano in its immediate vicinity, and knowing, as we do, the valuable deposits of sulphur and saltpetre which are lying unheeded within comparatively a stone's throw of this harbor, it needs not a prophetic eye to see the day when it will be filled with California liners seeking homeward freight.

Once taken possession of, either forcibly or by purchase, the state of Sonora will give such evidences of her agricultural and mineral wealth, as will put California and Australia to the blush, and the capital and emigration which will at once be attracted, will promise such a future as is little dreamed of.

The intense and unremitting heat, as I have before remarked, had a most enervating effect upon my health, so much so indeed, that I was becoming alarmingly reduced, and my energies fast evaporating; as for doing any business it was impossible, and I lolled about in my hammock, or on a cane sofa, anywhere indeed where there was a breeze.

One day, as I was stretched out in the consulate (being acting consul during the temporary absence of my uncle), I was listlessly looking over a North American newspaper, and wishing I might enjoy some of the invigorating breezes which were therein described, when a man whom we employed as a look-out, to report the arrival of vessels in the offing, came into the office and told me that there was an American schooner coming in ; without energy to go down on the mole to look at her, I continued my reading for a short time, and then dropped asleep. I was awakened by the entrance of a huge specimen of humanity, with a face *couleur de mahogany*, hair hanging down on his shoulders, immense beard and moustache, and arrayed in a blue shirt and pantaloons ; about as piratical a looking individual as one might ever expect to see. Inquiring of this amiable-looking gentleman what his business might be, and, at the same time, casting an uneasy look at several piles of doubloons upon the desk ; his reply was a loud guffaw ! upon which, being rather disgusted, I was on the point of signalizing the major-domo to eject him, when something in his eye arrested my attention ; scanning him from head to foot, the fact slowly dawned upon me that I knew the coon, and in an instant we were hugging each other, after the most approved old German style ; that piratical looking craft being no less a person than my old friend, Gus Ellis, the captain of the American schooner just arrived. If master Gus had dropped down from heaven I should not have been more surprised ; indeed one has to be buried for a year or so in some out of the way Mexican town, to thoroughly appreciate the pleasure of meeting an old friend.

Handing me his papers, as vice consul, I opened them, when, to my utter astonishment, I read thus :

"AMERICAN SCHOONER ALICE,
6 ⅞ tons Register;
A. V. H. ELLIS, Master;
R. B. CHILDS, Mate;
BENJ. YOUNG, Cook, and all hands.
Bound from San Francisco to Guaymas, Gulf of California."

I could hardly believe it possible that these three men had made a voyage of twenty-five hundred miles in a boat of six and seven-eighths tons! Yet so it was! there she lay at an anchor, and when the captain of the port's gig went alongside to board her, the captain of the port, Don Antonio Bustamante, a horridly fat old chap, by the way, in trying to get aboard, actually by his weight listed her so far over that he thought it prudent to retire to his own boat again.

Gus was a regular god-send to me, he was full of life and animation, being always jolly.

His first occupation was to rig two very fine boats that we had, in American style, and from that time for months our life was a round of excursions; running down to the different islands, we would wander around among their cool coves and caves, and loiter away the warm hours beneath their refreshing shades; then we would fish, then stand off for a few hours to sea; in fact, there was no end to our aquatic performances.

Gus, having a wonderful knack of picking up lingos, soon talked away as fast as any one, and commenced an indiscriminate attack upon the hearts of all the good-looking young girls about the place, and thus he whiled away his time between sailing and lòve-making.

The arrival of our piratical-looking friend was very opportune too, on our shores, for after being there some months, the difficulties between the Mexicans and the Frenchmen broke out, which necessitated the retiring aboard ship of almost all the families at the port, and my uncle at this juncture thinking, and rightly too, that the American flag would be no protection from outrage, at once embarked his family aboard a vessel belonging to himself, and sent them on a cruise outside. This was no small undertaking, for his family consisted of some twenty, including dependents, and only those who understand the ways of the people out there can conceive of the magnitude of the preparation necessary for such an exodus.

Here friend Ellis' services became invaluable; there was nothing the man could not do, where boats and vessels were concerned, and with his valuable aid, the family and their accompaniments were gotten on board, and through his energy, as forager, were kept well provisioned during the entire cruise. With his snug and fast yacht, he was enabled at any time to communicate with the shore, and kept the party afloat advised of all news of the belligerents.

Although my health was in a great measure restored, still it was not deemed politic to reënter upon my counting-house duties, and it was proposed that I should buy half of a vessel belonging to the house, and taking command of her, should trade on the coast; this was a business of all others the most congenial to me, and I was not long in accepting the proposal.

The vessel was a clipper schooner, and one of the most beautiful little craft without exception that my eyes ever rested upon; built in Boston, for a sea-going yacht, her model was perfection itself, and for strength, would favorably compare with any government vessel, her materials being live oak, and copper-fastened throughout, and her sailing qualities were first-rate ; indeed, during the eighteen months that I was in her, I never saw her match. On taking possession, I had her thoroughly overhauled in rigging, sails, etc., and her cabin most luxuriously fitted up, and when I got to sea, with my strong crew of Manila men, uniformed in the picturesque dress of their country, with my old French cook, a perfect gem in his department, and a fine breeze a-beam, skipping over the blue waves of the Pacific, I would not (as the sailors say) call the queen my grandmother.

Many a happy hour I have spent aboard of her, and many an anxious one too ; our trade was at all times rather a hazardous one, being generally occupied in a business, which was not in strict accordance with the revenue-laws, we were at any time liable to seizure ; great manœuvering was the consequence ; a considerable deal of brass, tact in quieting suspicion, and recklessness in case of exposure, were prime requisites.

There was a great deal that was delightful in it ; the house of every merchant on the coast was our home when in port ; our arrival was always a season of rejoicing among our friends, and sure to be followed by tertulias, and all that sort of thing, which of course was returned to them on board, and my vessel being a handy little craft, we would often "up anchor," and stand forty or fifty miles out to sea, with large parties of ladies on board, and that sort of thing smoothed down the asperities of a sea-life. Passengers we always had too, and in abundance, and jolly times we used to have with them, and on the smooth waters of the gulf, would often dance half the night away, our ball-room, the deck, our chandelier, the broad, bright, silvery moon.

Of gales, we had a plenty, and some pretty narrow escapes. Nowhere in the world do the autumnal hurricanes blow with greater violence, than on the southern coast of California, in the months of September and October; they continue but a short time, but while they last, their violence is terrific.

My little Maria, with her balance-reefed foresail, rode out one or two of them, when everything else was foundering around her; with hatches battened down, and the wheel lashed, she withstood the fury of the most terrific sea I ever beheld, for twenty mortal hours; to have said during that time, whether she was at the bottom of the ocean or on the top of it, would have been out of my power, for the crashing seas, that constantly broke over her, rendered it impossible for us to show ourselves on deck.

My voyages were generally as far to the southward as Acapulco, taking the ports of Mazatlan and San Blas, on the way down, occasionally touching in at La Paz and San José, on the Peninsula. Letting go anchor in either of these ports, getting everything snug, and giving charge to my mate, I would mount my horse, and scour away into the interior, perhaps two or three hundred miles, sell my cargo—buy another, and dispatch it on mule-back to the coast, in the meantime enjoying the hospitality of the many friends I was constantly making.

No one but an absolute stranger ever thinks of going to a hotel in Mexico; in fact, with the exception of the largest cities, there are none to be found, the only inns being what are called Mesons, a sort of stable for the cattle, with lodging-rooms for the muleteers, without a vestige of furniture, save a brick platform raised four or five feet from the floor, intended to serve as a bedstead, and generally speaking, windowless, infested with vermin, and atrociously filthy. These places are only frequented by muleteers, or unfortunates who have no friends and little money. When persons of any respectability find themselves in a strange place they immediately ride up to the house of the priest, who never refuses either to receive them or provide lodgings for them elsewhere. Many a time have I been indebted to a village curate for a solid meal and comfortable bed, without whose mediation or hospitality I should have passed the night supperless and without shelter. Whatever other faults they may have, the Mexican curates can never be called inhospitable.

My business frequently called me to Manzanillo, the seaport of the city of Colima, a place of forty thousand inhabitants, and the capital of one of the richest provinces of Mexico, lying some 150 miles in the interior. The port is perhaps as unhealthy a place as there is on the globe, so much so that no white man can reside there with impunity, and whole ships' companies often fall victims to the malarias and evaporations from the immense shallow lakes which surround it, and stretch away miles in the interior—vast reservoirs of green, stagnant water. Indeed it was pretty nearly certain death for a European to spend a night ashore. On anchoring I always gave orders to my mate to allow no one to go ashore, and in communicating with the shore, to make use of the native canoes. I also always caused to be served out to the men three times each day a wine-glass of spirits, with a half dozen grains of quinine, and by these precautions, and having heavy awnings fore and aft the vessel to shade the boys from exposure to the sun, managed to keep my vessel reasonably clear of the fever.

The ride from Manzanillo to Colima, though rather long

(being 150 miles), was not an unpleasant one. Starting with my servant a few hours before daybreak, we would travel along the sea some twenty or thirty miles before sunrise, thus leaving the heavy sand before the atmosphere became heated, daylight would find us in a beautifully undulating country, sprinkled with hamlets, diversified with plantations of cotton and sugar-cane, and groves of orange and of fig. Alighting at the first hut and waking its proprietor, stretched out in the doorway, we would order coffee ; after partaking of which we would mount again, and with hats slouched over our eyes, and downcast heads, would toil through the hot sun until eleven o'clock ; when, halting again, we would order a breakfast of fresh eggs, milk, and coffee, and then stretching ourselves on the ground, would snooze away till four o'clock; when, again mounting, we would away. Now we find ourselves in a mountainous region, and winding through many a defile, threading the spurs as they rise higher and higher, while away up in the clouds towered the volcano of Colima, 17,000 feet in the air, snow-capped—a visible beacon for many a score of leagues the country round.

Night finds us among the purple hills, their crests gilded and bathed in the golden effulgence of the rays of the setting sun. Dismounting and lighting a fire, and tethering our animals, after partaking of our frugal supper, we would roll ourselves in our sarapes and soon would be snoring away in concert with the whirring insects.

Soon after midnight we are off again. Suddenly we come upon a picturesque mountain torrent, and follow its banks as it winds through gorge after gorge, until reaching the table-land, it spreads into a broad river. The road leading across it is spanned by a splendid bridge, over half a mile in length—a noble monument of the energy and ingenuity of an American mechanic. This river, in summer fordable by animals, in winter becomes a swollen torrent, rushing along with great fury, and had borne off some half a dozen bridges constructed by English and French engineers, when a poor American carpenter happening that way, became convinced that he could build a bridge that would not yield. Some wealthy man hearing of him sent for him, and thinking favorably of his plans, succeeded in getting a contract for him. Without a cent of money, and scarcely speaking a word of the language, he went to work and in a little over a year, raised as handsome and as firm a structure as is to be found in the Mexican republic. Its length, if I remember rightly, was nearly 800 yards, with a width of thirty feet, and paved with stone.

Colima is a beautiful old town of heavy moorish architecture, embowered in gardens and surrounded by a highly cultivated country, framed by an amphitheatre of mountains, and watched over by its old namesake the volcano who, with smoking head, looks grimly down upon it.

A marked and beautiful feature is the prevalence of huertas, or large fruit gardens, which are scattered about, some of them of immense extent and filled with bananas, oranges, figs, cocoas, and endless varieties of rich, gay flowers, and parasitical vines clinging and wreathing themselves around the trees. In each of these huertas is a reservoir, built of masonry, through which clear water is constantly flowing, and here the families resort morning and evening to bathe.

The rides about the city and its environs are superb, and one may take a different direction every day for a year and discover new beauties. The favorite afternoon ride with the foreigners was out to the cotton factory, on the edge of a romantic little stream whose waters moved the machinery, a sweet spot surrounded by gardens, the whole under the superintendence of a Yankee (the same who built the bridge), and the only one in the whole district—a most unparalleled occurrence.

There is a large trade done in Colima, some four or five cargoes of European goods being disposed of each year to the merchants of the neighboring towns at a large profit. It is altogether in the hands of Germans, who, as a mercantile community, preponderate decidedly in this republic. Among them I found many warm friends and received no end of hospitality.

One evening in visiting at the house of some friends, I was introduced to a gentleman, a German, who spoke our language remarkably well, and in the course of conversation he mentioned that he had been in the United States. Presently I found that he knew many of my friends, and we were becoming very interested in exchanging reminiscences, when suddenly it flashed across my mind that his face was not unfamiliar, and in a moment more I recognized the features of a much-loved old teacher—a singular rencontre. He, formerly a German professor in Princeton College, and in a school in the vicinity, and I, his pupil, to meet in the heart of Mexico, far off the beaten track, where but few Americans had ever before been.

With a week's leisure hanging over me, I joined a party to inspect the crater of the volcano of Colima—no small undertaking! A week's provisions to be packed, mules to be chosen, guides for the ascent, and a rig-out of clothes suited to the low temperature of the summit.

The first day's journey brought us to the base; the weather

extremely hot and oppressive, the country around luxuriant in vegetation. At first, the ascent is easy, and the mules find little difficulty; as we rise, the character of the vegetation assumes different phases, and the earth gives evidence of its volcanic nature. Now we leave our mules, and, pike in hand, commence in earnest the ascent. The ground gradually becomes bare and destitute of verdure, sharp, jagged, and very broken. At each step the path becomes steeper and more difficult, and the air becomes rarified, and the cold very disagreeable. We judge our height to be now ten thousand feet.

Night approaches, and the view is superb; above us, all ice and snow, tinted and crimsoned by the sun's last ray; and the exquisite plains for leagues and leagues beyond bathed in the same rich glow! * * * A freezing night in an india-rubber tent—a glorious sunrise without a cloud.

Upward we push among the ice, and struggling to maintain our balance among loose masses of scoria, as a false step would launch us into eternity. Our heads become dizzy, and blood rushes to the surface, runs from our ears and noses; still we go on, benumbed with cold. Jamming our pike-staffs into the crevices of rock, a white steam issues of sulphurous odor. Hurrah! the crater is reached; and, bending our aching heads over it, we look down into a vast cauldron seething and bubbling with liquid lava, and are lost in wonderment and awe; but, worn out with fatigue, and with reeling brains, we soon bid it adieu.

ACAPULCO.

Acapulco, during the last century the most important point on the Pacific Ocean, as well as the strongest, from the fact of its being the depôt of treasure brought by the galleons from the East Indies, had in the present century dwindled into complete insignificance, with no remnant of its former greatness, save its magnificent fortress, garrisoned, alas! by a few ragged, bare-legged Mexican soldiers.

The discovery of California, however, was instrumental in rescuing it from certain decay, it being made the depot of coal and provisions for the numerous lines of steamers plying from Panama to San Francisco, thus improvising considerable trade, and the Acapulcaños, the vilest people in Mexico, awoke one morning and found themselves again famous.

Nature never formed a lovelier spot. A fine commodious harbor, almost land-locked, whose waters are clear and placid, rippling upon a white sand beach, shaded with cocoa groves, among which nestle the picturesque huts of the lower classes. A few yards further, the town is clustered together, crouching between high hills, on one of which is the far-famed fortress—a lasting monument of Spanish engineering—approached by a delightful promenade overlooking the town, planted with orange trees, forming a fragrant shade. The town itself is unimportant, containing a few squares of adobe buildings, a church, and a custom-house.

The American steamers stopping here on their upward and downward trips, throw into the town, for the space of at least twelve hours, from 1,000 to 1,500 passengers per month, who, while they waste a good deal of money, and in that way benefit the town, by their lawlessness, depredations, and rowdyisms, have so exasperated the natives that it is dangerous to move about unarmed. Imagine a horde of five hundred rough offscourings of San Francisco, graduated in every vice, disenthralled from the confinement of a ship's hold, vomited on the threshold of a little hamlet inhabited by people whom they hold in contempt : imagine, I say, this mob excited by drink, rushing about like demons, insulting women and bullying men, and committing all sorts of enormities, and then will you blame the people for taking the law in their own hands, and retaliating when opportunity offers ? Fights were affairs of every day occurrence, and generally resulting in bloodshed. No steamer ever stopped but that some of her passengers or crew were either cut or killed.

I witnessed many of these rencontres, and one in particular which struck me with great horror. I was lying beneath an awning on board my vessel, anchored close in shore, smoking a cheroot, and half dozing away a siesta, when a great row on the beach attracted my attention. Paying but little attention to it, however, I was about resuming my nap, when my mate came aft, begging I would send my boat's crew ashore to the assistance of a "pobre Americano" whom the natives were murdering.

Giving the necessary orders, I took up my glass, and discovered a man with a revolver in his hand, *backing* down to the beach, followed by a crowd of twenty greasers, brandishing knives. As they approached he levelled his weapon, keeping them at bay—then a rush was made at him—crack went his revolver, as the foremost man fell—a pause and great commotion—another rush, and down falls another—then a general rush is made, and two more fall to the ground—and, alas ! the poor American, overpowered by numbers, sinks gasping with a hundred stabs before my men could reach the beach.

Acapulco is only eight days mule travel from the capital,

and the road passes over a very rich section of country, in which is raised sufficient sugar to supply all western Mexico, and rice of a most superior quality. Its climate during the summer and fall months is very fatal to foreigners, malignant and congestive fevers attacking all unacclimated persons.

Its vicinity to the volcanos of Popocatapetl and Orizaba, render it liable to frequent earthquakes.

I witnessed one of the most severe ever felt there. It occurred on a beautiful moonlight night, after a day of suffocating heat, at ten o'clock in the evening, and to the loveliness of the night, can be ascribed the fact, that so few lives were lost, as the greater part of the inhabitants were enjoying the land breeze just setting in, and promenading in front of their doors. I myself had gone aboard ship, and was lolling in my hammock, when a sudden jerk or surge nearly threw me to the deck; rushing forward, I sang out to my people to pay out every inch of chain, in order to give her more play, then looking towards the beach, I saw the water had receded some distance, and was rushing shoreward again; this continued two or three minutes, accompanied by a murmuring sound, and then again all was still, the crashing sound telling of the destruction being dealt on land.

Jumping into a boat, we pulled ashore, and found things in a most lamentable state—men, women and children rushing about in desperate fear, while the smoke and dust, piles of broken wall and timber, bore dumb testimony of what had occurred; the earth in many places, was rent assunder, and a thick misty vapor exuded.

The climate, as I said before, was deadly to strangers, and a peculiarity of these southern climates is, that the disease rarely attacks sea-faring men while in port, but no sooner do they get to sea, than *down* they go with it. Thus it happened in my case. I had been lying with my vessel for two or three weeks, loading, and had been particularly careful of my crew, and had thus escaped a single case, but no sooner had I got clear of the land, than first one and then another of my men were taken, and before six days had elapsed, every man in the vessel, with the exception of the mate, a French doctor and myself, were under the effects of it, and we had already buried two poor fellows. The heat was most intense, not a breath of air was there, and for fifteen long days, we lay drifting helplessly about the ocean, the excessive heat driving us below; the birds took possession of our decks, and we had neither the power, or the energy to drive them away: on the tenth day out, we buried the third victim, and rarely have I seen so impressive a funeral service. We sewed him up in his hammock, and making fast an iron bar to his feet, laid him across the bulwark, while the doctor, a devout Catholic, read the service from his breviary; the awful stillness of the glassy and seething ocean, the haggard look of the men, debilitated and still under the effects of the fever, the flapping sails surging with the swell against the masts, and the long gaunt form of the corpse, perceptible through the canvas in which it was enveloped, were all accessories to as impressive a burial as ever I've witnessed by land or by water. The service concluded, and giving the order, all that remained of the poor fellow was launched into the deep, when horror of horrors, the iron bar made fast to his feet to take him down, got loose, and he, only half submerged, went bobbing up and down as far as we could see him, as the current swept him slowly away.

I had congratulated myself on my escape, when that very night I was attacked with one of the worst forms of the fever, which went at once to the brain. Day and night I lay sweltering in my little cabin, with a steam-engine pulse, raving and unconscious, but watched with a mother's care by the French doctor, who never left my side ; on the fourth day I regained my consciousness, and then all the horrors of my situation appeared vividly before me. I felt that I must die.

There is a certain stage of weakness and disease, in which every man can distinguish the near approach of death ; but to die thus !—in a miserable hole, with an atmosphere foul with bilge water—overrun with rats and cockroaches—without so much as a drop of cold water, or the friendly hand of a relative to soothe my dying pillow !—then the vision of the dead man, bobbing up and down over the glassy swells of the ocean, came vividly before me, and I shuddered with horror.

Speculating upon my situation, and dreamily dozing away the hours, I was called to my senses by the entrance of the doctor and the mate ; the doctor felt my pulse, gave me some powerful potion, and then very kindly told me that he had requested the mate to come down with him, in order that I might give him any directions that might suggest themselves to my mind relative to the disposition of my vessel, and a large amount of money that I had on board ; for he thought it his duty to tell me that the chances were strong against my recovery.

My first command to the mate was to get up some bar iron from the *run* of the vessel, and have it ready ; for I had no idea of floating on top of the sea, after being thrown overboard. I then made the necessary disposition of my property, and sank down overcome by the exertion, and never awoke again for twenty-four hours : that was the crisis of the disease, and on awaking, I found myself relieved, and rapidly recovered. Never will I forget the unwearied attention of the good Dr. C—— ; had I been his brother, he could not have taken better care of me. God bless him wherever he goes ! My mate was subsequently taken, and thus the doctor and myself were the only able men about the vessel, the rest of the crew being too debilitated to be of any use.

During all this time, we had been becalmed for fourteen mortal days ; on the fifteenth, however, a breeze sprung up, and the doctor lending me a hand, we got sail on the vessel, and shaped our course for the nearest port.

We made the harbor of San Blas, where, after getting everything snug, and providing for my sick men, I started off for the city of Tepic, a town celebrated for its fine climate, and some sixty miles in the interior. In order to avoid the awful heat, I resolved to make the journey through the night ; and, mounting my horse, I started off. All night I rode—first through the marshy plains along the seaside, then, as morning dawned, my road lay through a hilly country, till gradually making the ascent, I reached (about ten o'clock) the plateau on which the beautiful city of Tepic stands ; but I had overtaxed my strength, and, with scarcely power to reach the hotel, I sank down upon a cot, from which I never rose again for weeks ; excessive fatigue having occasioned a relapse. Here, too, I fell into the hands of a good Samaritan : a Dr. Rodgers, an American physician from Albany, living at the hotel, hearing a countryman of his was ill, came in to see me, and insisted upon my sharing part of his luxuriously-furnished rooms (the ordinary chamber furniture of a Mexican hotel consisting of a cot and a washstand, without a table, much less a carpet), and here I remained under his kind treatment for weeks.

Tepic, a flourishing and romantic-looking town, is situated on the grand highway between the Atlantic and Pacific oceans; Vera Cruz, the eastern, and Tepic, the western terminus, diligences running in connection between the two points, a distance of 200 miles. The town is located on a plateau some two thousand feet above the sea, and is blest with a most salubrious climate, and, thanks to the taste of its inhabitants for flowers, is beautified with many a garden perfuming the air.

The houses are generally of two stories, well built, and kept scrupulously white, giving the town an extremely tidy appearance. Its cathedral is an extensive building of no peculiar style of architecture, and fronts on a large plaza, which serves, as in all other Mexican cities, as a fruit-market, and on Sundays and other feast days it presents a most attractive appearance, as the rancheros and Indians squat beneath gigantic umbrellas, surrounded by piles of luscious and highly colored fruits. The "great guns" of Tepic are the members of the house of Barron, Forbes & Co., one of the oldest on the west coast, who, by their wealth and shrewdness, have acquired an incredible influence in the state, which extends itself even to the administration of government; and it would have been, at that time, a difficult matter to have passed a measure obnoxious to them through the legislature. The custom house was in their hands, and any arrangement Mr. Wm. Forbes chose to make was acquiesced in without question. During one of my visits, one of the upper employees in the custom house undertook to seize some forty mule loads of contraband goods belonging to the firm ; but his zeal cost him his situation, and sent him to prison for a short season.

Mr. Forbes represents her Majesty Queen Victoria and the President of the United States, as the consul of the respective countries.

To them belong some extensive cotton factories, having upwards of five thousand spindles in operation, and producing large quantities of cloth annually, netting to their owners incredible profits. This establishment is situated on the outskirts of the town, in a most romantic little glen, and is surrounded by the neat dwellings of the operatives, and circled by a rushing torrent, on whose banks is a superb garden, located in the most picturesque manner, containing all that is brilliant and exquisite in fruit or flower.

Light breezes waft the rainbow sprays of gurgling fountains across beds smiling with the most delicate and loveliest of flowers, which, refreshed by the moisture, gratefully emit overpowering fragrance. The coffee plant drops its crimson pods among the mammoth strawberries, and the apple and the orange lie on the ground together.

* * * * * *
* * * * * *

CHAPTER IX.

SANDWICH ISLANDS.

The Author goes to the Sandwich Islands—Embarks in a small Steam-boat—Narowly escapes Shipwreck—General Description of the Craft—Arrives at the Sandwich Islands—General Description—Is presented at Court—Queen not visible, very drunk—Princess Victoria, a dusky Negress, personates her Majesty—Dog Feasts—Impossible to restrain his Majesty's taste for Strong Waters—Description of Owyhee—All about the beautiful Cascade of Hailuku.

DETERMINING to go to China, I was looking around me for a chance, and had almost closed an agreement to go over in the "Isis," a large Dutch ship, when I happened to meet my old friend, Captain Gus Ellis, of Guaymas memory, the individual who commanded the celebrated schooner "Alice," before referred to. Captain Gus, after having given the Mexicans a series of lessons in boat sailing, and in the working of fore-and-afters generally; after having made love to and broken the hearts of a score of Mexican lasses; after having resigned his office as commissary-general to the beleagured citizens of Guaymas, who had taken ship to escape the kind attentions of the fillibusters, and, in short, after having used up all the excitements incidental to that very stirring period in the history of Sonora, had finally left there in a schooner which had been chartered to take up the aforesaid fillibusters, vanquished and in disgrace, to San Francisco. Since his arrival in California, he had turned his attention to *steam*, and any one who knows anything of San Francisco harbor in those days, will remember the redoubtable Gus, with his little "Fire-fly," rushing huge clippers about the bay, making miraculous escapes from being dashed into pieces by steamboats, or mashed into nothing by the great monsters he was tugging against strong currents to and from their anchorages. To give a little idea of the performances of this igneous insect, the "*Fire-fly*," I will relate a little incident which occurred while I was in San Francisco, which will not only illustrate the power of the little boat, but will give an insight into the character of my worthy commander.

The ship St. Patrick, a large vessel of a thousand tons, being assigned a berth at one of the upper wharves, it was necessary, in order to secure it, to occupy it forthwith, and the captain immediately sent word to Gus to bring round his little Fire-fly to his assistance. The tide was running very strong, as it always does in San Francisco, and although the little "Vapor," as the Spaniards have it, puffed and blew, and coughed most consumptively, yet the big ship made no headway, and her captain, in despair, was about hailing a rival tug, and informed Gus of the fact. That would never do! One effort more must be made. Singing out to the mate, who, by the way, was acting fireman, too, he says: "Childs, we must move that ship!" "Aye, aye, sir!" says Childs. "Childs, pitch in that barrel of tar, and I shall sit on the safety-valve!" "Aye, aye, sir!" says Childs, and he pokes away at his fires, and his captain composedly seats himself upon the lever of the safety-valve; the people aboard the ship all retiring below deck, in case of a blow up. The little Fire-fly gave one hard cough, two or three wheezes, then a mighty effort, and walked the thousand tons ship to her wharf in quick time. Gus, by his activity and ingenuity in towing ships in San Francisco harbor, had become quite notorious ; so much so, that the Hawaiian Steam Navigation Company, which had just organized, selected him from a crowd of shipmasters to take over their pioneer boat to run on the route among the Islands ; the requisites for that business being, skill in handling a steamer, rather more than ordinary daring in running one, and a man who, at the same time that he was popular, would have a moral and physical influence on the heterogeneous material of human flesh that he would be brought into connection with in the island trade.

By way of parenthesis, I must say, that my impression was that the steamer of which he spoke was a sea-going vessel, and that we would go over in short order ; but to my consternation, on presenting myself on board, I found a little mite of a boat, which had been brought out in the hold of a ship from the United States, and which had since been plying to Stockton, and in which, during several passages that I had made in her across the bay, I had even there felt not at ease when it was blowing heavily. She had been strengthened and sponsoned, and had had a couple of light spars stepped in her, to be sure, but for all that, the idea of making a voyage of two thousand miles in her was not agreeable ; however, I had agreed to go, and I was not inclined to back out. A good many friends came down to see us off, all bidding us good bye with the consoling reflection that they would never see us again.

In going out over the bar there was a heavy swell on, and

she behaved so badly that even then I began to lose the little confidence that I had in her. Our programme was to steam for three days, until we got off the coast, then to disconnect our engines, hoist our sails, and drift over to the Islands, always saving enough fuel to steam into harbor. After surging, pitching and rolling on the bar for an hour, we managed to clear it in safety, and laying our course so as to keep the wind abeam, we steamed off at the rate of six knots an hour.

As the sun went down the wind freshened up, and by midnight there was a clear gale blowing and a heavy sea rolling, we being obliged to run along in its trough to keep our sails full; the little thing rolled most tremendously, and at every surge the sea would swash over the main deck and through the cabins knee deep.

Being very much fatigued I turned in, and had hardly got asleep when the mate came down, and rousing me up told me that it was piping up harder, and that the ship had a strong list to windward, in spite of the gale blowing with full force upon our fore and aft sails, which of course should have had the effect of pressing her down to leeward; there was only one way to account for this, and that was that she was full of water and gradually settling, preparatory to going down (we had prepared ourselves for any such contingency with a fine lifeboat, in which was stowed a beaker of water, some bread, etc. etc., ready for an emergency). Springing up, I rushed out on deck, and going to the engine-room found that, sure enough, with only five feet hold, she had three feet of water in her, and that besides, her sponsons had also leaked full. Something had to be done at once. Going up to my friend's room and shaking him, I informed him of the state of affairs below, and that he had better turn out; very quietly rolling over on his other side, and telling me to go to the devil, he immediately began to snore—about as cool a proceeding, under the circumstances, as had ever come under my supervision. Going down on the main deck, we turned the boys out, and commenced shifting the deck-load of fuel to leeward! presently a sea struck her, and smashing in her companion doors, rushed across the deck, nearly carrying us all with it; things began now to look squally, and worst of all, the bilge pump choking, prevented the engine from keeping her free.

Manning the hand pumps we went below, and found on poking about up to our necks in water, or rather liquid filth, the component parts of which were coal dust, oil and dead rats, that the carpenters had left their chips on the kelson, when stepping the masts, and that these chips were all drawn in by the bilge pump, thus preventing it from acting, and a delightful job we had during the live-long night in keeping it free.

One of not the least amusing incidents of the gale on the first night out, was the part which Mr. Lighthall, of North River renown, and our engineer-in-chief, bore in endeavoring to save the craft and ourselves from annihilation.

Simultaneous with our exodus from our bunks in momentary expectation of the little craft making her last appearance *super-mare*, came old Lighthall, minus his inexpressibles, and in spite of his experience as engineer of every kind of boat, and in every kind of emergency under the sun (a better man or engineer never handled a starting bar), I must say that the old gentleman was badly scared. His first impulse was to seize a huge augur about six feet long, and to make frantic attempts to bore into anything and everything that presented itself, under the insane impression, that as there was so much water in the ship the best plan would be to *bore a hole* for it to escape. Now this would be excellent philosophy had the ship been on *land*, but being in mid-ocean, the supposition naturally suggested itself to friend Gus that those very holes *might possibly* let in more water than we might know what to do with, therefore, he delicately hinted to the old gentleman that he should amuse himself with some less dangerous method of evaporating his excitement; yet, nevertheless, it was necessary to keep a bright lookout upon the aforesaid augur, and many were the incipient borings that were nipped in the bud by the captain's watchful care, before attaining a dangerous depth.

The gale lasted two days, during which time it was difficult to tell whether we were above or below water. The ship was started at every joint, and, sitting in the cabin, with every lurch, the water would swash around our legs knee-deep. We hardly believed she would live it out, but there was no remedy for it. We could'nt alter her course to put in anywhere, as there was no point she would fetch nearer than her destination ; so we let her rip. On the third day the breeze lulled, and we disconnected her engines, and thus letting the paddle-wheels revolve, put her before the wind. It was but slow work, however ; with a fair wind, all sails set, and a large sea rolling after her, she never made over three knots. However, we were in no particular hurry, and took things mighty easy. The weather was perfect, the sun partially obscured by the light fleecy clouds always accompanying the trades, the atmosphere as soft and balmy as ever floated over southern Italy, and the dark blue rolling sea, cresting and foaming laughingly at our side, shooting forth avalanches of flying fish, albicore, and bonita, while now and then shoals of venerable old sperm whales would come spouting by, to the intense excitement of sundry old whalers aboard the steamer, who rushed frantically about decks, cursing their luck, that they had not the necessary apparatus for accepting their bold defiance.

A young moon, when we left, accompanied us over, and a series of more heavenly nights were never enjoyed by mortal or by Peri. Dreamingly stretched upon the deck, with the smoke of our cheroots curling over us, drinking in copious draughts of the combined loveliness of a moon-gilt sea and a moonlit sky, we talked of home and bygone scenes; many a sigh of sadness escaping us as we spoke of those whose star had set in our absence. And our hearts, too full for utterance, left us in silent contemplation of the past, when, soothed by the profound silence, unbroken save by the zephyr-breeze among the cordage, we gradually and peacefully would succumb to our drowsy feelings, and wander off to dream-land among the loved forms of long-separated friends.

It was a funny voyage throughout—a hare-brained sort of an undertaking; and I always was inclined to laugh at myself when I thought of it—a voyage of 2,000 miles, over, at times, a stormy sea—a little tub of a steamboat, hardly river-worthy, propelled by sails!!

Well, to tell the truth, she was the oddest-looking little affair that ever went to sea, a Chinese junk not excepted. Of course, under sail we could do nothing with her but let her drive before the wind, and I remember one night that a stupid fellow let her get aback, and a nice job we had to get her off again. We were sitting at the supper-table, when, feeling by the unusual motion that she was off her course, we went on deck to see what they had been doing with her. There she lay flat, aback. At once taking the usual method to box her off, we found, after repeated efforts, it would not work. Her paddle-boxes and saloons, acted upon by the wind as sails, counteracted all our efforts, and she would neither wear nor tack. After working all sorts of traverses, for an hour or so, and expending our curses and patience, a sea happening to strike her full on the port bow, gave her a cant to starboard, and her jib filling, and square sail braced well in by the port-braces, catching aback, drove her over to her course again. The name of this delectable vessel was the "Akamai," which, being interpreted from Kanaka into English, means "Good;" but whether it was intended to convey the idea that she was "good" for firewood, or "good" for *sea navigation*, never transpired. But, to make a long story short, after a voyage of some nineteen days, we arrived off the Island of Owyhee, the southernmost of the group; when again connecting our engines, and steaming up, after a fearful night of squalls and lightning, we ran in and anchored off the picturesque little town of Lahaina, on the island of Maui.

We came to an anchor off Lahaina a little before daybreak, and the sun had not risen over the highlands overhanging it, when hundreds of natives came flocking off to us, in every variety of boat, from a canoe to a ship's launch. Indeed, those who had not the means for procuring such conveyance, dashed boldly into the surf, and swam off to us, a distance of over a mile. Such a clatter I never listened to, nor did I ever witness such open-mouthed astonishment as these simple islanders expressed, on beholding our "floating house," as they termed our steamboat. No place was sacred from their intrusion, and before I was half dressed, my cabin was filled with a score of girls, laughing at the top of their voices, and examining everything with the utmost wonderment. The decks presented a lively appearance, crowded as they were with picturesque groups of men and women in their many-colored garments, while we were surrounded on every side with a flotilla of boats, filled with beautiful fruit, most grateful to the eye after our long voyage. It was amusing to see the swimming parties. Reaching the vessel, they would clamber up the sides, and, after satisfying their curiosity, overboard they would go again, like so many seals, and paddle away shoreward.

Lahaina is a stirring little place, straggling along a sand-beach, the romantic little huts half hidden by cocoanut groves, and defended from the foaming surf by a coral reef running along its entire length. Reaching the shore, we find a much larger place than we had supposed, and several prominent buildings, among which were the government house and a Protestant church. There was likewise a pretty good hotel, cosily located, where one could get a fair dinner, and then puff away his cheroot on its balcony, watching the pretty Mani belles as they gracefully tripped along ; or, should he prefer it, could swing his hammock beneath the noble cocoas, and snooze away, fanned by the soft trade wind.

The town, as I before observed, is embowered in groves of cocoa-nut and bread-fruit, which form long avenues, and beneath whose shade the picturesque cottages are ranged, affording a delightful tropical picture. Around their doors scores of girls were lounging, their beautiful forms enveloped in long, loose gowns, pendant from their shoulders, and their heads surmounted with the jauntiest little glazed hat, with a narrow rim, round the crown of which an ostrich feather tastefully floated.

These girls are grace personified, and the very perfection of physical beauty, and although copper-colored, still that is lost in their full expressive eye and animated features ; lolling upon a mat or cane sofa, they would motion you to a seat, when an impromptu flirtation would at once strike up in the most incomprehensible jargon of Kanaka and bad English. However, a squeeze of the hand or a gentle pressure of the waist always elucidates any abstruse remark.

Every man, woman or child who has ever written home concerning the Sandwich Islanders, have described their "surf-boards," and their astonishing skill in guiding them through a surf in which no civilized man could live, as also their excellence in swimming, and almost superhuman endurance in the water. Travellers are apt to term a Kanaka "half man half fish." I should say that he was "third man and two-thirds fish"—for no fish that swims the ocean could have any command over itself in breakers where the island girls and boys sport for hours, as perfectly at home as on the dry land.

The surf-board is a piece of thin plank, five or six feet long by about eighteen inches in breadth ; when the long, green swells are rolling in with terrific violence—with a din and crash that out-thunders thunder itself, then men, women, and children flock to the beach, and divesting themselves of their superfluous clothing, dash into the breakers, board in hand ; with a miraculous agility they dodge the heaviest rollers, plunging beneath them as they begin to crest, and reaching the outside breaker, prepare for their lightning ride shoreward.

Miraculous as their outward progress through a boiling surf, which no whale-boat would attempt, seemed to us, setting the force of suction and undertow completely at defiance, we felt a thrill of horror as we looked upon a couple of delicate-looking girls kneeling upon a frail board, rushing in, as if shot from a bomb, upon the crest of a great, green billow, which, raising his head as he came, appeared like a huge mountain of water; onward they came, just managing to keep in such a position as to avoid the break of the roller, and in less time than I have taken to describe, with screams of delight they dashed up to the very spot where we were standing. As swimmers they have no equals, men and women appearing to possess equal powers of endurance; and most astonishing facts of their aquatic feats are recorded, one of the most miraculous of which is worth repeating. A large native canoe, having on board a number of natives, left one of the southern islands bound to the northward; when only a part of the way across the Owyhee passage, where there is always a heavy cross-sea and furious currents, a squall struck and capsized her; among the passengers was a native woman, the daughter of a chief, with her husband, a white man; the others beings all Kanakas, they of course struck out for themselves towards shore, a distance of some thirty miles; but the white man could not swim, and his true-hearted wife directing him to put his arms upon her shoulders, struck out for the nearest land. For hours and hours they toiled along, the fond woman inspiriting the husband, refusing to leave him; all day and all night they buffetted the angry currents, till at last human nature gave way, and the white man gave up the ghost; still clinging to his cold clay, the widow toiled on, till at last, becoming insensible, her efforts relaxed, and she knew no more until she found herself resuscitated by some friendly hands, and on inquiry found that a favoring current had drifted her upon an island, where she had been discovered and brought to life by her deliverers.

Another instance, scarcely less remarkable, occurred during the period of my visit to Honolulu. At that time there were a large number of whaling vessels in port, many of which were short of men, and consequently sailors' wages were very high, and large advances were given to any Kanakas who would ship. One ship in particular, had lost the whole of one watch by desertion, and finally had succeeded in obtaining her complement; the men, all Kanakas, received their $100 each, as an advance, and went on board, and the ship got under weigh. All went on very well for the first day and night, and the captain was congratulating himself on his good luck. During the middle watch of the second night, however, stepping out on deck, the captain was astonished on finding no one about, and asking the man at the wheel what it meant, was told he didn't know what had become of the people, but presumed they had gone below.

Calling the mate, and mustering the crew, he found to his consternation that every Kanaka had disappeared; they must have deliberately jumped overboard, determining to swim ashore, a distance of sixty miles! On board whale-ships the mates do not usually stand a night-watch—the watch being generally in charge of one of the "boat steerers," and in this instance the "boat steerer" was a Kanaka, and they all went off together; the plan was probably hit upon before they left port—each man received his $100 advance, and then they deliberately formed their desperate plot for breaking their engagement.

Bidding our Maui friends good bye early one morning, we again got under weigh, and as the sun was setting, found ourselves abreast the Island of Oahu, the queen of the group, and the seat of government, the chief town of which is the city of Honolulu. There it lay before us, sentinelled on the one hand by Point Diamond, a huge bare mass of white rock, 600 feet high, and said to be hollow, and by the Devil's Punch-bowl, a lofty turreted mountain fortress overhanging it. At their feet, among the graceful foliage of bread-fruit and cocoanut, nestled the town, the most prominent of whose buildings was the great square stone native church. Within the reef, which forms a splendid natural basin for a harbor, lay three hundred sail of vessels, moored head and stern in tiers, mostly whalers, although here and there the lofty spars, out-topping all others, told of the presence of our Yankee clippers, while through the forest of masts, the tri-color and stars and stripes indicated the presence of French and American men-of-war.

Landing, one would fancy himself in a Yankee town, the houses, mostly built of wood, telling of their down-east origin, while their signs, in plain English, testified to the nationality of their owners, and the familiar sounds of Yankee dialect kept up the illusion that we were treading the streets of some Massachusetts seaport, which, however was quickly dispelled by observing names such as Kaaumanu and Nuauanu, painted on sign-boards at the corners of the streets, indicating their designation. Leaving the business part of the town, however, it loses in a measure its Yankee characteristics, and picturesque little cottages, built in a style of their own, embowered in shrubbery, delight the eye.

The dress of the native women attracts at once the eye of the stranger, being of the same style as that described in the preceding pages as worn by the girls of Lahaina; still there were brighter hues and much more taste displayed, and their rakish little hats, with pendant feathers, wore a more ton-ish look, as became the denizens of a metropolis. The half-castes affect the European modes, but wear their garments with a peculiarly witching way of their own. This class are all beautiful; they retain the full Asian eye, and the olive Asian tint of complexion, the rich glow of European blood rushing to the cheek, as also their liquid pronunciation, as they warble out our harsh English words. I always fell in love with them; but it was no selfish passion. I only wanted to be baptized a Mormon, marry the whole of them, and then retire, "en grand Turc," to one of the green oases of the Polynesian group. There was only one drawback: they would anoint themselves with cocoanut oil, and in that hot climate it immediately becomes rancid. Imagine the effluvia!

My friend with whom I was living was a "violent" artist, and wishing to make some sketches of these graceful creatures in their most witching postures, accordingly dispatched his "tamaree" for half a dozen Wyhenee houris whom he had noticed in his walks. His page being successful, at the appointed time in bounced five as beautiful and as graceful girls as ever caused art to tremble, laughingly, though noiselessly, into our apartments, with fingers on their lips motioning silence, as the Kaikos (Anglice, police) are extremely watchful of female vagaries, having the right of searching any bachelor's apartments suspected of harboring them. Turning the key, after a few preliminaries, the artist pro-

11*

ceeded to transfer to his canvas the exquisite points of Polynesian loveliness of form and feature, when a loud breathing outside the door admonished us that some one equally appreciative with ourselves was, uninvited, inspecting our operations through the key-hole. The young ladies immediately asserted that it was a Kaiko, and were in the utmost trepidation lest they should be all walked off to the fort for a day or two, and began taking measures for flight through a window. Meanwhile my friend suggested the expediency of filling a quill with snuff and blowing it through the keyhole. No sooner said than done, and then, such howls and curses I never heard from Kanaka lungs.

Pacifying the girls, my friend was proceeding with his study, when came a loud, thundering knock accompanied by an order to open at once in the king's name ; we told them to hold on a moment, and meanwhile bundling the girls out of the window, we piled all the moveable trunks and furniture against the door and invited the gentlemen to walk in, at the same time assuring them that if they did so it was at their own risk, as there were no Wyhenees about. They however determining to search for themselves, commenced preparations for storming the bungalow ; we meanwhile arming ourselves with a couple of immense clubs awaited their entrance. The door suddenly gave way, and in came three Kaikos ; without giving them time, however, for explanation we pitched into them club, in hand, when they went out quicker than they came in, and we did'nt relinquish the chase until they were clear of the grounds. The next day we were ordered before some official or other, but on stating the case, the Kaikos were severely reprimanded for interfering with quiet gentlemen, and our artist resumed his labors, the young ladies overjoyed at the discomfiture of their natural enemy the Kaikos.

An American cannot but feel his national pride tickled, on wandering through the Yankee like town of Honolulu, or on casting a glance over its harbor crowded with hundreds of sail of American shipping, from whose every peak, on a feast day, floats the stars and stripes—silent but flattering testimonials of the indomitable enterprise of his countrymen. Here in mid-ocean, thousands of miles from any continent, American influence has tamed and brought under the civilizing subjection of Christianity, the savage who comparatively but a few years since knew no joy so great as when feasting upon the remains of some unfortunate mariner thrown by the unmerciful waves upon his inhospitable shore.

Now, on the very spot where once were celebrated the hideous orgies of canabalistic feasts, rises the grateful incense of a thousand voices, chaunting in the same tone that sang the death-notes of their writhing victims, the same hymns of praise, which we in our childhood were taught to warble forth in our own dear native land, in thanksgiving to the only God. When on a Sabbath morn we hear the sweet bells murmuring through cocoa groves, and mingled with the roar of the long Pacific swells bursting upon the coral reef, and see lines of natives sauntering along in their picturesque though modest costumes, decorously wending thier way to the sanctuary, we feel an honest pride in the zeal and perseverance that has reclaimed the heathen from his sacrilege, and rescued this, fairest of Jehovah's works, this terrestrial paradise, from the brutal thraldom of paganism, and with reverential awe we acknowledge that mighty though unseen influence which upheld the poor missionary in his great work, and inwardly ejaculate, God is God, and there is none other like unto him. But we sicken when we think that the successors of those devoted men who so assiduously labored in reclaiming the savage from his degradation, taking advantage of the natural feeling of veneration which the blameless lives and self-sacrifice of their predecessors had given rise to in the minds of these simple islanders, have established an autocratic thraldom of which they themselves are the head, as despotic as is the government of the Russias, highly satisfactory to their own pride and love of power, but of incalculable injury to the interests of the religion of which they are the high priests, and tending by its restrictions and shallow and transparent hypocrisy, to undo inwardly, all that has been effected in the true conversion of the natives. With the government in their own hands, their power is unlimited ; the king a mere puppet, scarcely dares call his soul his own, but surrounded by the tinsel and pinchbeck paraphernalia of a ridiculous royalty, he moves as does his prototype on the chess-board, when and where these *republican* players may indicate.

With the talismanic word "Taboo," they have restricted the natives in a thousand harmless pleasures which at once tended to keep alive their nationality, and to preserve their natural elasticity of spirits, naturally depressed by their sense of inferiority to the whites. The king, a stout, copper-colored old gentleman of fifty years, is a man of strong common sense, and of some considerable acquirements, and had he been placed in any other position in life but of that of the Lord's anointed, would have probably cut a figure among his countrymen ; but surrounded by a spurious royalty, and hemmed in by forms and ceremonies imposed upon him by his republican ministers, and which are wholly distasteful, he strives like a school-boy wearied with his task, to escape his persecutors, and no opportunity is left unimproved, but that he immediately gets drunk, and lounges about the hotels, playing billiards, of which he is very fond, with any one who may present himself. For these little indiscretions he always paid dearly, however, for as soon as the ministers got possession of his body, they immediately put him under arrest—there remaining until he promised to do better. I myself have seen the old chap rolling around the streets with a bottle tucked under one arm and a Kanaka Wyheenie under the other, both gloriously drunk.

There is an ancient and honored custom of the Kanakas, which is the celebration, at a certain season of the year, of a feast, the principal feature of which is the roast-dog, on which they dote and which a whole mountain of taboos, thundered from the ministerial vatican, will not prevent them from eating; prince and peasant alike indulge in this luxury, and the king, who in this will not be thwarted, is assigned a little country seat where he can enjoy his canine festival without compromising his dignity, for although dog is the prominent eatable, strong waters flow abundantly, and the entertainment merges into a saturnalia and is kept up for days, and invariably results in the extreme illness of the royal family—his majesty generally leading off with an attack of *mania-potu*.

Having received through the kindness of a friend an invitation to a royal levee on one occasion, I gladly availed myself of the opportunity of seeing their majesties, and the Hawaiian aristocracy in full flower.

We arrived at the gateway of the palace grounds about eight o'clock, P.M., and on their being thrown open, passed up a broad avenue leading through a brilliantly lighted plantation, until we reached a circular opening in front of the palace. Here were drawn up a company of the Hawaiian guard, who presenting arms, the officer motioned us to proceed, and advancing a few paces, we ascended the steps of a wide portico which completely surrounded the palace. Sauntering about, enjoying the delightful air and the sweet music, we encountered many friends, when after exchanging salutations we proceeded to enter. The reception-room, a fine spacious apartment, was handsomely fitted up with modern furniture, the centre tables covered with late European and American publications, the étagères loaded with articles of vertu, gifts of foreign powers, and the walls hung with full-length portraits of H. M. Queen Victoria and of Louis Philippe, besides others of native chiefs; altogether a very appropriate and cosy room. The audience chamber leads out of this apartment, and was already filled with company, while others were awaiting their turn to be presented, and the courtiers were flying about in a high state of excitement and importance, marshalling their forces in proper order for entering the august presence. Mr. Wyllie, a Scotchman, and prime minister, in full court costume, led the way and announced in turn the humble aspirants for regal smiles. His majesty, flanked on the one hand by the Princess Royal Victoria, an extraordinarily dingy and thick-lipped young woman, and on the other by His Royal Highness the heir apparent, was seated on a Gothic chair placed on a slightly elevated platform, and was surrounded by several chiefs. As we marched by we were greeted with a low bow of recognition from their highnesses, after which, mingling with the crowd, we examined at leisure the royal household.

The enormous proportions of the chiefs were a source of wonder to us, indeed I am inclined to believe they are the largest men in the world; they are really colossal, their features, though large, beaming with intelligence, and bearing a most benignant expression.

The princess, Victoria (*vice* the queen, who was drunk), was very African in appearance, several shades darker than Kanakas usually are, and with very thick lips, she did not give us a very exalted idea of courtly beauty, nor indeed did we alter our convictions when we stood at her side at the supper-table, and saw her swooping up, with intense greediness, the very substantial plateful which we had the honor to set before her.

The young lady was attired in a very elegant dress of white satin, trimmed with expensive laces, and altogether got up in very fine style, considering she lives in the Sandwich Isles; but notwithstanding her furbelows, I hardly think she succeeded in captivating any of her guests.

The heir apparent (present king) was rather a fine-looking, well-built man, of, I should imagine, thirty-five years of age, with a very intelligent countenance, but unfortunately, very dark; he is said to be well educated, however, and to possess talent; he has great ideas of being the Lord's anointed, and spurns all overtures touching the selling out to the Americans of what he is pleased to term his birthright; he, moreover, does not love the Yankees overmuch, as they do not evince the same veneration and respect for his rank as do Europeans.

When in the United States, a few years ago, with my Lord Judd, he received little or no attention, which disgusted him, and on one occasion, his royal pride was excessively wounded.

One day, while in the city of New York, he was walking in Broadway, when two young men, happening to stroll along by him, the one said to the other: "There goes one of the Sandwich Island princes!" "Where?" "Why, yonder," indicating at the same time which was the august personage. "What!" said his companion, "that black nigger yonder! impossible!" His highness could not forget this, nor could Judd's oily tongue soothe his wounded pride.

In England he was fêted and courted, and some court beauties did not deem it a disgrace to have their waists encircled by his arm in a waltz.

The Hawaiian court, as may be imagined, is not very exclusive, and I must say that the assemblage, at the reception, was of a very mixed character; among the ladies present, I saw some females from California, who did not move in the very highest circles of that democratic city, and a host of skippers and ship chandlers' wives, who looked as if they had lain in a state of torpidity for a century or two, and had emerged for the occasion; there was some considerable beauty among the half-castes, however, several of whom were very vivacious and agreeable; the men part of the assembly was made up of the élite of the city, *i. e.* the wholesale storekeepers (those who sell oil by the barrel—those selling by the gallon being excluded), the hotel keepers, and the whole posse of missionaries, consuls, etc., etc. These affairs are, however, conducted with a great deal of decorum, and if the women are vulgar, and if the men do favor whale oil rather than Macassar, still we must confess that, considering its farcical nature, the dignity of the court was exceedingly well maintained, and that the "Spouter" captains and their shell-back wives conducted themselves with as much humble grace, as if they had been accustomed to "drawing-rooms" during their previous life.

Saturday is the grand gala day among the Sandwich Islanders—the missionary sceptre is then sheathed, and the native breathes free again, that the bug-bear taboo is taken off his favorite pastimes. Rushing to the surf, he plunges in, and careless, sports among the mountain combers; tired of aquatic sports, anointing himself with cocoanut oil, and loosely throwing on his clothing and springing upon his horse, he scours away over the plains like a liberated school-boy. The Waiatiti plains, which spread out from the suburbs, and the Nuuana valley, are the principal rides, and on Saturday afternoon are filled with mounted Kanakas, men and women, tastily attired, flying along with frightful impetuosity, totally reckless of the consequences of collision or anything else; the women ride astraddle, but enveloping their limbs in a roll of bright-colored calico, with their long flowing gowns and jaunty little hats, present a most picturesque appearance. Sweeping past you with horse at full run, with flowing robes, the very personifications of Di Vernon, they challenge you to a race, and it behooves you to look to your seat, for whether you will or not, your horses, educated never to allow anything to pass them, themselves accept the proposal, and on the instant, start off at their topmost speed. The Nuuana valley gradually ascends for some five or six miles; running through a country under a high state of cultivation, and lined with pretty little villas, the views of the city and harbor, and islands adjacent at different points of elevation, are superb The ragged summit of the Punch-bowl, and the crystallized and hollow mountain of Point Diamond, overhanging the green, wide-spreading plains, dotted here and there with hut and villa, the town beyond, with its white houses half hidden by the cocoanuts, and the forests of masts and cordage rising from the hidden hulls of the shipping, form as pretty a landscape as one may chance to see.

Owyhee, the southernmost island of the group, is decidedly the finest, being the largest, best irrigated, and most productive; the scenery too is most romantic, and from its summit two huge volcanos, Maunaloa and Maunakea, the Gog and Magog of Polynesia, belch forth from their troubled bowels a continuous volume of flame, and smoke, and burning lava. Their craters are said to be the finest in the world, Vesuvius not *holding* a *candle* to them—are visited by all who have an opportunity, and who inevitably return, deeply impressed with the *awfulness* of these nature's greatest wonders.

What apter illustration of the Bible's hell, than that vast crater, whose superficial extent is greater than that occupied by the two largest cities in the world, heaving, and bubbling, and hissing with eternal fires, and with crashes of a thousand thunder-claps, hurling immense masses of rock and liquid lava high into the air?

Not far from Hilo, the principal port of Owyhee, is a most romantic cataract, whose silvery waters collected from the mountain-brooks leaping merrily down from the volcano's embraces, dash gaily over a precipice, and mingle with those of a fountain-like basin, sixty feet below; this is the charming cascade of Waialuku, as romantic a fall in its natural accompaniments of jagged rock and luxurious verdure, as exists in the world. Many an afternoon, with a plentiful supply of cigars, we would stroll off to it, and throwing ourselves, scarcely out of the dash of its spray, beneath its shade, would listen to its joyous music. Many an island beauty, hither wends her way to display her agility in the acrobatic exercise of diving and tumbling from the fearful height of three-score feet, from the summit of the fall to the basin of the cascade, yet they thought it nothing, and artistic groups constantly appeared in graceful pose, before taking their aërio-aquatic leap. The face of the precipice was covered with lithe forms of boys and girls striving for the ascent; laughingly floating around the basin, they would challenge us to catch them, and when having seduced us into accepting their banter, would seize upon and nearly drown us, until almost suffocated we cried their mercy. Imagine a laughing waterfall, glistening in the sun's rays, frolicking over masses of broken moss-grown rock, on either side dense shrubbery of luxuriant growth, below a reservoir of crystal water, discovering beneath a white and pebbly bottom. Picture to yourself, this quiet sheet rippled by the splashing of a score of water-nymphs with elfin locks, straggling over their exquisitely formed shoulders, as darting from above, they come shooting down like falling stars from a height of sixty feet, and you form some idea of the Waialuku cascade, on a summer's afternoon; a very pool of Siloam, one bath in whose troubled waters, like the font of old, invigorates and revivifies.

The fate of the Kanaka like that of the North American Indian, is sealed; he is a doomed man, and it will be but a question of a very few years, when his race will be completely absorbed by the Anglo-Americans. Like the Indian, they fade away before the approach of the white man, not by violence or ill-usage, but the relentless decree of fate, and disease fulfills their inevitable destiny.

During the year 1849–50 the measles, hooping-cough, and influenza, swept off some 9,000 natives; estimating the population at 80,000, this was more than one-eighth of their entire number. Since then, death has been gradually but surely doing its work, with the powerful auxiliaries of syphilis, small pox, and fevers, to so great an extent, that the mortality considerably exceeds the births. From a loose calculation, founded upon facts derived from authentic sources, I should judge that disease, emigration and infanticide, will in less than a century leave these islands without an aboriginal inhabitant.

Essentially American in feeling and institutions, these islands must, necessarily, eventually fall under the rule of the Americans, in spite of English intrigue, or French bravado, and their importance as an acquisition can scarcely be over estimated.

As an inter-oceanic depot between our western sea-board and the Indies, they are a prime requisite, and no thinking man will doubt, but that the moment the Pacific railroad is definitely fixed upon, schemes of steam navigation will be broached on a scale, such as the world has never dreamed ; for with the Chinese ports within forty-five days from our Atlantic sea-board, who will dream of exposing the delicate and costly fabrics of the east to the dangers of a Cape Horn, or Good Hope voyage, not to speak of the immense saving of interest on the capital employed ; and such steam communication once established, these islands would of necessity belong to us, for the very population necessary for the transaction of the business and the supply of such an enterprise, would outnumber the present inhabitants of the group, and would of course for their own protection seek admittance into the American Union.

As a naval station it has not its equal ; her harbors will accommodate the fleets of the world, and are possessed of natural docks for refitting, and besides are capable of the highest state of defence. With a climate of unprecedented salubrity, and a soil bearing almost spontaneously all the products of temperate and tropic clime, these islands possess advantages for military and naval depots, such a combination of which are not to be found in the world.

CHAPTER X.

MANILA.

Take Ship for Manila—Arrive there—Working Ship in narrow Places—First Impressions—Banca—River Passig—Hotel—Ancient Appearance of the City—Heterogeneous Masses of Population and Peculiarities—The Chinese—Their immense Numbers—Their Industry—Their Accumulative Propensities—Natives—Their Dress and Customs—Sports—Mania for Cock-fighting—Calzada—Beautiful Drive—Grace and Beauty of Women—Lovely Music—Cigar Factories—Vast assemblage of Workwomen—Pine-apple Cloth—Remarks upon Trade, and Natural Advantages of the Island.

Leaving the Sandwich Islands in a fine clipper ship, we flew away over to the China Seas, at the entrance to which we were saluted with a fierce typhoon, and on the 28th of December, we made the light on the island of "Corregidor," at the entrance to the harbor of Manila; we had a splendid breeze just abaft the beam until we got to within twelve or fifteen miles of the mouth of the harbor, when the wind suddenly shifting, headed us off on every tack; anxious, however, to get in, we crowded on all sail, and at it we went, and by dint of taking advantage of every favorable puff, we managed, little by little, to shorten our distance. It is a beautiful sight to see a clipper ship of a thousand tons, with a spanking breeze working up through a narrow channel; scarcely is she about on one tack, before she must go in stays for another, and as may be imagined, on board all is excitement, and every one kept actively employed ; as our barometer showed signs of bad weather, we felt it important to get in that night, and, therefore, every nerve was strained to get the most out of the vessel that we could, and in order to make the most of a favorable slant we would often shave the reef so closely that the slightest mistake in manœuvering would have lost the ship ; the crew never left their stations from day-light till dark. I was stationed at the wheel to "con" it, that is, to see that the helmsman did his duty, and I watched with great pleasure the "pilot-boat" qualities of our ship.

The entrance is fine, high mountain ranges on either hand clothed with tropic verdure, at their feet snow-white beaches, foaming with glistening breakers, which seemed to dash their spray on the very thresholds of the pretty little bamboo huts, which here and there peeped out from the forest ; the island of the Corregidor rising mid-way between the two shores, crowned with fortifications and steepled with a lighthouse, gives character to the scene. About dark, just when we were thinking that we would be obliged to stay outside all night, we got a favorable breeze, and rapidly shot inside the island. Darkness came down upon us, but the bright flashes of the revolving lantern made us sure enough of our position to venture in ; so squaring, away we went flying up the bay. Just before the bell struck 4 (10 o'clock P.M.,) the lookout forward sung out "Land close aboard !" when luffing up in the wind, letting everything fly, we let go an anchor, which brought us up all-standing, when, sure enough, within only a few lengths of us lay a long, black object ; what it was we could not imagine, but as our lead gave us plenty of water, we did not trouble ourselves. Daylight, however, solved the problem, it proving an immense battery, made of timber and brushwood, used by the natives as a fishery.

At daylight, or shortly after, a pinnace with a long, brass swivel-gun mounted midships, and pulled by twenty Manila-men arrayed in their picturesque costume of blue and white, with red sashes and heavy brown straw hats, like an inverted pan, the crown terminating in a peak or steeple, tipped with brass, came alongside. From her stern sheets (covered with heavy wooden awnings, and luxuriously furnished), three officers in Spanish uniform came aboard. Our papers were produced, and very strictly scanned ; our crew inspected, when we were given permission to communicate with shore. Calling a banca—a boat used in those waters, much resembling a Venetian gondola, with its long, black hull sharp at either end, 'midships an arched awning made of bamboo, shading cane sofas on which the passengers recline ; (the bogadores, or rowers, sit one at either end, and with their paddles they send the light fabric flying like a bird over the heavy swells which roll in at the mouth of the river)—we stepped in, and taking our places, ordered the "patron" to shove off.

The approach to the town is not prepossessing—the heavy masonry of its walls and fortifications, stained with age and weather, the massive, awkward-looking church towers, and the red-tiled roofs of the dwellings, giving rather a sombre coloring to the scene. Entering the river Pasig, prolonged into the bay by two stone piers, at the extremity of one of which is a lighthouse, and at the other a small fortification, and paddling up among the many small craft, of European and Indian build, we pulled up at the guard house where, after undergoing an examination, we were permitted to continue on our way.

Landing by a stone stairway, and entering a marine store, we passed out of it up a broad staircase into the saloon of "the hotel." Immense rooms, whose lofty ceilings and bare waxed floors looked most refreshing after the excessive glare and heat without; shaded corridors with cane divans, inviting to repose, most favorably impressed us. A Chinaman, the major-domo or factotum of the establishment, coming forward, begged us to be seated, and, clapping his hands, gave orders to some of his satellites to bring iced drinks, cool fruits, and cheroots; and as we refreshed ourselves, gave us all the news and gossip of the place. Then, conducting us to our apartments, the picture of neatness and comfort, he left us to make our toilet for dinner. Kept by a Frenchman, long a resident of the Indies, in the most liberal manner, with a capital *table d'hôte*, and everything on the most liberal scale, this was decidedly the best hotel I ever saw in the East. Situated on the river, and commanding a fine view of the bay, its balconies in the evening were a most delicious retreat. With a handful of cheroots and iced drink, and a lighted joss-stick by my side, I have passed many an hour in pleasant reverie, only distracted by strains of lovely music stealing through the embrasures of the fortifications on the other side of the river, or by the deep and harmonious peal of the cathedral bells. On one's arrival at the hotel, a body servant is assigned him, and from that moment he is your very shadow. Waking at night, you see him through your half-opened eyes fanning you; looking over your shoulder at table, he anticipates your wants; and in driving out, he mounts the box and sits beside the coachman.

The city of Manila is divided into two distinct sections—the city proper and the suburbs. The city proper contains all the public buildings, customhouse, arsenals, barracks, and governmental offices, and likewise the residences of all in any way connected with the administration of the government, and is surrounded by wall and ditch, heavily fortified, which separate it from the other portions of the city. This, however, is by far the lesser section, containing not over five thousand inhabitants, all Spaniards, while the suburbs contain at least one hundred thousand. Here all foreigners as well as the artizans dwell, and consequently all is bustle and activity. Its principal streets, the Escolta and the Rosario, are lined with shops, crammed from floor to ceiling with every imaginable article of utility or luxury, while outside their doors are itinerant venders, tailors, carpenters, cooks, etc., all assiduously plying their callings. The Chinamen are the principal tradesmen, and they are as indefatigable here as in their own country, never a moment idle, but always on the watch to make money.

Particular trades occupy a distinct section. That occupied by the shoemakers struck me most forcibly: the shops, mere dens about nine feet square, were literally stuffed inside and out with every variety of shoe (the Manila people being fanciful in their feet coverings, and wearing an immense number of them), while the only available space would be occupied by the cobbler and his journeymen, who, nearly naked, the perspiration rolling down them, might be seen from daylight till late at night sewing away, scarcely lifting their eyes. The stores—some of them kept by Europeans—are really elegant. The public buildings of Manila are none of them worthy of note. The residences are built in the old Spanish style: below, the masonry very heavy, while above, everything is exceedingly light and airy, from the excessive heat and fear of earthquakes. The churches are built in a combination of the Moorish and Spanish style, which gives a certain romantic air to the city.

The large proportion of Chinese population renders it necessary to put them under certain restrictions. Each one has his name registered on his arrival, and pays a tribute during his residence, regulated according to his employment, and a captain or head, chosen by themselves, settles all their disputes, collects the tribute for each one, and is responsible for their conduct. Almost the entire provincial trade is carried on by them ; their commercial relations extending throughout the group. The principal man living in the city has his agents established throughout the provinces, and keeps them supplied with goods, which he buys at from six to eight months' credit from the European importer. The amount sold to one of these Chinamen is often very large, as high as sixty to one hundred thousand dollars per annum, and all on credit, which is scrupulously responded to.

The natives are swarthy in color, of medium size, and exceedingly robust, though lithe and active. They are very intelligent, readily catching at European ideas, but not having the perseverance of the Chinese, are outdone by them in mechanical and commercial pursuits. In temperament quiet, taking the world easily, but when excited, violent to frenzy, stopping at nothing to gratify revenge. Singularly enough, they possess none of the characteristics of feature or character of the Chinese, although so near neighbors. Indeed, there exists a strong antipathy between the two people. This class of the population are employed either in agricultural or in sea-faring pursuits. Making most capital sailors, quick and active, and ready upon an emergency, they are preferred by all ship-masters trading in eastern seas. They invariably go in companies of five or six, accompanied by a contramaestre, who makes their bargains for wages, and through him they receive their orders when aboard ship. Although generally quiet, steady men, woe be unto the ship-master who treats them inhumanly; for when roused, they are devils incarnate. Many of them act as house-servants, and acquit themselves well; and likewise as mechanics, and when they are not too lazy to work, they succeed admirably.

They are passionately addicted to amusements, and fond of music and dancing, but gaming is necessary to their very existence, more particularly cock fighting, which they carry to the greatest excess; see the Manila man where you will he has his cock; walking, under his arm; sitting, tied to the leg of his chair, and every leisure hour is devoted to training and caressing him; at every corner there is a cock-pit, and every afternoon is spent in matching one bird against another. They fight them with long gaffs made of steel, and sharp as a razor, these are about four inches long, and slightly crooked, looking like a miniature scythe; of course, with such weapons as these, the fight does not last long; the second or third round generally results in the death of one or other of the combatants. I remember while lying in the harbor, and having occasion to caulk the vessel, some fifty or sixty men were sent off to us, and every man of them brought his cock with him; our decks were like a farmyard, such a crowing never was heard, and at noon, when the men knocked off work, little circles were formed, and in a few minutes the combats commenced, and raged without intermission till the gangs were turned to. On complaining to the "boss," he said it would be useless to attempt to prevent it, as the men would rather lose the job than come off without their birds.

The residences of the agricultural population are most singular affairs, looking more like large bird-cages than anything else, and as a general thing, located on marshy ground. In order to avoid the malarias, and the numerous reptiles and insects, they are built of bamboo, and elevated on poles, some fifteen or twenty feet from the ground, only accessible by a ladder, or more commonly by a long notched pole, which the inmates are obliged to *shin* up and down ; made of bamboo, they are light and airy, and I may add, after getting used to them, remarkably comfortable.

The Mestizos form a large element in the population of Manila, constituting the middle class ; being half breeds, the issue of a cross between the Spaniard and the Indian, they assume a superiority over the latter, though looked down upon by the former. Of a light olive color, with great vivacity of expression, graceful in figure, with fine hair, and possessing the large, soft black eye peculiar to the tropics, they are most interesting in appearance, and although, as I said before, looked down upon by the old Spaniards, still, as a general thing, they mingle with them upon terms of a certain equality; the stately Don oftentimes yielding to the influence of the fascinations of some lovely Mestiza, and waving the distinction of *caste*, leads her to the altar. The females are of an extremely graceful and elegant carriage, and almost intuitively acquire to proficiency, the accomplishments of dancing and music ; their dress is extremely unique and striking—a little shirt, made of piña cloth, with wide short sleeves, worn loose and unbound to the figure, reaching to the waist, round which a petticoat is girt, made of silk, striped or checked, of gay colors, or of cotton cloth, no stockings, their little feet inserted in slight slippers without heels, and embroidered in gold lace; they never wear bonnets, their long and beautiful hair being sufficient protection to their head. The men wear trowsers fastened by a scarf, very wide, and for festive occasions, made of striped silk; the shirt made of piña cloth, the bosom elaborately embroidered, is worn outside the pantaloons, looking as if the person hadn't finished dressing himself; a high hat, either of beaver or of straw, and heelless slippers. The Indian wears pantaloons, wide and loose, half way down the knee, made of a coarse, blue cloth, a shirt of the same material, and an immense straw hat, like an inverted basin, with a little peak, which is generally tipped with brass.

The European ladies, though retaining the fashions of Paris as a standard, manage to make important modifications to meet the exigencies of a hot climate; and, as they loll listlessly on the cushions of their coaches, as they every evening roll up and down the cool *Calzada*, their swelling forms, enveloped in clouds of delicate pine-apple cloth, and their dark tresses caressing their fair cheeks, they appear among the dusky forms moving around them, as aërial beings through the dim twilight.

The Calzada is a beautiful drive of about a mile in length, running along in the rear of the fortifications, and terminating at the bay, affording a fine view of its extended waters, as well as of the shipping and the lofty mountains beyond; the island of the Corregidor is likewise visible, its revolving light throwing periodical flashes over the dark waters. This is the grand rendezvous of beauty and fashion ; and every one who pretends to respectability drives up after dinner, and, falling into line, slowly trots up and down, saluting his friends, and admiring the ladies. As it grows later, a general halt is made at the bay end of the drive ; and, while the band of some one of the regiments is performing delightful music, the gentlemen dismount and pay their respects to the ladies.

The attention of the stranger is continually attracted by the beautiful pine-apple fabric, manufactured into handkerchiefs, dresses, and the like, which is so much used here, and which is so entirely unknown to him ; it is made from a peculiar kind of pine-apple ; the finest kind is very beautiful, and is, perhaps, superior to any other fabric in the evenness of its texture ; it is of a rich yellow color, and is embroidered in the most tasteful manner. In preparing it, it is of so delicate a nature that the windows are covered with gauze-screens, to prevent the air from circulating and injuring the web. Some of the finest specimens sell for fabulously high prices. The ordinary work, however, is not expensive, a handsomely embroidered pocket-handkerchief selling for eight to ten dollars ; collars at from five to twenty dollars, according to quality.

Tobacco is very extensively cultivated, and, being a government monopoly, yields a large revenue. The only style of cigar made there is the cheroot ; a long, smooth cigar, tapering from one end, and both ends cut square off. The manufacture of cigars is monopolized by government, and the factories are worth visiting. The one which I visited was divided into six or seven different apartments, in which were employed somewhere about 6,000 women; they were seated at small tables about two feet high, by six long, and two or three broad ; each woman had a pile of tobacco in front of her, and worked away most assiduously, producing from 150 to 200 cigars per day. Witnessing the operation of rolling them does not improve one's relish for smoking. Saliva is rather too extensively used, and the smell of garlic from several thousand breaths would seem to flavor them. The women were most diabolically ugly, and looked very cunningly upon us, as if they would like to exact tribute for our visit. Some years previously, a midshipman ventured in alone, when he was caught, stripped of all his clothing, and held *naked* until he agreed to pay a stipulated ransom. These cigars are very much esteemed all over the Indies, and, being mild in flavor and slightly narcotic, they would seem to be better adapted to the enervated constitutions of the East Indians than the stronger flavored tobacco of Cuba. There are now made up large numbers of cigars in the form of Havanas of an inferior tobacco, on account of being freed in this way from the government tax.

The Philippine Islands were a great acquisition to the Spanish crown, not only from their vast extent, but from their geographical position, being as it were a key to the China seas. Situated within the tropics, their fertile soil is irrigated by the condensed vapors swept over them by the northern and southern monsoons, which alternate successively with the seasons, making them capable of producing almost every article known in tropic commerce, and thereby creating a trade, which affords the mother country a large revenue. So little is known outside of the commercial world of the value of their productions, that it might be as well to enumerate some of the more important of them.

The Manila hemp, which has so world-wide a reputation, is,

unlike the European plant, the product of a species of the plantain tree, and is produced from the bark ; the fibres are separated by a species of iron comb ; after drying, it is made up into bales of 280 pounds ; it is then shipped to the port of Manila, where, being repacked, it is made into bales, which are hydraulically pressed, and are then ready for foreign shipment. The best article is of a long and fine white fibre, well dried and glossy ; the darker colors are considered inferior, and are not shipped, being used for home consumption. The amount shipped, during the year of my visit, to Europe, America, Australia, India and China, was about eight thousand tons! Sugar is also an important article of export, although the mills for mashing the cane and expressing the juice are of primitive style, and very inadequate to the trade ; the sugar varies very much in quality, according to the district from which it is brought ; the largest export is made to Great Britain, although large quantities are consumed in China and British India. The Manila cheroot is quite a prominent article of commerce of the islands, and a source of large revenue to the government; being a monopoly, the government tariff for their disposal is fixed as follows (but, I believe, rather more with the view to weight than to quality) : The firsts are sold at fourteen dollars per thousand ; the seconds are sold at eight dollars per thousand ; the thirds are sold at six dollars seventy-five cents per thousand ; the shipments amounting to some seventy millions annually.

Rice is very largely culivated throughout the islands, more particularly in Luzon, being the staple article of food of the entire native population, as well as of the Chinese ; it differs very much, of course, in quality, whether grown in the upland districts or in the marshes ; but little, however, is exported.

Indigo is exported to the United States, although not in large quantities; the crop being a very precarious one, and requiring an immense deal of attention, is not a favorite with the agriculturists, although the quality of that sent to the United States is said to be very superior.

Coffee is not largely cultivated, but is of a very superior quality and is greatly esteemed, being considered by the French as fully equal to the Java; the exportation, however, is not large.

The natives of the provinces of Luzon, and the islands composing the archipelago, consume a large amount of European manufactures, which are supplied them by the Chinese traders, who receive in return the following articles, many of which are entirely unknown to our commerce: The edible bird's nests are the more highly esteemed, and are classified as two sorts—white and feathered—the first being the most valuable, and worth its weight in silver; the feathered sort, so called because the edible substance of which the Chinamen make soup, is covered by down and feathers, is much lower in price. Béche-la-mar is a sort of fish found on coral reefs, and when cured and dried looks like a cucumber, but black and dirty-looking; it is also used by the Chinamen for making soup, and is really very delicious when well prepared. There are some thirty different varieties, and it is worth from twenty to thirty dollars the hundred weight.

Pearl shells, also, enter largely into the trade, as well as the pearl, and small quantities of gold dust.

A custom among the natives and Chinese, which strikes the stranger as very remarkable, is the use of the betel nut by the whole native and Chinese population, to such an extent that it forms a source of revenue to the government. A prepared leaf, called a buyo, is spread over with lime, and a piece of the nut is placed within, it is then rolled up, put in the mouth, and chewed as tobacco is with the Americans. It is a most filthy habit, the whole mouth, as well as the teeth, being discolored by the reddish-black liquid formed of the masticated nut and saliva. This article is sold everywhere, and at every few steps the pedlar offers it to one. The taste is very peculiar, pungent but not at all agreeable.

The Philippines are, as I have before remarked, a valuable possession to the Spaniard, not only on account of the revenue received, but from their commanding position in the Eastern seas; and their very contiguity to the vast and populous empire of China ensures a certain and profitable market for their products, whenever the absurdly restrictive policy which has always held anything like commercial energy in check, shall be abandoned; but the Spaniard looks with an evil eye upon foreign enterprise, and uses all his influence to keep it under.

The whole of the import trade is in the hands of a few British and American merchants, who have been established there for many years, and who are most liberal in their dealings, and friendly towards the existing government; but, notwithstanding, they are looked upon with dislike, jealousy and suspicion, and made to feel that they are only tolerated.

My stay at Manila was not very protracted, and having made several short voyages down to Singapore and to the islands of the archipelago, which proved disastrous, I at last made arrangements to go over to China in a heavy clipper ship bound to Hong-Kong.

CHAPTER XI.

CHINA.

Approach to China—Junks—Pirates—Limoon Passage—Pilot—Hong-Kong—My pecuniary Prospects—Falling into pleasant Places—Meeting an old Friend—Going up Canton River—A fast Boat—Engagement with Pirates—Stink-pots and their Effects—Am Lucky—Take Command of a Vessel—Fit her out—Buy her myself—Sell Half of her—Dispatch her to Australia—Wander over China—Macao—Poet Camoens.

THE reflecting man must approach the coast of China with a feeling akin to positive awe. The Christian pilgrim to Jerusalem, as he kneels in reverential attitude as the spires of the Holy City rise for the first time before him, through the morning mists, looks upon them with sentiments of the liveliest love and reverence; of love, for those ruined towers once looked upon the passion of our Lord; of reverence, for their remote antiquity as relics of ages long gone by. With how much greater reverence, then, should one approach a land whose existence can be traced for four thousand years; which at the time of Christ's advent upon earth could already count back twenty centuries, and which during all the convulsions which have torn the world has maintained intact its form of government, its customs, its laws, and its religion?

While Europe was floundering in the depths of barbarism—

while the Vandals were encamped amid the Seven Hills of the Imperial City, and the classic towers of Greece were blackening with barbarian fires—while ignorance and superstition had spread their dark pall over the eastern world, and ghostly monks, in the dim light of conventual cells were laboriously tracing their black-lettered manuscripts—while the arts and sciences were abandoned for war and rapine, at the extreme East flourished the Chinese empire, which, like the sacred "Nile," burying itself beneath the desert sands, and running a course of a thousand miles, again becomes a broad, flowing stream,—so the Chinese nation, coeval with the flood, plunged beneath the sands of time and only reappeared to the world after being concealed for a thousand years.

While to the westward all was oppression, ignorance, and chaos, here, at the extremest east lay a flourishing empire, whose people claiming an antiquity thousands of years before our era, living under the same government, adhering to the same customs and belief which their earliest ancestry had sanctioned, had arrived at the last point of intellectual refinement, *learning* being the sole test of political preferment.

Emperor after emperor—dynasty after dynasty had passed over them, ruling hundreds of millions of contented men with autocratic sway; not derived, however, from victorious armies or from accident of birth, but relying solely on the strength of their moral and intellectual attributes. Here all was peace and prosperity. The once arid plains, watered by artificial streams, led down from the far-off mountains, smiled before the neat hamlet of the thrifty husbandman. The mountain torrent dashing over precipitous heights, was made to turn the busy wheel which bruised the cane and ground the corn ; printing-presses threw off their thousand pages of Confucian lore, while the mariner, guided by the compass (which the philosophic brain of some ingenious countryman had invented—a boon to the world), stood boldly among the dangerous seas which washed his coasts. Her soldiers, disdaining the clumsy weapons of their enemies, thundered with gunpowder at the daring Tartars who ventured in their territories.

In the art of government the Chinese can challenge the world. Century after century—dynasty after dynasty have succeeded each other—peace and plenty reigning. Patriarchal in its form, the emperor is worshipped as the father of his people, the originator of all the blessings that are vouchsafed to them. Each year, as the welcome sun returning warms the cold earth, the monarch guides his golden plough, furrowing up the ground, and planting the yellow seed, and imploring the divine blessing on the harvest ; thus, giving an example of industry to his people. For centuries living separate from the world, their only feuds were with the Tartars, nomadic tribes, who, in their wanderings, occasionally overstepping the bounds of prudence, made forays into Chinese territory; being of a warlike turn, it was not found an easy task to eject them. Gradually they grew more formidable, and, as a precaution, that huge monument of human industry and perseverance, the Chinese Wall, was built.

Year after year, the Tartar element infused itself, to a greater degree, in the Chinese population, and turbulence and riots were its fruits.

Looking with contempt upon the effeminate Chinese, a strong feeling of antipathy was begotten, and as this increased, powerful plots were discovered, the magnitude of which caused the throne itself to tremble.

After years of effort, the Tartars at last gained the ascendency, and revolutionized the country. Essentially a corrupt people, they were not satisfied with gaining supreme power, but endeavored to grind down the Chinese to the most abject conformity to their own peculiar prejudices.

Up to the time of their subjection, the Chinese wore flowing locks; their conquerors forced them to shave them off. Many for non-compliance lost their heads altogether! In dress, too, they insisted upon vital changes, forbidding the use of certain colors.

Disdaining the virtue of Chinese philosophers, they violated the sanctity of the literary tribunals, and although affecting reverence for intellectual superiority, they cared not to abide by its rigid tests, but introduced venality to sway the voice of arbitration in the halls of literature. Corruption and deceit became, thenceforth, a synonym of Chinese character, and has, during the Mantchou-Tartar dynasty, pervaded the whole system of government.

Subjection to a foreign yoke has caused a succession of ineffectual efforts to rid themselves of it; and as each plot is laid bare, and each revolt successfully subdued, the hatred of the two races becomes more ungovernable.

Secret societies have sprung up out of this state of things to a most astonishing extent; and scarcely a hamlet but that has its political club, whose members are bound to secrecy by the most terrible oaths, while regularly organized societies, on a grander scale, permeate the whole length and breadth of the land. The association of the Triads is the most extensive and powerful known among the Chinese, and is the mainspring of all the political movements which agitate the country. More widely extended, and as loyal as the followers of Ignatius Loyola, they penetrate the palace of the emperor and the hut of the peasant; while no sacrifice is too great for its votaries to make, no torments are agonizing enough to cause them to betray the secrets of their order. Every effort has been made to exterminate them, and they are persecuted with the most unparalleled ferocity. In a single province, during the prevalence of rebellions, five hundred have been known to fall daily before the sword of the executioner. At Canton, any foreigner may witness, for the sum of one dollar, on almost any day of the week, these massacres, which appear to be perpetually taking place. The criminals are brought down in gangs; the executioners ranged in rows; as soon as the signal is given the work begins—there is a dull crunching sound. Chop, chop, chop. No second blow is ever dealt; for the dexterous man-slayers are educated to their work. Three seconds a head suffice. In one minute, five executioners clear off a hundred lives.

The most serious revolt that has ever threatened the Mantchou-Tartar dynasty is, at the present moment, in full tide of successful operation, and its armies are even now thundering before the very walls of imperial Pekin.

The prime mover and originator of this gigantic plot, which counts its supporters by millions, and who is now designated by his followers as the "Eldest son of God," was of a most obscure origin. Born in the heart of the empire; son of a poor agriculturist, whose efforts were barely sufficient for the support of his family.

Tai-Ping-Wang early became ambitious of eminence as a literary character, and thus eligible to the rank of mandarin- The poverty of his parents rendered it impossible to afford him any education beyond that accorded to the poorest Chinaman ; for, independent of its cost, the poor farmer could not afford to lose the labor of his son, whom he was obliged to support. The son, however, made use of every spare moment in the interval of toil to add to his store of knowledge, and at last, renounced the laborious life of husbandman to become a school-master. This was a congenial occupation, and enabled him to prepare for his examination before the literary tribunal of his district. After years of toil, he presented himself to the examiners, and, to his consternation and that of his family, was dismissed as incompetent.

Broken-hearted he resolved to go to Canton, where he could have better advantages for study, and, at the same time, try his chance before a different tribunal ; without money, through a country which has no facilities for travel, he set off alone on a journey of hundreds of miles in length, and after hardships and sufferings which only those who have one great aim in life can undergo, he arrived at his destination, and became the adherent or servant of an American missionary, one of whose tracts, published in the Chinese tongue, had by some accident been discovered among some rubbish in his obscure village, and which having attracted his attention by its promises of future happiness to the believer, he determined to seek out its author and enlist under his banner. Once under the protection of the missionary, he became a sort of a lay-assistant, meanwhile, using every effort with a view to a second literary trial ; years passed by, and at last the important day came round ; he was presented for examination and again failed! Bowed down by the weight of his misfortunes, he wandered back to his far-off home, where, like the prodigal son, he was received again with open arms by his poor but affectionate parents. Worn out in body and in mind by exposure, anxiety and excessive application, his nature could stand no longer, and he was seized with a violent protracted fever, which for a long time threatened his life.

During his illness he had frequent visions—revelations of the future in all its glory; in his delirium, angels from heaven anointed him the Son of God, and gave him supreme command over his countrymen. Returning strength found him a firm believer in the reality of the visions which his delirium had produced, and fancying himself the chosen of God—the embodiment of the Father and the Son, which he had read of in missionary tracts, he endeavored to make proselytes of all his family and friends. At first he was laughed at, then hooted at as a crazy man and reviled, and at last persecuted as a seditious person, preaching wrong doctrines. Persecution brought him followers, as it always has done, and in a few years the crazy convalescent found himself quite a popular leader in his own country—a sort of "Joe Smith," and possessing considerable influence.

His doctrines were very obscure, tinged with the principal features of the Christian creed; he insisted, however, on temperance in every respect—on the strictest morality, prohibiting the use of opium, and requiring his disciples to cut off their pig-tails, and leave their heads unshorn.

Anything approaching to the supernatural, even in our own country, where, through the advantages of universal education, all are supposed to be capable of penetrating the thin veil of trickery which covers the motives of its originators, is eagerly seized upon, and the more astoundingly impious the pretensions of its inventor, the greater the number of its votaries. What wonder, then, that in a country so ripe for revolution, where superstition and ignorance reign supreme—where any change must be beneficial to the masses, that Tai-Ping-Wang, who aspired to be the "Son of God," the "All Powerful," who could work miracles, and do all sorts of supernatural things—who promised eternal happiness to all who would follow him—who, unlike other leaders, showed a marked sympathy with the poor and suffering—what wonder that he, under these circumstances, should attract, in a country whose population is as the sands on the sea-shore, an army of adherents? From far and near they came and joined themselves to the standard, I was almost going to say of the cross, till at last that band of outlaws, with a crazy fanatic for a leader, has swelled into an army of millions of men, before whose advance the imperial troops recoil in dread. Possessed of the finest provinces of China, with a large standing army, in good discipline, and in many instances armed with effective weapons, it is a matter of strong probability that the *poor farmer's son*—the *country schoolmaster*—the *plucked scholar*—the *crazy fanatic*—the *Tai-Ping-Wang*—the *Eldest Son* of God, may soon sit on the imperial throne, and drive back to the worship of their Grand Lama, the Mantchou Tartars who have so long trodden the Chinese in the dust.

The reigning emperor, Hein Tung, ascended the throne in 1851, in the forty-sixth year of his age. He is the seventh emperor of the reigning or Mantchou Tartar dynasty, whose chief Tchoutchi was proclaimed in 1644 A.D. The family of the emperor is composed of four sons and a daughter. The elder, Yeh Wei, heir to the throne, is now nineteen years old ; the young prince is well educated, but, like his father, hates with a deadly hatred all foreigners. The ministers are fourteen in number, and are possessed of enormous power, and are divided into two distinct classes. The first and most important are the cabinet ministers, four in number, the other ten being charged with the government of the provinces. They transmit to those at Pekin all documents which interest the emperor, and they become, in a measure, his masters. It may be easily understood how, with such ministers, the emperor can know nothing of what is going on in the world, and that no fact is ever communicated to him in its true light ; consequently, he is utterly ignorant of all that is passing in his kingdom, that his ministers do not wish him to become acquainted with ; this will account for the difficulty which our envoys have met with in endeavoring to treat with the Court of Pekin, for it is manifestly to the advantage of the minister to keep his master from coming in contact with men, who once brought in connection with the supreme head of the government, would very soon expose to him the trickery of its underlings, costing them, if not their heads, at least their rank.

A cordon of junks, employed in fishing, lines the shores of China at a distance of sixty or seventy miles from it. These boats go in pairs, and dragging a seine between them share the produce of their mutual labor ; these junks are sometimes very large, the average size being about a couple of hundred tons, and are manned by several families who own them jointly and are supported by the proceeds of the sales of fish. It is a strange sight, on first approaching the coast, to see myriads of these picturesque-looking craft, cruising in pairs and dashing about under the influence of the strong monsoon generally blowing; indeed it is only due to the extraordinary dexterity of the Chinese in managing their craft that they do not constantly come in collision with each other and sink. It is not a very pleasant sensation on being caught among them on a dark night, in an unwarned merchantman, to feel that each and every one of these fishermen is ready upon an emergency to turn pirate, and that, thoroughly armed, they only want the impulse. to make them pounce upon and massacre you without remorse Making the land, on nearing a port, a mite of a sampan (Chinese boat) the frailest, prettiest looking little thing imaginable, comes dancing under your stern, looking like a mere feather on the billow. Hailing your vessel, the Chinaman singing out enquires in the dialect of the coast, "Captain, wantchee pilot"? "Aye, aye," says the master, never deigning to back a top sail to let the poor devil get aboard ; but there is no necessity for it, for no sooner does the fellow get an affirmative answer, than, making a tack or two, he swings under your bow, and just as you are holding your breath, thinking that you have run over him, he pops up over the bow and presents himself to you for duty. Looking around to see what has become of the sampan, you spy it towing astern, and the old women and children (wife and family of the pilot), calmly eating their dinner or supper, as if perfectly contented with themselves and things generally. My first entrance into China was made through the Limoon passage into Hong-Kong harbor, a narrow strait dividing the Island of Hong-Kong from the main.

The afternoon was a beautiful one, and the bright sunbeams shining on the green mountain side looked cheerful and inviting, more especially as the previous week had been dark and stormy. Quickly we threaded our way among the hundred junks which, reefed down to the brisk breeze then blowing, were bobbing up and down, apparently in inextricable confusion.

As we drew nearer in with the land, the smaller sampans briskly skipping over the waves, came dancing around us Shooting in the narrow channel scarce a mile wide in some places, we watched with anxiety to see how our pilot would handle our heavy ship, but soon found that she was in competent hands, as he worked her gradually up. The passage is a deep cut through the mountains, a volcanic chasm, the lofty hills rising up on either side clothed in a lovely verdure, generally uninhabited, though here and there was a cluster of fishermen's huts hidden in some secure little haven.

As we advanced, the land on the island showed signs of civilization ; a tall mass of stone buildings we were informed was a hospital where the garrison, debilitated by the heat of Hong-Kong, were sent to recuperate. Just as it had got fairly dark, we shot through the narrows and opened the broad bay of Hong-Kong ; the dark peak of Victoria soared up to the black sky, while around its base the thousand lamps glittering, and running up the mountain side, indicated the whereabouts of the city.

Winding through the shipping, steamers, junks, heavy men-of-war and lorchas, we luffed into the wind, when splash went the anchor ! and then I felt myself to be really in China.

My duty through with, I lit my cheroot and, avoiding others, took a meditative walk in the waist.

Here was I in China, the jabbering of the hundred bumboatmen in the sampans hovering around me convinced me of that, while the clang of numberless gongs on board some newly-arrived fleet told me that I could be nowhere else.

My meditations were however of a practical character ; as I hinted before, my expedition down to Singapore was not a lucrative one, and not "to put too fine a point upon it," as Dickens would say, I was left with scarcely a cent to bless myself with.

So that on my arrival at Hong-Kong my services had only brought me in some twenty dollars, which was the extent of my finances : this in itself was a fact worthy of some consideration, and it required all the sedative influence of my cheroot to console me under my adverse circumstances. Fifteen or twenty thousand miles away from home, a stranger in a strange land, without a soul I had ever before laid eyes upon, was not a pleasant reflection; but like Mr. Micawber, I was hopeful that something would turn up, and that if I couldn't get command of a vessel and go into her cabin, why I must e'en ship before the mast and go into her forecastle. So disposing of the matter in that manner, I drew my jacket close around me and stowing myself in the quarter-boat, lay listening to the delightful band which was playing on the quarter-deck of the British ship of the line laying not far from us, until I gradually fell asleep, but a smart shower driving down from the mountain soon aroused me, and drove me to my cabin.

Hong-Kong harbor is as lively a looking place as I know of anywhere, indeed I do not remember in all my wanderings to have been more favorably impressed with any view than I was with that which the rising sun unfolded on the morning following the night of my arrival.

It was a bright Sunday morning in January, the air was

cool and bracing, and although so very early, the northeast monsoon blew a stiff breeze over the bay, causing a considerable sea, and forcing the hundred sampans dancing about us to take a reef in their bamboo sails.

Overhanging our mast heads, frowned down upon us the peak of Victoria, whose base forms the island of Hong-Kong, and plastered as it were against its eastern extremity was the city, seemingly as if the houses had been thrown at the mountain's side and had stuck fast on its precipitous sides, for it is only when approaching it closely that the eye can discern any level spot on which one would suppose a house could be erected. Indeed, after all, there are but few enough of them, only the width of a single street, and after it, streets rise one above another on terraces, one being obliged in going through the city to make numberless ascents and descents, up and down stairs, which in that warm climate is not at all a desirable mode of progression.

This terracing of the mountain side gives the town a most picturesque look. Indeed, one seldom sees more startling effects produced by grouping of houses on level ledges, or perching of churches or ornamental buildings on uncertain-looking crags, than he does at Hong-Kong; and at night, as the ranges of lighted lamps rise, one above another, with here and there a galaxy of brighter lights issuing from the gothic panes of the cathedral, the windows of the government house, or mayhap from the Hindoo burial-place, illuminated for ceremonial, the effect is very fine and beautiful.

The spacious bay, extending for several miles, from the Limoon on the one extremity to Green Island on the other, and stretching across from the foot of the mountain to the hilly shores of the Kowloon on the main, bears upon its bosom about as varied a fleet of vessels as ever crowded the waters of any bay.

The lion and the lamb lie down together. Under the very shadows of the fleet of men-of-war stationed here for no other purpose in the world than to exterminate the pirates, lay scores of junks, whose sole and only business in the world is to rob the weaker, though ostensibly engaged in fishing. Being heavily armed, they hunt down and pillage all other craft not so strong as they are. They are not particular about the flag, but show equal favors to all. Their own countrymen they have a weakness for; but their bloodthirsty ferocity is more particularly excited when brought in contact with the Fanqui, or foreigner. Not content with robbing, they torture and murder all who fall in their power. It seems an impossibility to exterminate them, for so numerous are they, that although hundreds are yearly destroyed, thousands of others are ready to take their places. In the harbor of Hong-Kong itself, under the very guns of the frigates, vessels have been boarded and pillaged without exciting a suspicion of what was going on.

A case occurred, when I was in Hong-Kong, of unparalleled audacity and barbarity. A pretty little brig, an opium clipper, being ready for sea, the captain went on board, accompanied by several friends, myself among the number, to speed him on his voyage with their good wishes and a parting glass.

The style of craft being new to me, I examined into everything much more closely than I otherwise would have done, and going into a little armory, I found the mate superin tending the cleaning of some muskets. In conversation with him regarding the necessity of so heavy an armament, he rather carelessly replied that he wished there was not an arm aboard ship, as they were very troublesome to keep in order, and were rarely used ; and I noticed, at the same time, that after having them burnished up, they were not recharged. I extended my walk forward among the crew, and although I noticed several Manilamen and Chinese, who had not the best faces in the world, still I remember that I was impressed with their contentment, and with the idea that they were a very orderly and well disciplined set of men.

Shaking hands with our friend the skipper, we passed over the side and went ashore. Not three hours had elapsed (we hardly thought the vessel had weighed anchor—in fact, she had never got outside the harbor) before we were horrified by the report that the brig was being brought in by a man-of-war's boat, and that every white man had been murdered by the Chinese and Manilamen, who had revenged themselves and then escaped in the boats.

Jumping into my boat, I pulled aboard, and witnessed the most horrible sight it has ever been my illfortune to look upon ; the captain, covered with wounds, was lying stark and dead, and his faithful dog, also mortally wounded, was stretched upon his bosom, with a faint low wail, and licking his master's face ; the mates too, lay weltering in their blood, their torn clothes and fractured furniture showing that they had not given in without a struggle.

The cabin, which we had left the picture of neatness and comfort, was a ruin ; every article of furniture, dashed into a thousand pieces, testified to the desperate struggle its inmates had made for their lives; and a barometer, a very heavy instrument, and very strongly secured, had, in their desperation, been wrenched from its fastenings, showing the superhuman strength possessed by man when struggling for life. It was evident that the Chinese and Manilamen had deliberately concocted their plot before leaving the harbor, either for revenge, or for the purpose of gaining the advanced wages; and they had, doubtless, predicated their success upon the carelessness of the mate in not charging the firearms. This was done in open daylight, almost under the very guns of the man-of-war, and yet the perpetrators escaped. The English jurisdiction only extends half way across the bay, so that as long as these pirates keep on their side of the harbor, and do not molest the Europeans, the men-of-war do not interfere, and one may often hear heavy firing, and see the flash of guns at midnight, the result of an engagement between these precious rascals and an intended victim.

Merchant ships of all nations frequently fall victims to these outlaws, who, heavily armed, lie in wait for the unwary, and once in their power, there is no hope; torture and assassination are sure to follow capture.

My first step on going ashore was to look around me to see what I could do to make the pot boil, for I had no idea of letting people know that I was, as they say in California, "dead broke." Knocking around among the shipmasters, I found that there was a scarcity of officers, and that high wages were being paid to respectable men, as mates, especially for Coolie ships, of which there were a great number fitting out, bound for Australia and California. Fixing upon a pretty clipper brig as the most desirable, I made application to the captain, and was accepted, *sur le champ*, as the Frenchman have it, was paid $100 advance, and what was best of all, was informed that my services would not be required for a fortnight, thus giving me an opportunity for seeing Macao and Canton, and enjoying myself generally. Cat-like, and with my usual good luck, I had fallen upon my feet, and among good Samaritans, having taken lodgings at the City Hotel, kept upon the Americo-Anglo-Chinese plan, by one Marcus Shaw, as good-hearted a little Englishman as ever drank toddy, with spacious billiard rooms, and bowling saloons; it was the resort of the fancy of Hong-Kong, *i. e.* the army and navy officers, and shipmasters generally.

Arriving quite late at night, I went directly to my room without meeting mine host; indeed, for that matter no foreigner at the head of an establishment of that sort, ever takes the slightest apparent interest in the conducting of it; his Chinese comprador receives the guests, provides for them, presents his bill and receives payment, very often without the party ever seeing the landlord.

Next morning, on opening my eyes, I saw, standing motionless by my bedside, a knowing-looking Chinaman holding a tray on which were the component parts for an eye opener in the way of a brandy cocktail, with a little "chit," (Anglice note) from mine host, requesting the pleasure of my company to breakfast at his private table at eleven, and begging me to consider the boy as my peculiar attendant.

John, after mixing me a most reviving potion, readjusted my mosquito bar, and leaving me to finish my nap, proceeded to open my boxes and to arrange my clothes for the day's toilet.

I was at first rather astonished, and watched master John

through my half-closed eye, but soon found that he knew what he was about, so I rolled over for another nap. At ten I was again awakened by Ganymede, when, declining a repetition of the cocktail, I proceeded with my toilet, and presented myself to mine host in his private apartments, where, for the first time, I had the pleasure of seeing him.

After being introduced to his wife, we proceeded to discuss the most sumptuous repast I had tasted in the East. After breakfast I was told to consider myself perfectly at home in these apartments and not to think of dining at the table d'hôte; but that his dinner was served at seven, and that he would take it as a personal favor if I would consider myself a standing guest. This attention was quite overwhelming, inasmuch as I was quite at a loss to account for it; but accepting it as a special dispensation of Providence in my behalf, I thanked my entertainer, and having nothing particular to do, proceeded to cultivate the acquaintance of his very pretty wife, and examined the contents of his library.

Time passed pleasantly enough; the billiard tables were first-rate, and the bowling alleys *à la mode de* New York, while mine host's table and wines, not to speak of his guests, generally good fellows from the garrison, were unexceptionably jolly.

Notwithstanding the delightful manner in which time was slipping by, I had always staring me in the face the disagreeable necessity I should be under of soon going aboard ship to lead a gang of ruffianly sailors, which occupation would not be in pleasant contrast with the life I was leading

Lounging about the streets one day, I met, to my astonishment, an old friend, Ned S——, who had just come over from California. He was greatly surprised at seeing me, and on finding out how I was situated and my intentions, how I had taken the "bull by the horns," he entered a solemn protest upon my going off on any wild-goose chase, and insisted that I should apply to the master of the vessel that I had shipped aboard of to rescind the contract.

A week after my arrival, together with my friend Ned, and half a dozen others desirous to see the Chinese waters in the vicinity of Canton to advantage, eschewing steam, after a long consultation, we determined on chartering a fast boat, a vessel of some thirty tons, between a sampan and a junk, with a very pretty model, schooner rigged in the Chinese style, of bamboo sail, etc. etc. This expedition was considered by prudent folks to be what insurance people consider extra hazardous, owing to the great numbers of pirates that infest these waters; but as these fast boats always go heavily armed with, at least, two six-pounders, and as we were each provided with a cutlass, a revolver and a rifle, we had the vanity to consider ourselves a match for a hundred coolies with any number of stink-pots or two-handed swords.

By way of parenthesis, it might be well to state, that these stink-pots are a very effective weapon, and by no means belie their name, for a viler odor than they emit when they burst upon an enemy's deck never offended nautical olfactories.

Having equipped our craft, armory and larder, we proceeded to elect our officers, for some system was necessary in case of a sudden attack. The rank assigned me was that of second-lieutenant, of which distinction I was utterly unworthy, as my notions of military tactics were extremely dim, while I was about as familiar with the use of the sword as I was of a chop-stick. However, I bore my honors meekly; endeavored to assume a very dignified demeanor, and drew up my recruits in position after the most approved West Point style. My company consisted of four Chinese boys, our servants, men of mighty valor, two Englishmen, a Frenchman, and two or three coolies, hands belonging to the junk.

My efforts to drill them into something like unity of action were laughable ; and endeavoring to teach Master John Coolie how to load and fire a rifle, I came very near converting myself into a target; for, after teaching him to load once or twice, I told him to do it on his own hook, when, to my utter consternation, he pointed the rifle just sufficiently elevated to cover my head, shut his eyes and let drive ; the ball struck in a beam over my head, about six inches above the level of the cranium, and my fist struck Master John under the chin, which sent him flying into the caboose, to the consternation of the cook.

We were only called into active service but on two occasions. The first time was about midnight ; we were sailing quietly along among a lot of junks, and all were asleep but the Chinaman at the helm and the sentry, who, I am sure, was not more than half awake, if he was so at all ; suddenly, however, feeling, I suppose, the responsibility of his situation, he pulled open his eyes, when, to his consternation, he found a junk close aboard us, and by way of giving the alarm, let drive with his revolver right into the crowd on her decks. Whether or not, in the first instance, she had meditated hostilities we never knew ; but, probably, taking us for a *bonâ-fide* corsair, she fired away a big gun point blank at us, and then rained upon us a perfect shower of stink-pots,* which emitted an odor some-

* The stink-pot is a small hand-grenade, filled with sulphur, which, bursting on an enemy's deck, momentarily suffocates all in its vicinity.

thing like that which is said to prevail in the infernal regions, although I, for my own part, do not believe his horned majesty ever smelt anything half so overpowering.

Aroused by the first alarm, we rushed pell-mell on deck, each with his weapons in his hands, and the companion ladder being narrow, in our hot haste we came very near being jammed immovably together.

If it had not been so serious a matter, it would have been a comical sight to have witnessed a dozen men, sans-culottes, rushing up a narrow stairway, each carrying a small armament. I remember very distinctly that the man who followed me up the ladder had a musket with a fixed bayonet, which, in his anxiety to get up, he thrust into my thigh, thus drawing the first blood on our side.

Reaching the deck, we found that the China boys had just poured in a broadside with their two six pounders, and had evidently disconcerted our assailants. Without *comment*, we kept up a steady fire upon him with our small arms, so much so that Master Chinaman lost no time in getting under cover, and began to find out that he was barking up the wrong tree ; evidently counting upon an easy conquest of a fishing boat, never dreaming of a score of western devils lying in wait for him ; so, after treating us to a few more stink-pots, he squared away and left us victorious, without our having the slightest desire to follow him.

Mustering our forces, we counted noses, and found that, though much begrimed with gunpowder and half suffocated with the stink-pots, there was not a single man wounded, with the exception of myself, for I had just begun to find out that the poke I got behind from the bayonet of my friend coming up the companion-way was painful, although not serious, and that I was losing considerable blood ; free applications of water and linen bandages very soon set me all right again.

Assembling in the cabin, we told of our doughty deeds over a big tin pail of punch, which was brewed by our steward in honor of our victory ; there mighty feats of valor were recounted; the oftener the glasses were replenished the doughtier were the deeds that were done, and the more eloquent the toasts in honor of the illustrious wounded.

The rage of our Coolie captain was beyond description when he found that his foremast was chipped, and that his galley had been burglariously entered by a brace of six pound shots, to the utter destruction of all his cooking utensils; and to have heard his unpronouncable execrations as he swayed to and fro on his cane stool would doubtless have been awful, had we been able to understand them.

Notwithstanding our piratical encounter at the outset of our voyage, we had a delightful trip. Booming along with a leading breeze, we coasted the many green islets studding the mouth of the Canton River, and, on the next morning after our departure, found ourselves under the muzzles of the guns of the Bogue forts, where the river contracts into a very narrow pass ; these fortifications run along the base of the mountains, on either side of the river, while a wall extends all the way to their summit, the batteries being along the edge the water. This renders them very effective, as far as ships go, but as their rear is not all defended, they could very easily be taken, by landing a force which would march up the other side of the hill, and getting their guns into position, play away upon the batteries below. During the opium war, the English adopted this plan with success, much, however, to the disgust of the Chinamen, who insisted that this was not a *fair way of fighting*.

Entering the narrow passage, we soon came upon the town of Whampoa, whose heights are crowned with an imposing-looking pagoda, half covered with ivy. This is at the head of ship navigation, and here all vessels take in cargo. The presence of forty or fifty vessels naturally creates a large trade; and besides the traders, there are half a dozen hulks or *chops* moored, which serve as chandlers' stores.

The distance to Canton is about seven miles, but the river is not navigable for vessels drawing a heavy draft of water. we sailed slowly up, and viewed admiringly the green fields, the fresh-looking groves, the villages, and the tall pagodas, as they loomed up in the mist. Just after dusk, we found ourselves nearing the city. Approaching the city of Canton in the dim moonlight, we find ourselves rapidly gliding through a maze of intricate passages, and are thunderstruck with the intrepidity of our helmsman, as he guides our awkward-looking craft, under full headway, among the hundreds and thousands of vessels which lay moored on the bosom of the river. First we came up with some enormous junks, looking half European, half Chinese, which lay in tiers, partly submerged, along the edge of the river. These craft were built to fight the English during the opium war; for, the celestials finding their own craft insufficient to cope with the *Western* devils, thought they would imitate their vessels, and forthwith built some huge craft, very nearly resembling the English frigates, but which the Fanqui (foreigners) took the liberty of sinking as soon as completed. Further along we come upon some immense floating structures, looking like lofty warehouses, and which indeed are such, to a certain extent, but which are also used as canal boats, conveying grain from one end of the empire to another.

Now we come upon a compact mass of boats of every class and description, and in them permanently reside the floating population of the city of Canton, numbering over 300,000 souls! These people are born, marry, and die, and, in a word, begin and end their existence on the water, and they seldom dream of setting foot on land.

These boats, twenty to thirty deep, regularly intersected by avenues, cover miles, and have their wants supplied by ambulatory salesmen, who ply on the watery streets. Of this vast population, some dwell in decorated river-boats used for every purpose of license and luxury; for theatres, for concerts, for feats, for gambling, for lust, for opium-smoking. Some craft are employed in conveying passengers, and in a state of constant activity; some are moored, whose proprietors have pursuits as varied as those of the land population. Some are of enormous size, magazines for salt and rice. Some are called *centipedes*, from having a hundred rowers, and which act as express-boats, flying quickly to and fro; besides the smug boats, with their heavy armaments, the mandarin boats, the lorcha, and the little sampan, pulled by women, and flying from ship to ship, begging a fare.

Returning from my excursion to Canton, I had the disagreeable necessity of going aboard ship, as per agreement, staring me in the face, and I was getting my sea-rig for a long and rough cruise, when, one morning, my friend Ned bounced into my room, and, half hauling me out of bed, by way of awakening me, informed me that he had just purchased the brigantine F——, formerly an opium-clipper, and that he would be glad if I would take command! It did not take long for me to dress that morning. Of course, I accepted at once, with the proviso, that Captain L—— would rescind my engagement as officer of his vessel, which I knew he would do, with great pleasure, for he was a *first-chop* man, as the Chinamen would say. We struck a bargain seriatim. I was to go aboard at once, take charge, and get her ready for sea, to take a cargo of Coolies for Sydney, and was to have $150 per month, and a month's wages in advance to pay my bills. This was unlooked-for good luck, and I felt as proud as a pashaw with three tails.

Walking down to the mole, I hailed a sampan, and in five minutes stood upon the deck of my new command. She was a beauty, for although very old, yet she was clipper in proportion, every inch of her, and as prettily sparred and as jaunty a little craft as I ever saw in the water.

Doffing my shore rig, I went to work at once, and with my boy, Achun, the very best and most honest Chinaman, I do believe, that ever lived, and a gang of Coolie riggers and stevedores, in a fortnight I announced my craft ready for sea. During this time we were anchored in the roadstead, and as the northeast monsoon was blowing unusually strong, I had to keep a bright look-out that she did not drag; during the day-time, there was no danger of it, as the Chinamen at work on board were always on the look-out, but at sunset, they all went ashore, leaving master Achun and myself alone; consequently, the duty of keeping watch devolved upon myself, and many a long and stormy night have I promenaded her decks, in doubt whether or not to let go a second anchor. I had four dogs as companions, all pups however, but vigilant little rascals, constantly yelping and barking if a boat passed within a quarter of a mile of us ; in fact, they were getting to be so great a nuisance, that I had partially made up my mind to present the whole batch to my sampan man for his Christmas dinner ; but, fortunately, my design was never carried out; indeed my humane forbearance saved my life, in this wise : One dark, stormy, blowy night, after having spent three or four hours on deck, paying out chain, I at last let go my second anchor in disgust, and turned in. Scarcely were my eyes shut, when all four dogs commenced a simultaneous yelp ; in vain I sung out to them to keep quiet—the more they barked ; till at last, becoming alarmed lest something extraordinary should have occurred, I seized my pistol and a lantern, and rushed out again into the storm. The wind was piping a hurricane—the brig was surging and tugging at her anchors, as if she would part her chains, and the sea was a perfect glare of ghostly phosphorescent light, but notwithstanding the excitement of the dogs, there was nothing to be seen. I patted them and tried to quiet them, but they would not be pacified, and continued a low, uneasy growl. I searched the vessel on deck and below, but could find nothing suspicious, yet I felt uncomfortable, knowing what a charming locality I was in, with the uncertainty whether or not the junk lying astern was a pirate or a lawful trader. Finding nothing, and bestowing an ill-humored kick upon the most vociferous of the dogs, I descended into my cabin, when, after barricading the door and placing my cocked pistol and a big knife on the table by my head, I disposed myself for a nap. My cabin was aft and between decks, and under it was the run of the vessel, which was used as a cabin store-room, and a hatchway under the cabin table led down into it, so that a person below need only shove the hatch off with his hand, and jump on the cabin floor; this opening was covered by my chest, which I had inadvertently placed there out of the way. Never dreaming of searching this place, I was soon asleep from sheer fatigue; the next day, having occasion for a spar which I had remembered seeing down in the run, I dispatched a couple of boys below to get it up; in a moment, up they rushed with eyes distended and hair standing straight up, yelling out, "Man-ee, Man-ee." Seizing my knife, I drove them down to show me what they had seen, when, to my consternation, I found a Malay, with great glaring eyes, stowed away directly under my cabin, which, with a little effort, he might have entered at pleasure. Sending a boy up for my revolver, cocking it and taking aim at his head, I invited him out of his hiding-place, assuring him that a second bidding would be accompanied with a leaden argument.

Crawling out, he displayed about as forbidding an appearance as ever did an Indian thug; abject and quivering with fear, but his wicked eyes flashing at ill-suppressed spite; walking him on deck, and relieving him of a villainous-looking kris with a keen blade and jagged back—a tap from a heaver sent him headlong into the sea; where he went I did not take the trouble to look, but there is no doubt he swam ashore, as the gallows was too plainly marked on his brow for him to be drowned; where he came from, I cannot imagine, but suppose he swam off with the intention of murder and robbery, which he would in all probability have accomplished, had it not been for the puppies. The next day, I invested a whole string of cash in dog meat for their benefit, and they had a regular tuck-out, so much so, that a little Newfoundland got a fit from indigestion, and departed this life in a convulsion.

My pretty little brig was transformed by the carpenter into a regular ark, for, expecting to carry a large number of passengers, a house six feet high was run from the foremast chock aft. In order to save room, instead of taking my water in casks, I had teak-wood tanks built, corresponding to the model of the vessel, and an awful job I had in stowing them and filling them, and in getting aboard the provisions and fuel for the voyage; working with a gang of ship coolies, who could not understand a word of English, I was obliged, in order to explain myself, to take hold and give a practical illustration of my meaning, and I am sure my best friend would not have known had he seen me in my costume of blue shirt and canvas breeches, begrimed with tar and dust.

On purchasing the vessel, my friend Ned had at once chartered her for a voyage to Australia for as much as she had cost him, the charterer to make necessary alterations, and to find provisions and water, thus virtually getting the brig for nothing, for the charter money was to be paid down as soon as the alterations were commenced, and which on being paid, was immediately handed over to the owner as purchase money, leaving Ned sole owner of a brig, worth at least $5,000, and for which he had not paid a single cent.

Ready for sea, the government measurer came on board, and to our dismay, reported her as only having capacity for 60 passengers; this was absurd, for she could accommodate double that number without any inconvenience. The Chinese charterer was desperately cut down, but he had no recourse, for the charter party read, "as many passengers only as the law allows;" there was no way of getting over it. After cursing to the extent of his ability, he offered me $3,000 if I would put the vessel under the Chinese flag (I was then sailing under the English colors) and take 120 instead of 60 passengers. I told him that I had nothing to say in the matter, but would consult my owner. Jumping into my boat, I laid the case before my friend Ned, when he told me that he would leave it altogether with me, but, that as he had paid nothing for the vessel, if I would give him $1,500 he would sign a quit-claim in my favor. Meeting the charterer, I informed him that I would accede to his proposition, providing he would pay me $1,500 down, and the balance on the day of sailing. He at once accepted the terms, when, counting out the dollars, I immediately passed them over to friend Ned, receiving a bill of sale of the brig.

So here I was, in three weeks after my arrival penniless in China, the master and owner of a snug vessel.

Getting ready for sea, we got our *chop*, or ship's papers (an immense roll of parchment inscribed with Chinese characters), and setting our flag, a huge banner of blue silk, with half a dozen red streamers attached, we dropped down to Green Island, out of English jurisdiction, in order to be out of reach of the passenger laws.

Getting an offer for half the vessel, I disposed of a part, and putting the proceeds in my pocket, together with the $1,500, balance of the charter money, I put another man in my place as captain, and proceeded with a pocket full of rocks, as the saying goes, to make a tour of China, intending to take a steamer down to Australia, in order to anticipate the arrival of the brig and dispose of her there. Making rather a longer stay however in China than I had intended, the vessel got to Singapore before I did, and after taking in water and provisions, was wrecked on her way through the straits of Sunda. The particulars of the disaster I never heard ; all that I know is, that between the captain and the charterer, there were considerably over the stipulated number of passengers, and I am inclined to think, that the captain was not sorry when she stranded, thus relieving him of the responsibility of striking out into the stormy Indian ocean, in an old vessel, with a great excess of passengers.

One of the loveliest places in China is the city of Macao, and it is the resort of the Canton merchants, whither, enervated by the extreme heat of the factories, they retire to recuperate among its delightful retreats.

MACAO.

The mere fact of Macao being the burial-place of Camoens, the sweet poet of the Portuguese, would invest it with the mantle of immortality.

Among its most interesting memorials is the grotto of Camoens, a rudely constructed temple standing on the brink of a precipice commanding a most glorious prospect over the peninsula, and here he wrote his famous "Lusiad."

The son of a ship-captain, he was born at Lisbon in 1524, and being placed at college at Coimbra he fell passionately in love with a lady of the palace, and was banished on this account to Santarem. Here he poured forth his spirit of poetry, and bewailed his broken hopes in numbers which are compared to Dante and to Tasso.

Despair preying on his mind, he enlisted and fought at Morocco. In the midst of battle he wrote his immortal verses. At the siege of Cuta he lost an eye while gallantly fighting; but no notice being taken of his bravery, or his misfortune, he became disgusted and embarked for India, and finally settled in Macao.

Leisure was found at length for the embodiment of his great conception, and selecting Vasco de Gama's Indian expedition as the subject, he devoted the best years of his life to the composition of the "Lusiad," whose versification is so charming and harmonious that not only the minds of the cultivated, but the common people were enraptured with it, and committed portions of it to memory.

Macao, once the stronghold of the Portuguese in the East in their palmy days of naval supremacy, has now dwindled into complete insignificance as far as commercial or political importance is concerned; and although its elegant structures, and its romantic harbor still remain, the town Macao is only known to a few valetudinarians who resort there to escape the stifling heat of Canton or of Hong-Kong.

It is indeed a lovely spot, and as imposing as it is lovely. The Praya Grande, a fine esplanade, runs along the beach, faced by elegant stone structures, built after the style of the last century, combining European solidity with oriental elegance. Among them is the palace of the governor, the English factories and the custom houses. Gazing upon these splendid piles of buildings one can scarcely realize that they are almost unoccupied, and that with all these facilities for business there is absolutely nothing doing.

Beyond the praya there is a heterogeneous mass of dwellings, palatial buildings with massive walls and lofty ceilings, embowered in shrubbery emitting the loveliest perfumes. These dwellings, too, are only occupied part of each year by merchants from Canton and Hong Kong, who come here to rusticate.

Beyond this is the China quarter, very unimposing, but containing an immense number of inhabitants.

There are many magnificent gardens growing the rarest flowers and the most delicious fruits, while from their terraces stretch away enchanting views seaward. It is in one of these lovely paradises in which is located the grove of Camoens, and who could wonder at his inspiration on so peerless a spot?

The inhabitants appear to partake of the dead-and-alive appearance of the whole place—a cross between the Chinese and the Portuguese, the majority of them are almost revolting to look upon. Nevertheless, there is some pure blood, and among the Portuguese there is a great deal of intelligence and beauty.

Kneeling at early dawn before the altars of San José in that most romantic little chapel, on looking about me I have seen peering through those graceful coquettish veils as lovely eyes and as soft as ever gleamed from Spanish maid. Indeed glances shot on the first morning that I from curiosity attended mass, made me thereafter a devotee at the same shrine.

Taking leave of China, I embarked in the steamer Pekin for Singapore, where I arrived after a pleasant passage of six days.

CHAPTER XII.

SINGAPORE.

Leave for Singapore—China Sea—Shocking Contrast—Chinese, their Improved Condition—Assimilating to Europeans—Game of Ten-pins as played by Chinamen—London Hotel—Public Drive—The Gurries and other Equipages—Pretty Residences—Interior—Valuable Estates—Numbers of Tigers—Their fondness for Chinamen—The moving Population and its Materiel—Peninsular and Oriental Steam Service—Leave for Australia.

No city in the East presents more diversified objects of attraction than does Singapore. The moment one opens its broad bay his attention is diverted on every hand by strange and picturesque objects. On the one side are moored tier on tier of immense Chinese junks with their forests of fragile-looking masts, decorated with tiny, gay-colored streamers; with their lofty sterns, on which are crowded noisy groups of coolies hurrying to and fro like bees in a hive; with their long pointed bows, on either side of which glares a great eye, without which appendage no vessel ever goes to sea. These immense constructions, of hundreds of tons' capacity, leave China loaded with silks and teas at the commencement of the northeast monsoon, and sweeping down before its blasts, soon arrive at Singapore. When once moored in safety, their hundred owners at once transform them into shops, or floating bazaars, and barter their merchandise for the spices and ivory of the Indies, until the southwest monsoon sets in six months later, when they again up-sail, and after a terrific ringing of gongs and a propitiatory burning of paper to their good god "Joss," they leave for home again.

Beyond the junks lie the awkward embarkations of the Cochin Chinese, who, in their attempts to imitate the European structures, have not only signally failed, but have fallen behind their China brethren in the sea-going qualities of their vessels.

Not the least noticeable object is the Malay proa, which is constantly flitting across the vision—a very ideal of all that is beautiful in nautical structure; with tapering ends and swelling sides, and flowing lateen sails, it skips over the long swells and whirls about as if a thing of life. This proa is a sort of marine cab, and flits from one ship to another soliciting a fare, looking like an albatross on extended wing, while the boatman, enveloped in the white folds of his flowing robe, with the picturesque turban covering his brow, appears to direct the movements of his aërio-aquatic car merely through volition, for no one ever saw them make an effort.

Around you on all sides float the flags of every nation under the sun. The cross of St. George, in its field of white or red; the lovely *fleur-de-lis*, the Danish cross, the German towers, the Prussian eagle, the Yankee gridiron, and the golden banner of Spain, wave over an infinity of shipping as varied in model and outline as the colors which designate their nationality.

Looking shoreward, the houses peeping from the midst of spice and palm trees, seem to have been built without regard to each other, but picturesquely grouped by an artistic hand.

Jutting forth from the long rampart, like a wall surrounding the town, comes the fortress masked by the densest foliage, the long, black guns creeping forth from among flowering vines like Satan from Paradise.

On going ashore, one's attention is kept on the *qui vive* by the contrasts which present themselves in quick succession. A promenade winding through avenues of spice and palm facing the bay, and guarded by a sea-wall tells of English energy. Bright lamps, throwing their long shadows into the dense shrubbery, reveal the dusky Sepoy—child of the soil, arrayed in British red, and doing sentinel's duty. A clattering gig, occupied by two corpulent gentlemen with shaved heads and long pig-tails, with flowing robes, heralds the approach of affluent Chinese merchants. A little gurrie or cab peculiar to the place, attended by a Sycee coachman, who runs alongside the horse, instead of mounting the box, quickly passes by, but not before revealing a lovely face, whose exquisite features and marble brow sends a thrill of sweet remembrance through the exile's heart, and tells of the presence of European beauty. Trotting along on his high-bred horse, comes the stately Englishman, as stiff and starch as if pacing Rotten Row, while sauntering along is seen the Hindoo in his pure white robe and crimson turban. The Mussulman, likewise arrayed in white; the Parsee, in his crimson cap and flowing ringlets; the Persian, in his striped silks, and the Arab, in his head-dress of flowing silk.

Admiringly, we pass along the promenade and enter the extensive grounds of the London Hotel, when, attracted by a thundering noise, proceeding from a long shed-like building, brilliantly lighted up, we enter in, and to our amazement see before us, an *American bowling saloon,* complete in all its appointments ; but what amazes us more is to see a dozen Chinamen contesting a game with all the eagerness and heat displayed by American players. They were fast-looking boys, those Celestials, several of them, indeed, extremely handsome, and dressed in the extreme "Mode de Pekin." Their efforts to win were amazing, and still more diverting was it to see the precision with which they poised their ball before throwing it, as if their lives depended upon the accuracy of their aim ; and the insane hubbub that followed a ten-strike ! Imagine twelve Chinamen, all shouting at the top of their voices ! They played very well, and as the pins were knocked down, the boy who officiated would sing out in Malay the number fallen, and I cannot forget the enthusiasm which the announcement of "Stoppar," *Anglice* "ten," always elicited fron the long tails.

The London Hotel is quite an imposing structure, being built of white stone, with a tall portico supported by pillars. It shows very well, situated as it is in the midst of handsome grounds. The sleeping apartments are agreeable and airy, and the dining-room constructed by itself, separated from the house of lattice-work, is a paragon of coolness. I made out to pass a very pleasant fortnight within its walls, sleeping through the heat of the day, and in the evening, after dinner, smoking my cheroot on its balcony, talking with people from all over the world, who had met here as a centering point in transit to the four quarters of the globe—the conversation, a regular pot-pourri, an olla-podrida, perfectly suited to the place in its spiciness. The smart Yankee, with national volubility telling of what he had seen in Canton—the English valetudinarian, with leave from his regiment in Bengal, en route for Australia to brace his enervated constitution, cursing Indian malarias, and sighing for the cool breezes of Scotland—the Dutchman, bound for Java, and the Spaniard for Manila, all joined together by temporary ties of intimacy, cemented by the freemasonry of hotel atmosphere, and making as jovial a party as if we had known each other from our boyhood.

A creek intersects the town, dividing the commercial city from that portion devoted to dwelling houses. These latter, which look so prettily from the bay, lose none of their attractive features when viewed—as sauntering through the long avenues on which they border, we strive to penetrate the soft, half-illuminated obscurity which appears to pervade them, built in Anglo-Indian style, within large spaces of ground, planted with exquisite shrubbery, lit up with transparent paper lanterns, and furnished with eastern luxuriance and lightness, and cooled with the omnipresent *punka*, which, laden with a thousand perfumes, induces a most delightful drowsiness.

The commercial town presents quite a European appearance, with its fine warehouses and its showy shops. And well it may! for the business transactions of this point are second to none in importance in the East. The harbor, commodious and entirely free from gales; its position is central, the key to the Indies, and its liberal revenue laws, exacting no duties, render it the nucleus of the whole eastern trade. Its chief articles of exports are drugs of all kinds, tins, spices, sugars, and tortoise-shell, while hundreds of vessels constantly discharging there, exempt from duty, every commodity under the sun, make it a mart for the merchants of

China, Australia, and the Phillipine Islands, who thus purchase to greater advantage than they could by a direct importation.

The largest element of the population of Singapore is the Chinese, who comprise nearly two-thirds of its whole number of inhabitants, and to their energy and activity may be ascribed the wonderful prosperity of this island.

The Chinese appear here to lose, in a greater degree, their natural characteristics of penuriousness and trickery, than in any other country to which they migrate. In Manila, for instance, the Chinese artisan works with unabated zeal from early dawn to midnight, and although amassing large sums of money, he never spends one penny more than is absolutely necessary for his support, never allowing himself recreation or repose, and thinking it a part of his creed to take advantage whenever he can do so undetected. The higher classes of merchants are honest, indeed, but are quite as economical, and as much averse to the indulgence of luxuries, as their poorer brethren. This feeling, so natural in a Chinaman, and so peculiarly characteristic, appears to have been entirely revolutionized in Singapore, and I can only account for it in this way. In Manila, and in the other parts of the East wherever they have taken up their abode, they have been looked upon with envy and suspicion, and as fair game for all sorts of extortion, and there is no imaginable tax, however burdensome, but what has been imposed upon them. Looked down upon as brutes, they had no desire (feeling the impossibility of so doing) to elevate themselves socially, but consoled with the reflection, that those that persecuted them could not compete with them, they have gone on quietly accumulating, until having sufficient to satisfy their wants, they return home again. In Singapore the Chinaman pays no heavier tax, nor is debarred from any privilege which the European enjoys, and on evincing a desire to better his condition by honesty and liberal dealings, he is at once taken by the hand by the older residents, and the poor coolie who landed only a few years before, with a little rice and his bamboo his only earthly possessions, soon finds himself a wealthy and respected man. Feeling that he has a position, and living on terms of equality with his English neighbor, and moving in a far higher rank than he could attain in his own country, he loses all desire to hoard, and enters into social relations with those around him. At his table may be met many English guests, his purse lightens at the call of distress, and he enters, *con amore*, into all the amusements of the day.

The billiard table and the bowling alley are both extensively patronized, and on the public drives may each afternoon be seen, in their well appointed equipages, the wealthier merchants rolling along, complacently nodding to their European acquaintances.

Singapore is an island of only thirty miles in length, separated from the Malayan peninsula by a narrow channel, five or six miles in width. Only a few years since, its whole surface was an impenetrable jungle, but now it smiles throughout its whole length with plantations of rice, sugar-cane, indigo and spices, from the cultivation of which the planters realize large sums. Some of the suburban residences are kept up with unheard of splendor, with all the semblances of royal magnificence. Indeed, one wandering among their fairy halls, enriched with all that is luxurious from further India and from China—floating with perfumes, agitated with gorgeous fans of oriental plumage, moved by unseen hands—recalls to his mind the wondrous tales of the " Arabian Nights."

One great drawback to a country residence on this island, is the superabundance of the Bengal tigers, whose fiercest nature appears here to be developed ; crouching in the jungle by the road-side, they pounce upon the unwary traveller, or the laborer in the field, and with one stroke of the paw, deprive him of life, and then, secreting his body in the thicket, they glut upon it at leisure.

So great is the dread inspired by these ferocious animals, that a standing reward of $50 is offered for their skin ; but, notwithstanding the *greatness of the sum*, which appears to the poor Malay an everlasting fortune, it is impossible to exterminate them. Breeding in the impenetrable wilds of the mainland, they swim the narrow strait, and prowl about the plantations till, surfeited with their prey, they again jump into the stream and seek their lairs.

So great was the consternation caused by an unusual number of deaths by tigers in 1852, averaging considerably more than one man per diem, and so loud the complaints of the inhabitants, that a joint stock company was formed in California, consisting of thirty men, armed with revolver and bowie knife, who, incited by the reward of $50 per head, were ready to embark and sail across half the world of waters, and wage war with the wild beasts of India.

What adds most to the variety, and constant and camelion-like changes of the society of Singapore, consists in its being the central depot of that mighty organization, "The *Peninsular and Oriental Steam Navigation Company*." This gigantic association possesses more steam vessels than does the British Navy in itself, and its ramifications are more extended than any other private enterprise in the world ; it has in its employ more than two thousand five hundred people, and its salaries amount to half a million dollars ; four hundred coal ships are constantly employed in transporting fuel to the different stations between England and Hong-Kong, and 100,000 tons are consumed at a cost of over one million dollars annually. The ships of this company from the Red Sea, from Calcutta, from Australia, and from the Philippines, pour semi-monthly an incongruous mass of people into the island, who, bound to some one of these destinations, await here the appropriate vessel for pursuing their voyage ; this tends to give an exceeding deal of life to the city, and likewise leaves an immense deal of money in it, for passengers after being cooped up for weeks in a steamer, on being emancipated, are proverbially lavish in their expenditures.

The great overland mail from England, touching at Bombay and Ceylon, meets here the steamers from Calcutta, from Hong-Kong, and Manila, and receiving from them their passengers bound for England, transfers to them the passengers she brought out, and returns again on her long voyage up the Red Sea, while the other boats leave immediately with their passengers and mails for their several destinations. The extreme regularity with which all this immense machinery is kept in motion is really wonderful, while the discipline and order maintained on board the ships is worthy of the highest commendation.

After a delightful voyage in one of the finest of the Peninsular and Oriental Company's ships to the Red Sea, touching at Madras, Ceylon, and Bombay, I again returned to Singapore and took passage from thence in the screw ship for Australia, touching at Batavia.

CHAPTER XIII.

MELBOURNE.

Melbourne and its Appearance—My Impressions—Its Society—Wide Streets—Its Hotels—Beautiful Suburbs—Compared to California—Its Climate—Its Stability—I meet an old Friend—Speculation—Buy a Schooner—Trade to Otaheite—The Boomerang—Getting ready—My Crew—Description of a gang of Cut-throats—Mate Mutinies—Meets his Deserts—Delights of the Voyage.

It was a lovely day on which we first sighted the headlands of Port Philip, and steaming in with a strong flood tide, we rapidly passed in through the golden gate, when before us lay the vast expanse of water known as Port Philip. The distance from the heads to the anchorage in a direct line, is, if I remember rightly, about forty miles, while the détour which vessels of a heavy draft of water are obliged to make, lengthens it to upwards of seventy miles. We, however, took the short cut; and following up the channel, with the reef on either side which could be readily distinguished by the eye, we went puffing merrily up.

The channel was filled with shipping bound in and out, from the stately clipper to the heavy old coal ship of the English Channel; and it was a gay sight to see them beating down or scudding up the narrow strait, passing consequently close to us, and, as they approached, either by signal or speaking-trumpet, inquiring the news. Passing the light-ship, and leaving the flourishing town of Geelong astern, we soon gained our anchorage in Hobson's Bay, after threading our way slowly through and among hundreds of vessels from every land under the sun. It was a lively scene, indeed! and just such a one as I had witnessed in the year 1849, when I first entered the harbor of San Francisco. On our port hand the river Yarra-Yarra disembogued itself into the bay—and it, too, for several miles, was completely blocked with smaller craft.

On this river, eight miles from its mouth, is situated the city of Melbourne. Entering it, the town strikes one most favorably; its broad streets, its handsome stone houses, its ever-varying stream of population, made up of every grade of society, from the peasant to the peer, arrayed in every variety of apparel, from the broad-brimmed hat and flannel shirt of the miner, to the white kids and broadcloth of the exquisite. You are amazed to see so vast a concourse of people, but are still more surprised when, on inquiring, you are informed that the population of this new city already exceeds 80,000 inhabitants! You wander on through streets of extraordinary width, lined with substantially built houses, filled with well-dressed people, ornamented with brilliant shops; and, were it not for the eight yoke ox-team toiling heavily along, or the crowds of rough, Esau-looking individuals elbowing by you in a most independent style, or the profusion of extravagance shown in everything and by every one, you might imagine yourself in a thriving country town in England. Great Collins street is a splendid avenue, traversing the city laterally, and is the grand business centre—its width being about equal to that of the London Strand or the New York Bowery—and along its whole length fine shops, showy hotels, and theatres, are located, and at either end churches and parks.

There are several fine hotels, one of which, a showy and spa cious building in Great Collins street, is really an elegant affair, and got up on the American plan, having that very Yankee-like adjunct, a bridal chamber, furnished in the most luxurious style with satin, rosewood, Valenciennes lace, tapestry curtains, Turkey carpets, etc.; the charge, if I recollect rightly, was a hundred dollars or twenty pounds for its occupancy for a single night! exclusive of servants' fees—a liveried footman standing outside the door at night to attend to the wants of its occupants. Vulgar miners, who have become suddenly rich, coming down from the "diggings to get married," often avail themselves of these luxurious lodgings. This house was kept by two brothers, Americans, I think, from New Orleans; the lower floor was occupied by drinking saloons and by an immense concert room, in which I saw a band of Yankee negro minstrels perform. Speaking of drinking saloons reminds me of a custom which has recently been introduced there from Yankee-land, of having a regular bar-room, and allowing the customers when they call for a drink to help themselves from the decanter, which formerly was not the case: for the English drinking community, not having a very nice sense of honor, if allowed to pour out for themselves, would perhaps fill their glass, and thus take more than their money's worth, and therefore it has heretofore, in the old country and in the colonies, been the custom for the bar-keepers to pour out a sixpenny worth in a glass, and hand it to the customer. But, since the gold discovery, there had been such a large infusion of Yankee blood, that they would not stand any such usage as that, and insisted upon helping themselves. The publicans were at their wits' end; they didn't want to lose the Yankee custom, for they were famous and frequent drinkers, so they hit upon a plan: they invented a name for the drink which *they* poured out for the customer, and another name for the one which he poured out *for himself*—the former, called a "tod," cost less than the latter, called a "nobbler." The idea took famously, and every or any hour in the day your friend would slap you on the back and ask you to go and have a nobbler; and eventually this became a slang word all over Australia.

The Port Philip Club Hotel, on Flinders street, was a very fair house, but it seemed to me that its guests were principally fast young bachelors; at any rate, the charges were enormous.

The suburbs of the city are most extensive and beautiful, stretching away on all sides to a considerable distance; and, from their peculiar build, and from not being so densely settled, with fine gardens and lawns, they presented a very picturesque appearance. On the east, communicating with the city by a fine avenue, lies Collingwood, a place of some considerable size, with half a dozen churches and a theatre. A short distance from, but really connected with it, is Richmond, also handsomely built, with several churches and public buildings. Praharan, still further along, is not less beautiful though not so substantially built, and St. Kilda, on the borders of the bay and commanding an elegant view of it, is the seat of many of the wealthier merchants, who have there their marine villas.

Along the banks of the Yarra-Yarra are many beautiful residences, to which the merchants retire after the fatigue and excitement of a business day in Melbourne; with these suburbs there is a constant communication kept up by coaches, or omnibuses, and a person need never be at a loss to reach either at any hour during day or night.

I was greatly struck with the similarities and dissimilarities in the state of affairs as existing in San Francisco and Melbourne. The same headlong race for gold characterized both places; the same heterogeneous masses of society thrown together, and at once amalgamating; the same variety of language, and of costume; with both of them, the same rainy season succeeded by an intensely dry, and hot one, and both lying in the same latitude, the one north, and the other south of the equator; the one about the same distance east, and the other about the same distance west of the meridian of Greenwich.

The dissimilarities are as marked as are the analogies. In Melbourne everything has a solid and substantial look, which betrays care and deliberation in construction, and the wharves and public buildings are on a grand scale. In California, the town mostly constructed of wood and the buildings hastily thrown together without regard to uniformity, gives one an idea of extreme insecurity; as for government works or wharves, excepting mere temporary scaffoldings, there are none.

The administration of justice in Melbourne is most strictly and faithfully performed as impartially as in the old country, and public works are not neglected, the streets and dwellings being lighted with gas, and a pure crystal water introduced by an extensive aqueduct.

In San Francisco justice is administered by gamblers and bribed villains, the streets are ungraded and unlit, while every drop of water that is drank is brought from over the bay, ten miles distant. In Melbourne the streets are guarded by a well organized police, and the highways scoured by a mounted arm of the same service.

In California, the police are notoriously the most corrupt and dangerous of her citizens, elected from the shoulder-striking fraternity, as a reward in controlling elections for unworthy aspirants, whom they aided by their bullying and rascally designs.

In Melbourne, the high officers of state are appointed by the home-government; men of rank and position at home, they bring out with them their families, maintaining their accustomed style of living, and thus giving a tone to society.

In passing along the streets, one encounters crowds of women, the majority evidently in quest of menial positions, and elegant equipages rolling by filled with well-dressed women and children.

How different from San Francisco; then there were scarcely any females, and one passing along the street, was she ever so plain or vulgar, caused an immense sensation, while as for ladies, the only females who could figure in a coach were the public women of the town.

Mid-day in California is midnight in Melbourne; in the one place the magnetic needle points to the north, at the other to the south; here the barometer falls before the approach of a storm, there the rising mercury denotes one.

In California the flowers breathe the most delicious perfumes, in Australia they are bright and beautiful, but have no odor; the birds are of the most exquisite plumage, but give forth no soft notes in song, while the woods of California are perfect sylvan choirs.

Having seen all I cared to see of Australia, I determined

upon leaving it, and falling in with a China acquaintance, he proposed I should take an interest in and charge of a topsail schooner which he had just bought, and make a voyage in her to Tahiti. Always open to an offer, and ready like friend Micawber for whatever turned up, I proceeded with him to the bay to inspect the craft.

She was a queer specimen of naval architecture, of no very beautiful proportions, Sidney built, of a wood with an unpronounceable name, and from her appearance I judged that she had been unacquainted with broom or scrubbing brush since the day she was launched. Her sails were in a most deplorable condition, and presented the appearance of a whaleman's breeches after a five years' cruise, and I very much doubt if they had any of the original cloth in them.

However, I was in no wise particular, so at once made terms with the owner, and proceeded to get ready for sea. At that time wages were most exorbitantly high, and as money was not plenty with either owner or "skipper," I overhauled my sea rig and went to work myself, and by dint of hard labor, got the "Boomerang" into a livable condition, and having got aboard sundry barrels of Sidney bread and beef, and, last but not least, having shipped my crew, I announced my frigate ready for sea.

The "materiel" of the crew is worth describing. My mate, a drunken, quarrelsome brute, from the Solway; the cook, a cross between a Lascar and a Coolie, looking like neither, but partaking of the bad qualities of both; and my four foremast hands, one a Manilaman, with a huge sabre-cut across his nose and cheek, a reward of piracy probably, most richly deserved; an old English man-of-war's man, who knew more than anybody else, yet knew nothing; a Swede, the only reliable man aboard the vessel, and a Mahoneese, the most villainous looking wretch that I ever set my eyes on, with a squint that was horrible to behold.

When the shipping-master brought these gentry aboard, I asked him whether he thought I was going to sea with such a set of cut-throats? Well, said he, there isn't another man on the beach that would go in the schooner, so you will either have to take these or none. I accepted the alternative, and forthwith ordered the mate to get her under way, with many misgivings however.

Going off with a fine breeze, I began to think the vessel "a singed cat," and was glad to find that she sailed tolerably well on the wind, considering her model, and being particularly anxious to test her capability for carrying sail, although it was blowing a stiff breeze, I ordered the mate to loose her fore-top-gallant-sail. I had previously noticed that the brute did not receive my orders with any alacrity, and I made up my mind that either Mr. Mate or myself must conquer, and that at once, for to yield an inch to him would have invited my four other beauties to mutiny. Singing out to him from aft, to loose the sail, he pretended not to hear me, but proceeded with his work, in stowing the anchors, the men looking toward me to see the result. Jumping down into the cabin, and putting my revolver into my pocket, and seizing an iron bar, which lay on the transom, I went again on deck, and taking a turn or two, I again sung out, Mr. ——, send some one up to loose that fore-top-gallant-sail. No answer! Springing forward and confronting him, I repeated my order. Looking me full in the face, with a leer he said, "she's as much sail on her noo as she needs, hasn't she, b'ys? The words were no sooner out of his mouth, than the iron bar came in contact with his skull, and down he fell, bleeding like a bullock; then drawing my pistol, I threatened the first man who *winked* disobediently, to blow his brains out. In five minutes the sail was loosed and set, and for days, everything went on as orderly and quietly, as aboard a man-of-war.

The mate did not get around again for some time, but was always respectful, and apparently subdued, giving me a wide berth, for I gave him to understand, that a mutinous look would be the death of him.

Our voyage progressed but slowly; the weather was very bad, with heavy gales accompanied by large seas, which at times making a clean breach over us, rendered it unsafe to go on deck without being lashed to the rigging. No one can imagine the state of our little cubby-hole of a cabin, overrun with vermin, cockroaches, bugs, rats and centipedes; the water leaking through the half-caulked deck kept everything dripping wet; indeed, my bedding was half the time floating in the bunk. I had no one to share its delights: the mate's company I had dispensed with since the first day out, and, consequently, I was alone in my glory.

I often wished myself forward in the forecastle among the men, for their quarters were infinitely better than mine. Having no mate that I could trust to, I rarely left the deck, more particularly as there were no attractions below, but wrapping myself in an india-rubber poncho and stowing myself in a quarter boat, would snooze away, ready at a moment's notice in case of change of wind or anything else that might occur.

Not being overburdened with cash on leaving Australia, my instruments were not on an extensive scale, being confined to a sextant, an incorrect compass, and a general chart; with such imperfect appliances for ascertaining my position, and none to assist me with whom I could compare, all this tended to increase my uneasiness, and together with the unpleasant suspicion that the mate and the man-of-war's-man were hatching a mutiny, my situation was not an enviable one.

Onward we rolled, accompanied by continual gales; our provisions, bad in the first instance, damaged by salt water, became unfit to eat, and the water casks on deck being stove, we were on an allowance of a pint a day, which, saturated as we were with brine, almost crazed us.

At this juncture I had recourse to a distilling apparatus, which alleviated somewhat our suffering. Having a large copper boiler on board, we iron strapped its top, and boring a hole in it, soldered on a long spout: over this spout we suspended a large tin funnel, and filling the boiler with salt water got up steam. The vapor pouring through its spout filled the funnel, which being continually cooled by sea water, condensed the steam which ran off into a receiver below: this appliance gave us a little additional allowance, and partially alleviated our burning thirst.

We longed for the green shores and luscious fruits of the Polynesian Isles, and one bright morning we sighted the lofty mountains of Tahiti, whose peaks soared away ten thousand feet in air, while the lowlands at their base jutted into the dark blue sea, fringed with snow-white foam.

Drawing in with the land, a rushing breeze straining our rotten canvas and making everything crack again, bore us bravely on towards the coral entrance, when, gliding in and clewing up our sails, we let go an anchor in the beautiful basin of Papetee.

CHAPTER XIV.

POLYNESIA.

Arrival at Otaheite—Lovely Harbor—Its general Scenery—Strange to find it in possession of red-legged Frenchmen—Beauty of the Island—Its magnificent Verdure—Picturesque Dwellings of the Natives—Ship a new Crew—Cruise among the Islands—Fill up with Cargo, and sail again for Australia—The Voyage—Sydney—Its Harbor—Its Elegant Buildings, public and private—Dashing Appearance of Population—Leave for Melbourne.

THE Otaheite whose tropic loveliness and whose beauteous maidens seduced the seamen of the "Bounty" from their loyalty a century ago is now a very, very different place from what it then was. The same musical surf beats in mournful measures upon its coral barriers; the same old breadfruit and banana trees wave their massive foliage, and the same blue mountains overhang the same bright shining valleys as in days of yore, but still, alas! how great the change. Those gentle islanders once so innocent, so pure, so happy—lords of their isles, dreamed life away in graceful independence, now, alas, tainted with disease, inoculated with hypocrisy from their infancy, the fruit of jesuitical interference, they dare not even call the soil their own, but must bow in reverence to the hated tricolor. Usurping the lovely grass-house, rises the cabaret, issuing from beneath whose roof, low, ribald songs in French patois mar the divine presence of nature, holding here her favorite court.

Its principal port, Papeetee, is one of the loveliest spots in Polynesia, with its coral ramparts, crested with foaming billows on the one hand, and on the other long rows of modest cots embowered in groves of palm and breadfruit, while, dividing its entrance, lies a gem of an island grown up with the most luxuriant foliage, masking a heavy battery erected by the French. This exquisite spot is walled in on the one side by the purple mountains of Emao, and on the other by the sparkling ocean.

Since the French have taken possession, however, by their merciless rule they have driven the better class of natives from their settlements, while the poorer classes, tainted by their licentiousness, hover about the skirts of the white man, abject and loathsome.

Since the discovery of gold in California and in Australia, scores of vessels, freighted with the vilest beings, have touched here for provisions; this, while it has given great impulse commercially to the town, has had a most fatal moral influence upon it.

These wretches, many of them criminals of the deepest dye, escaped from the prisons of Norfolk Island and Botany Bay, have disseminated seeds of vice and disease which will cost the good missionaries ages to eradicate.

Licentiousness runs riot in spite of taboo and ecclesiastical anathema; indeed it seems inherent in Polynesian blood. In walking along its streets one might well imagine himself in some little Mediterranean port, in the south of France, with its cabarets, its billiard rooms and cafés, and above all, its red-legged soldiers, with their small waists, expanded breeches, and clanking sabres. Then, too, there are barber shops, and tailor shops, and blacksmith shops, and an infinite variety of groggeries of all kinds.

However, these "desecrations" are found only in close propinquity to the landing-place. But in strolling along the Broom road, shaded by noble trees hiding picturesque little Polynesian villas, one's spirits become raised as he leaves the heavy atmosphere of trade and drunken sailors, and can quietly and undisturbedly admire nature in her most favored kingdom. Successions of beautiful gardens, emitting overpowering fragrance, bounded by groves of breadfruit, banana and oranges, overhung by the lofty and graceful cocoa-nut. Cross-paths zig-zagging off into the plantations, revealing glimpses of little paradises too modest to expose themselves to view. Processions of islanders, wending their way hither and thither, rolling out in *alta voce* unceasing strings of their vowelly language; the girls, many of them very beautiful, though not very virtuous, dressed in the picturesque, though *Frenchy* garb recently adopted, tripping laughingly along, coquettishly endeavoring to attract attention by affecting coyness. The young ladies dress in silks and satins, or in calico and cotton, as it may suit the purse of their particular male friend; but whether it be silk or whether it be cotton, they are the same joyous, light-hearted beings, and trip merrily along without thought or care. At nine o'clock the bugles sound forth the summons for the natives to retire to their home, and then all is still again.

As soon as my vessel's anchor was down, my precious crew, who had only shipped by the run, immediately jumped into canoes and paddled off ashore, leaving the schooner to her fate, and I must say I never experienced a more delightful sensation than when they were once fairly over the side. As they passed under her stern the mate saluted me with a parting curse, while the Malay waved his kris menacingly at me ; but these being the usual performances of discharged seamen, an idiosyncrasy of character, a sort of letting off steam, which from expediency had been held in during the voyage, I thought nothing of it—merely informing my friend the mate, that if he ever came within sight of me ashore I should take the liberty of blowing his brains out. I had no trouble with them, however, as they all immediately got gloriously drunk, were put in the stocks, and ultimately all shipped on board an English whaleman—I wish the skipper joy of them. In their stead I succeeded in shipping three fine fellows, Americans, and two Kanakas, and never were better men on board ship—good tempered, sober, and attentive to their duty, all went on harmoniously and pleasantly.

Having made all the necessary arrangements, we again got under way, and in turn visited the Marquesas and Austral groups, picking up among them an assorted cargo of pearl shell, sandal wood, cocoa-nut oil, lime juice, live stock and fruit.

It was a pleasant life this cruising around, among these primitive groups, hospitably entertained among the hidden domestic paradises of these children of nature, feasting on delicious fruits, bathing in the silvery surf, and for hours gazing down into the depths of the clear blue sea, from whose pebbly bottom arose in a thousand beautiful and fantastic forms, the many-colored coral, presenting the effect of lovely gardens, amid whose smiling grottoes thousands of bright-hued fish gracefully glided.

The kindness and unaffected generosity of these people were really wonderful, taking into consideration the wretched set of beings who have for the last half century been wandering about their islands taking advantage of them in every possible manner, robbing them and betraying their confidence. Notwithstanding all this, no stranger ever enters the picturesque, though simple hut of the native, but he is at once welcomed with the hospitable "Alofa" and importuned to partake of bed and board until he chooses to depart.

Many a time have I, wearied with my rambles, entered the domain of a person on whom I had never before set my eyes, and throwing myself on a mat, and unceremoniously beckoning a girl to bring me a young cocoanut to drink, and resting my head upon her shoulder, have in a moment fallen asleep, as peacefully as if I were not partaking of the hospitalities of a man whose father, perhaps himself, had feasted on the remains of many a poor shipwrecked mariner. The girls are the most fearless children of nature, with the greatest flow of the kindliest humor that I have ever met with in any country, with their fanciful robes flowing loosely about them, and their glossy black hair gracefully floating in the wind, among whose locks were entwined sprigs of dew spangled jessamine, and their soft dark eyes dilating with excitement; they would accompany us in our walks, and hand in hand would bound on before us like young fawns gambolling about among the trees, and if they saw that we noticed a particular fruit or flower, starting off at full speed to pluck it.

While in bathing they would sport about us like Nereids, much to the consternation of those of us who were not proficients in the art of swimming, for they had no mercy on any awkwardness.

Taking a last look at the beautiful Island of Tahiti, and having concluded all my business arrangements ashore, I shipped into my boat and in a minute was alongside the "Boomerang."

The schooner's appearance was very much changed for the better, since our arrival—my new Yankee mate having labored to great advantage with paint brush, scrubbing brush and sail needle.

She was pretty heavily laden, to be sure, and the deck load of fruit and swine was no particular improvement on the original, but notwithstanding it was pleasant to see a good-natured, honest set of men around one, in place of the cut-throats that I just got rid of.

Up comes the anchor with a "Cheerily, men O!" from her bed among the mermaids. "Hove short, sir!" sings out the mate. "Heave away lively then. Run up the jib! Lee fore top sail brace! b-lay! to'-galln' and royal braces well!—Lay aft here—one of you take the wheel; and you Mr. Pilot take charge."

Here we are again on the blue water, cresting and foaming under the influence of the strong trade wind.

Discharging our pilot, we once more say adieu to old Tahiti, and then turn our thoughts upon our voyage.

Days and weeks roll by; a heavy gale relieves us of our deck load, and the poor grunters feed the sharks instead of hungry Australians.

The old schooner leaks like a sieve; pump, pump, pump, still all goes on pleasantly; the rats and vermin were all smoked out in Papeetee, so that the cabins are livable, and the mate (an extremely intelligent man, an alumnus of Yale College) and myself revived many a pleasant reminiscence over a glass of grog and a cheroot. We had a wearisome voyage so far as time went, but I must say that, in spite of all anxiety, I was rather sorry when we made the land off Sydney.

However, the idea of a run on shore after a long voyage, is always pleasant, and above all, a change of living, for although we had fared sumptuously on roast bread-fruit, fried bananas and fresh pork, still we eagerly looked forward to a well-cooked dinner in one of the crack restaurants in Sydney.

However conversant a person may be with the rapid strides the English have made in civilizing and colonizing their possessions in Australia, he must gaze with undisguised wonderment upon the elegant and substantial appearance of the beautiful city of Sydney. Even though he may come direct from that miracle of a city, San Francisco, which sprung up from a wilderness almost in a single night, still he feels that he has left behind him a mere settlers' village, compared to this magnificent city.

Entering between rocky headlands, the bay stretches away for half a dozen miles before you, circled by lofty, wooded hills, indented with verdant coves; the heights, highly cultivated, are adorned with picturesque country seats, and a still loftier eminence is crowned by a fine lighthouse, and drawing further in, the government-house, of castellated build, comes into view. On the port-hand, lies the old town, running up a steep slope, the houses apparently built one upon the top of the other, in every variety of style, present a very pretty feature. Around about you are hundreds of craft, some lying at anchor, with sails furled, taking in and discharging cargo, others cutting across your bows and under your stern, while occasionally a little steamer, puffing volumes of black smoke, will shoot past you. Approaching the town more closely, long lines of warehouses are disclosed, and the wharves, with piles of merchandise and with busy throngs moving about them, attract your attention.

Once on shore and refreshed with a bath and with a well-cooked and well-served meal at one of the sumptuous hotels, you set out for a walk, and striking into George street, the Broadway of Sydney, a splendid avenue longer and wider than its celebrated prototype, your eyes are distended in utter amazement at the elegant shops, with their magnificent displays of the fabrics and wares of every land under the sun; the sidewalks, filled with beautiful and well-dressed women and with exquisites, got up in the last mode-de-Paris, with cane and quizzing-glass, who look little of the Australian emigrant; elegant equipages dash by with coachmen and footmen gaudily liveried, and tandems of superior appointments, driven by men "bang up" in appearance, dexterously thread their way among the crowds of vehicles passing and repassing in quick succession. The style of building is certainly very superior, and the material, a light freestone, gives the houses a bright and cheerful look. You enter an elegant café, and calling for an ice, you sit down, and resting, ask yourself am I really in Australia? Before you are the banks and insurance offices, and crowds of business men are hurrying to and fro with as much earnestness as in Wall street. Block after block of private residences stretch away in all directions, and the fresh beautiful children, walking and playing before them, send a gush of home recollections through one's mind. Fifth Avenue, however beautiful, must be very elegant to surpass some of the Sydney streets ; there is nothing half so bright, half so elegant in London.

The suburbs stretch away for miles, with miles of suburban villas, and Pyrmorne and Balmain, with their picturesque cottages and terraced heights, produced a strong impression and envious feelings in the mind of one who for five years had been thrown by fate among the riff-raff of creation.

In spite of Sydney having formerly been a criminal station, and in spite of the element infused into its society by pardoned convicts becoming wealthy and powerful, and having a strong influence in the affairs of the colony—notwithstanding all this, there is at present an exceedingly good society in the province. The vast trade carried on between it and the mother country, the attractions produced by the gold mania, and the field offered for aspirants to political preferment, not to mention the immense number of government officers—civil, naval and military—who are appointed for an indefinite period and who come out with their families and settle down permanently in their new home—all this has tended to bring into the colony a large element of refinement and respectability. Most of these people, moving in the higher walks of life at home, at once fraternize here and give an elevated tone to society, which is of a necessity extremely exclusive. The governorship of the colony of Australia is a highly prized gift of the home government, and is eagerly sought after by those high in rank, who together with families and suite form quite a brilliant court. During the season, Sydney is exceedingly gay, the entertainments being on a magnificent scale, balls, concerts and the like following each other in rapid succession; and as far as appearances go, it would be a difficult matter to say whether one was at Almacks or at the government house in Australia.

My stay was short in Sydney; having settled up my business and bidding good bye to the old "Boomerang," I got on board a steamer bound for Melbourne, and in three days was again ploughing the waters of Hobson's Bay.

CHAPTER XV.

VOYAGE IN SOUTH PACIFIC.

Take Passage in a Brig—Find I am *sold*—Captain and all Hands get Drunk—Captain and all Hands *stay* Drunk—Work Ship myself—Furious Gales—Ship dismasted—Nothing to eat—General Filthiness—Touch at Pitcairn's Island—Get jammed in between the Trades and Equatorial Calms—Reach the Coast—Ninety day Passage—Wind up with a grand Shindy.

HAVING determined to go over to the coast of South America, I looked around me for a chance, and happening upon a notice of the sailing of an English brig, "The Balmoral," for Callao, in Peru, I at once took passage in her, without even going down to the port to take a look at her, not caring a great deal what kind of a ship she was, as long as she would carry me over in safety. Indeed, the experience of the previous year had not made me very exacting in point of accommodation.

Settling up all my affairs at Melbourne, and taking a steamer down to the port, I hired a small boat, and after considerable trouble, succeeded in finding my brig. Pulling alongside, I in vain hailed the deck for some one to heave a rope or to help me with my luggage; so mounting the ladder, I scrambled up the side, and jumping on deck, took a survey as to how the land lay. In vain I looked about me for officers or crew; not a man was to be seen; so overhauling the yard-arm tackle, I hoisted in my own plunder, and paying the boatman, walked aft into the cabin. During my wanderings about the world, I had fallen in with a good many forlorn craft; but I had never met a more perfect type of what a sailor calls a *ballyhoo*, than was this one. In model she looked like a Dutch galiot; her rigging untarred, and hanging in a bight, swayed to and fro in the wind; her decks, rough and greasy, appeared never to have been washed down, and the cabin was in a state of dire confusion, the rats making a violent stampede as I entered.

Finding no one around, I at once took possession, and arranging my boxes to my satisfaction, made a tour of inspection. The cabin was absolutely bare of furniture, but there were two state-rooms, and in one of them I discovered some bedding, an old quadrant, and two or three books on navigation. This looked like *occupation*, so I came to the conclusion that the old thing *was inhabited*, although temporarily deserted. Peering into the pantries, I found some hard-tack, a piece of cheese, and pipes and tobacco; with these I at once proceeded to make merry, and having supped to my satisfaction, I stretched myself out for a nap, and soon was snoozing away as comfortably as possible.

Somewhere about nine o'clock in the evening, I was awakened by a terrible racket, when, lighting a lantern, and looking over the side, I found a boat with some half dozen men in her, all drunk, alongside, and each man swearing to the extent of his ability. Inquiring who the amiable party might be, I was informed by the drunkest man of the party that *he was skipper of that brig*, and wanted to know who the devil *I was*. After great difficulty, all these worthies got aboard, when no sooner had they touched the deck, than they commenced an indiscriminate fight. Stepping into the rigging, by way of security, and hanging my lantern so as to let its rays fall upon the belligerents, I let them fight it out, looking very complacently down from my eyrie, and occasionally lending them a word of encouragement. By degrees, overcome with their exertions, they fell down, one by one, on deck, and in half an hour the whole party were asleep, with the exception of the captain, who stumbled aft into the cabin, where I at once followed him. Presenting myself as a passenger, he appeared to feel very much mortified at the state I had caught him in, but begged that I would not mind him, and would proceed to make myself as comfortable as circumstances would allow, and, furthermore, adding that the agent had no right to take passengers in such a vessel, as she was in every way unfit.

Seven days did we linger in the harbor before we finally got off, during which time the crew were never sober, and the skipper generally about *three sheets in the wind.* Cook there was none, nor steward either, the government boat having claimed both of those gentlemen as *escaped convicts.* The consequence was, that whoever wanted anything to eat was at liberty to go and cook it himself.

Just before we got under weigh, the mate, a great, red-headed, overgrown Scotchman, came aboard with his wife, rather a pretty west of England lassie, with a brogue so broad it was next to impossible to understand what she said at all; but like all Englishwomen of that class, she was fond of her cups, and so my lord and lady were both *boosy.* This was a glorious prospect for me: a drunken crew, a drunken captain, and a drunken fellow-passenger, and *she a woman!*

No sooner were we well clear of our anchorage, than I found

that I was *in for it*, and that although I had paid an enormous passage, still that I should have as much hard work and *more* anxiety than if I had shipped regularly as a foremast hand.

By a rule of the port, as also of San Francisco, owing to the dearth of sailors, enormous wages were paid, as high sometimes as $100 per month, and sometimes *so much* was given by the run or for the whole voyage—for instance, $300 to China, $400 to the coast, and so on ; and the sailors, in order to guard against fraud on the part of shipowners, insisted on having the money paid in advance, on the *capstan head*, as they termed it, before clearing the harbor ; consequently, just as we had got well outside the heads, the men came aft in a body, and demanded their wages ; being too much overcome to attend to business, the master took a huge bag of gold from between the mattresses of his bed, and handing it to me without counting, he begged me to pay off the men ; willing to oblige, I did as he desired, paying each of the boys from $200 to $300 apiece.

No sooner were the men paid off than they broke out into open mutiny; they would execute no order unless they felt so disposed ; and, in fact, would be governed by no one but myself, and it was not always, by any means, that they would be influenced by me ; these beauties, however, insisted that *I* had been imposed upon in coming aboard this old craft as a passenger, and conceived that *I* had a common cause for discontent with them, and consequently, I suppose, felt that I was entitled to some consideration ; it was well for us all that this feeling did exist, for I verily believe that otherwise the ship would never have reached her destination, for many a time when threats and entreaties would avail nothing, have I prevailed upon those lawless scoundrels to execute an order which, unfulfilled, would have caused the dismasting of the vessel.

The brig was an exceedingly dull sailor, and being light, with no cargo, and but little ballast in her, it was not prudent to carry much sail on her ; indeed, had the ship been ever so staunch, we would not have dared to lug sail on her, for it was always extremely problematical, whether or not after we had prevailed upon the men to set a sail, they could be induced to take it in again. After the first ten days out, it seemed as if all parties, forward and aft, had determined to have a *good time*, each in his own peculiar way, and not to exexert himself more than was absolutely necessary ; with this understanding, the lofty sails were permanently furled, and reefs taken in the topsails, so that with the exception of relieving the wheel, there was absolutely nothing to be done, for both washing down decks and mending sails were voted superflous, and night-watches a bore; the state of things on board may be better imagined than described—no head—no discipline—all drunk from morning till night, blow high or blow low, the only symptom of life about the ship was evinced by the man at the wheel, who generally tried to keep awake during his trick at the helm ; the mate and his precious wife devoted themselves to the rum cask, so that I did not have the pleasure of their society very often ; as I said before, our cook and steward were both seized upon by the police before leaving port, so that we remained minus those important personages. Not caring to perform the duties of scullion myself, I chose from among the crew an Italian, the least filthy of the gang, and installed him forthwith into his *doctorate ;* his duties were not multifarious, for the ship's stores consisted of sundry barrels of beef and pork, a couple of flour, a bag or so of coffee, and a few boxes of red-herring, so there was no very great field for displaying his culinary talents, even had he possessed them; indeed I do not think he was a disciple of Soyer, for he was evidently ashamed of his new profession. Our table was varied with beef and pork for breakfast, and pork and beef for dinner, with a cup of thick coffee or a glass of rum to wash it down; this was our only fare for three long months, with the exception of some vegetables, purchased subsequently at Pitcairn's Island.

The weather, on first leaving port, was tolerable good, but after we had been outside for ten or fifteen days, we had a succession of remarkably heavy gales, which, with our mutinous crew and drunken officers, made it a very serious affair for the ship. My plan was to sleep as much in the day time as possible, and in the evening to light my pipe, when the weather was at all bad, and to remain on deck the greater part of the night. With the hearty approbation of the skipper, I had taken whole charge of the craft, and made or took in sail at discretion, that is, when I could prevail upon the boys to execute my orders. I recollect on one occasion we had got jammed in on the coast of New Zealand, and had had for days a succession of terrific gales. Close reefing the topsails and furling the courses, I hove her too, and the people, disgusted with the long continuance of the gale, lashing the wheel, had gone below to await a change of wind; for a couple of days and nights I scarcely ever left the deck; but the third night, soaked with rain and sea water, and thoroughly fagged out, I roused out the captain, who did not happen to be dead drunk, and persuaded him to stand watch the rest of the night; throwing myself down on the transom in the cabin, I was soon in dream-land, never waking up until the *cook* brought me my coffee in the morning. Going out on deck-I found the gale to be little less than a hurricane, the sea wild and irregular, while to the windward a thick haze and cloud-bank, rapidly rising, looked very ominous. At once directing the attention of the captain to it, I advised him to furl the main topsail altogether, and to run her off before the wind; but the drunken rascal said, "Let's have our coffee first, *mon, whar's* the use of being in *sick* a hurry ?" Worn out with previous anxiety and watching, and disgusted with things generally, and the captain particularly, I lit my pipe and sat down composedly to see what the result would be ; as for myself, I can truly say that I did not care *one sou* what happened to her, I had arrived at that state of mind which makes one perfectly indifferent to all casualties, whatever their nature. I had not been many minutes seated, when, as I had surmised, the squall struck her with terrific violence; then came a tremendous crash, and down came fore and main royal masts, the foretop-gallant mast and foretop mast and the jib-boom, alongside. This was a nice mess ! especially as at the same time a couple of seas boarded her, sweeping her deck fore and aft. Getting her off before the wind, we managed to muster all hands, and went to work with a will to clear the wreck, which pleasant job we got through with about midnight.

For weeks this weather lasted, and we went wallowing along through heavy seas, and battling tremendous gales. Our nautical instruments consisted of an old-fashioned English sextant about fifty years old, and a quadrant, also very aged, and *no chronometer*. The consequence was, that we had to rely altogether upon lunar distances for longitude, and this was my chief amusement; day and night I was at it, and no star ever was in distance, but what I had a shy at it.

What a tedious, wretched voyage this was, to be sure! Heavy gales day after day, week after week. No companions, and a terrible feeling of anxiety and responsibility. For weeks I never left the deck; at night usually sleeping with my heavy coat wrapped around me under the lee of the trunk-cabin on deck.

The old brig, not a very beautiful specimen of naval architecture in the first place, after being dismasted was about as ungainly a looking object as one might often meet with; but it did not appear to make any great difference in her sailing qualities. She went rolling and pitching about all the same, never making over four knots the hour. As the voyage wore on, the men became more uncontrollable and would positively do nothing unless it was deemed by them absolutely necessary. Here we were in the stormiest part of the South Pacific, in a dismasted brig, with a drunken captain, a drunken mate, and a drunken and mutinous crew. The ship being under as short sail as was practicable, there was no call for actual exertion on the part of the men with the exception of their trick at the wheel, and even while steering it was necessary to watch them sharp, lest they should get the ship aback. During this part of the voyage we had some terrific weather. So much so that at one time I was fearful that the little brig would be overwhelmed with the enormous seas which constantly combed and broke around us. One night, worn down with fatigue and suffering from the effects of constant wetting with salt water, I resolved to *turn in*, let the ship sink or swim, as the case might be. I had hardly lain down when a tremendous sea came aboard of us, sweeping everything movable from the decks and carrying off with it a couple of our precious crew, and filling our cabin four feet deep with water; waking from my sleep, I heard the rushing sea and felt the shock, and thought sure enough our time had come; but notwithstanding the serious aspect of affairs, I burst out into a hearty laugh (the first I had uttered since leaving Melbourne) at the sight which presented itself before me. The gale was from the southwest and blowing a hurricane, and a full moon threw her rays into the cabin, giving everything a ghastly hue; wallowing on the floor, up to her neck in water and screeching at the top of her voice, was the wife of the mate. She thought she was gone, and was struggling and praying away at a terrific rate, while her drunken *rib*, fairly sobered by the sea which floated him out of his bunk, was "*sans culottes*," seeking his beloved amid the broken furniture, which smashed about as the ship rolled and pitched, and swept them from one side to the other, with great force. Thus the voyage wore on, a constant gale blowing, the vessel wet and uncomfortable, and the provisions, spoiled and bad as they were, gradually becoming more and more scant. Drifting about the ocean and finding ourselves not very far from Pitcairn's Island we resolved to bear up for it and recruit.

PITCAIRN'S ISLAND.

In one of the most remote corners of the Pacific ocean, far, far out of any beaten track which vessels are wont to take in crossing from Asia to America, and hundreds of miles away from any other land, in latitude twenty-five degrees south, and one hundred and thirty degrees west longitude, lies a rocky islet, scarce seven miles in circumference, against whose precipitous sides a furious surf constantly beats, which threatens death and destruction to the daring mariner who ventures within its boiling caldron. Yet this spot, this speck upon an unknown ocean, so inhospitable, so inaccessible, is invested with a deep and thrilling interest, and the greatest English poet has thrown over it a mantle of romance; for, in his poem of the "Island," Lord Byron has given to the world the tragic settlement of "Pitcairn's Island."

I give the story, though few there are who are not familiar with that most interesting romance of naval history, "The Mutiny of the Bounty." For the facts I am indebted to my friend, Capt. Dillon, of H. M. S. "Cocatrice."

In the year 1789, His Majesty's ship "Bounty," Captain Bligh, while in the vicinity of the island of Otaheite, one of the Polynesian group, was taken possession of by a part of her crew, who had mutinied, headed by one Fletcher Christian, and her commander, with all those not favorable to the insurrection, were cast adrift in an open boat. The mutineers, twenty-five in number, were supposed to have made sail towards Tahiti, and as soon as the occurrence became known to the English admiralty, an expedition was sent out to capture them there, but on its arrival, it was found that nine of the most criminal of the mutineers had some time previously set sail, taking with them each his Tahitian wife, intending to seek some uninhabited island, where, having established themselves, to break up the ship, so that no trace of them should be left. Here all clue of them was lost, and it was not until twenty-five years after that anything further was heard of them, and it was in this wise: In the year 1813, two captains of the Britith navy, cruising in their respective ships in the vicinity of Pitcairn's

Island, and in utter ignorance of its occupancy, were not a little astonished on nearing it, to find it regularly laid out in plantations and built up with neatly constructed cabins ; on bearing down for the island and closely approaching it, several natives were observed with a canoe on their shoulders making for the beach, and presently launching it through a very heavy surf; but their astonishment can be more easily imagined than described, when, on nearing the ship, one of the natives called out in plain English, "Won't you heave us a rope ?" The first man on board was Thursday October Christian, a son of the leader of the mutiny ; his only dress a piece of cloth around his loins and a straw hat ornamented with cock feathers. His companion was named George Young, an interesting youth of sixteen years. Being extremely interested in these young men, the commander invited them into his cabin, and causing food to be set before them begged them to partake, when, to his utter amazement, they both rose to their feet, and assuming a devotional posture, one of them in a low distinct voice repeated, "For what we are going to receive, may the Lord make us truly thankful." After hearing their story, the officers accompanied them ashore, accomplishing with great difficulty a landing through the surf, when they were met by Adams, the only surviving mutineer, who conducted them to his residence, and on being informed that their visit was wholly unintentional and had no reference to the mutiny, testified the greatest joy on once more beholding his countrymen. The colony had increased to about forty-six persons, mostly grown up people, forming a most interesting community ; their chief, John Adams, who, although a mutineer, was possessed of a frank and noble heart, and the solitude and tranquillity that had ensued since the many and dreadful scenes through which he had passed, had disposed his mind to repentance. Feeling his wickedness and the weight of his sins to hang heavily upon him, he had determined on a thorough change of life, and faithfully had he carried out his resolution ; he instructed the young community growing up around him, to the best of his ability ; he inculcated in them the strictest principles of moral rectitude, and unfolded to them, as they became able to comprehend it, the plan of salvation. The children acquired such a thirst for scriptural knowledge that he had at first little else to do than answer their interrogatories and put them in the right way ; as they grew up, they acquired fixed habits of morality and piety, and they soon formed a happy and well-regulated society, the merit of which belongs to Adams, and tends to redeem the errors of his former life. He died honored and respected, in the year 1829, aged sixty-five years.

At the time of my visit to this " happy land," there was but one of the original settlers left on the island, an aged Tahitian woman, tottering on the verge of the grave, a widow of one of the mutineers ; there were two men and seven women of the first generation, and three of the latter, daughters of old Adams ; the rest were the issue of the second and third generations. We found them exceedingly industrious and of frugal habits, the men and women both engaged in agricultural pursuits, while some of the former were good mechanics ; their mode of dress, assimilating somewhat to our own, is obtained from vessels touching there occasionally, in exchange for fresh provisions.

The men are firmly built and stalwart in appearance, with fine eyes and expressive countenances ; they all speak English fluently, indeed, it is their native tongue, but they give it the full liquid sound, which is peculiar to the Polynesian idioms. In character, they are extremely docile, and live in the utmost harmony, requiring but little restraint, thanks to their early training and the religious element which runs through them. The women are rather slight, but with forms of the most exquisite mould; their countenances, beaming with vivacity and intelligence, are lit up with the full Asian eye, which shows great depth of fervid passion, tempered however with the most chaste expression ; admirable women they are; virtuous and industrious as wives, and fond and affectionate as mothers, they, on their ocean-bound rock, remotest of the human family, set an example which the world would do well to follow.

How true is it that the " Lord moves in a mysterious way his wonders to perform !" Here, on a barren rock unknown to all the world beside, sought out by blood-dyed criminals to hide their guilt, has he raised up an altar from which the purest incense arises, around which, with one accord, all assemble and offer up hymns of the most heartfelt praise. Strange, that to the offspring of the pirate, should be vouchsafed a peace of mind and a purity of heart, such as is seldom if ever known in this world of sin and sorrow.

Leaving Pitcairn's Island, we, with our usual ill-luck, got jammed in among the southeast trade-winds, and made a very long passage, but succeeded at last in reaching Peru. By way of winding up a most disagreeable voyage, and in perfect keeping with it, the closing scene was quite tragic. Arriving in the evening, the men immediately got into a boat and went on shore, leaving their clothes behind them to return for them in the morning. The next morning I was awakened from my sleep by a most diabolical noise, when, half awake, I rushed out on deck, and, before I knew it, was in the midst of a bloody fight; half a dozen men were amusing themselves beating the captain, who was defending himself with a capstan bar, while the good-for-nothing, drunken mate was looking on, evidently enjoying the sport. Incensed at his cowardly apathy, I called upon him to come to his master's assistance, but was answered only by a laugh ; when, losing all command of myself, I, in a moment, became engaged with him. While pummelling each other to the extent of our ability, one or two of the men, not yet actively employed, and very hostile to the mate, at once jumped upon him, thus leaving me free to go to the captain's assistance. Half blinded with blood, and seizing an axe, in two jumps I was alongside of him ; but there my recollection ended, for a blow from behind with an iron belaying pin laid me "*hors de combat*," and it was not till some hours afterwards that I came to my senses, and found myself stretched on the cabin floor, stiff with bruises and weak from loss of blood. The captain was beyond recognition, while the mate and his lovely wife had each a pair of beautiful black eyes and swollen faces. The result of the affair was, that we were not able to go ashore for several days.

CHAPTER XVI.

WEST COAST.

The Author goes Ashore—Finances at a Low Ebb—Seeks Employment—Becomes a Night Watchman, at ten Dollars per Night and Grog—Gets Command of a Ship—Is transferred to a Steamer—Pleasant Voyages—The Surf—Is Chartered by Government—Callao—Its improved Condition—Frequent Revolutions—Presidential Candidates—The Ins and the Outs—Coolie Trade defended.

BIDDING adieu to the old craft, I moved my effects ashore, and, in so doing, spent my last dollar. So here I was again, a broken merchant; but, as men were scarce, and wages enormously high, I wasn't uneasy—for, even if the worst came to the worst, I could without difficulty get a berth. But I hoped for better things; for I was certain that with my ability to speak the language, and my knowledge of the coast and numerous acquaintances, I could always find lucrative employment.

Taking lodgings, I at once went to work beating up acquaintances, and, as luck would have it, fell upon an old friend with whom I had had business connection in California, and to whom, on a previous voyage, I had consigned my vessel. My friend G—— was in full tide of an active business, and very kindly offered to do anything for me that lay in his power; and, giving me access to his purse, thus I was relieved from the unpleasant idea of being *hard up*, and fell for a second time into the hands of *good Samaritans.*

Lounging about, I soon became tired of waiting for employment, and begged my friend G—— to give me something to do, by way of keeping my hand in ; and, accordingly, he informed me that in case I was so inclined, he had several ships in harbor which required watchmen, and that it being a difficult matter to get any one sufficiently trustworthy, he would pay me ten dollars per night to act in that capacity. Nothing loath, I at once acceded to his proposal, and forthwith entered upon my new duties. Pulling off in my little gig, about nine in the evening, to the ship designated, I would report myself to the officer of the deck; bidding my boys to let my boat drop astern, and to make themselves comfortable in her for the night. I would then relieve the officer in charge, who would go below and leave me to my solitary walk and reflections ; and, as I paced up and down the lonely deck, I would often smile to think what my friends at home would say to my new avocation as night watch. Oftentimes, some kind-hearted skipper would send his steward on deck to ask the watchman if he *wouldn't* come down and have a *glass of grog*, which invitation the watchman would always politely accept ; and, on appearing in the cabin, would always, with becoming humility, doff his tarpaulin, and drink to the health of the benevolent skipper and of his friends assembled.

My pay as night watch gave me sufficient spending money, and enabled me to enjoy myself moderately ; and thus between trips to Lima, and various other excursions, a month flew away pleasantly enough.

At this juncture, a large American ship being bought by a

native firm, some one was wanted to take charge of her, and, through the good offices of my friend G——, I was the lucky individual, and, at an early date, was duly installed. I had not been many days aboard, however, when a friend mentioned to me that a coast steamer, owned by the same concern, would soon be wanting a captain, as the present incumbent was entirely too slow, and, consequently, was going to be ousted from his position. Now, if there was any one position that I aspired to at that time, it was the command of a steamer on that coast; for, having traded on it as master and supercargo of sailing vessels, I was anxious to try steam *versus* sail.

My knowledge of the coast and the language here stood me in good stead, and, notwithstanding numerous and powerful opponents, I was duly installed as master of the Peruvian steamer "Villa de Huacho." Previous to taking command, however, I was informed that it would be necessary to undergo an examination before the marine board to test my qualifications. This frightful ordeal having been gone through with, I was presented with a budget of documents, constituting me a "*Piloto de la Marina Peruana,*" etc., etc., etc.; which documents were all figured off with armorial seals and signatures, and for which I paid the nice little sum of forty dollars. The steamer, a small side-wheel boat of American build, was under the Peruvian colors, and traded up and down the coast from Paita as far down as Arica, touching in at every little nook and corner on the route.

Leaving Callao, at night, we would get under weigh and running down the coast, touch in at Cerro-azul and the Chincha Islands, arriving at Pisco the following evening; or going north, leaving Callao we would touch in at Huacho, Casma, Lambayeque,

Huanchaco, and Payta, and returning, call in at the same ports, making the voyage in a week or ten days. Our cargoes were very varied, consisting principally of the products of the country, and our passengers, of small traders and the planters living along the coast. It was a pleasant trade to be in, the weather always serene, never warm or cold, while the only drawbacks to navigation, were the dense fogs prevailing in the winter time. Running into a little harbor, we would come to an anchor, and while awaiting for cargo we would scour away into the interior, visiting many friends.

A great drawback to the coasting trade is the absence of good harbors, there being only two or three worthy of the name along the whole coast. At Pisco, a principal port, the surf rolls in, for several hundred yards rendering the landing very unsafe; indeed, during the full and change of the moon, the surf breaks so heavily that no boat can live in it. During the time that I was trading there, I came near losing several passengers and had my boats capsized on various occasions.

The ports of Lambayeque, and Huanchaco, the only outlets of a rich and fertile country in which large quantities of rice, sugar, and cotton are raised, in no respect deserve the name of harbors, for on their beaches beats as terrific a surf as I ever witnessed, breaking for nearly half a mile from the shore.

No boat can live in the breakers, and these places are only accessible by means of balsas, huge rafts constructed of a light, buoyant wood, and on top of the logs, some five or six feet high, is raised a platform, on which the passengers and freight are placed ; these rafts are propelled by sails, and are the only means of transport through this boiling surf. It is a pretty ticklish business the first time one attempts the voyage, for although the Indians perfectly understand their management, still it is very frightful to get half way among these terrific breakers, rolling, foaming around you with a deafening crash and apparently determined on overwhelming you. I must own up to being badly scared on first going ashore at Lambayeque; indeed it's a *very*, *very* dangerous amusement, for on two different occasions I knew of the rafts being broken up and passengers and freight all being lost.

During the last few months that I remained on the coast, I was under government charter and was principally engaged in carrying troops and dispatches to different ports, and on one occasion was ordered to Huanchaco with a load of gunpowder. Having had a serious attack of fever, I was then slowly convalescing, and being still weak from its effects, my duties devolved upon my mate, an old whaler and a very competent man ; previous to going to my room on the night before making the harbor, I gave the mate the course and told him he need not wake me until the custom house-boat came alongside.

The next morning, on awakening, I was surprised to find the ship rolling heavily and going along under half head of steam. Stepping out on deck, I found we were in the ground-swell and running slowly down the edge of the breakers, and that we were some six miles beyond our port. Singing out to the mate (who by the by had never been there before), I begged to know where he was going to ? He told me that he was looking for the port ! that he had come to, at the place designated on the chart as the port, but as there were no houses there and a dangerous surf breaking out a mile or so from the beach, that he was sure that that could not be the place, for no boat could possibly communicate with the shore ! Informing him of his mistake, I ordered the ship to be put about, and we found ourselves in a short time at anchor, rolling guards under in the heavy ground swell.

As I looked shoreward I really could not blame my mate for not coming to an anchor in the first instance. The only thing indicating a settlement being a huge cross prominently placed upon a bluff as a land-mark, and a few fishermen's shanties scattered along the beach, while between the beach and the anchorage line upon line of bristling combers rolled in, cresting and breaking with the noise of a park of artillery; and little would one suppose that the commerce of a large town (Trujillo) was all carried through these dangerous breakers. I mention this circumstance to give an idea of the energy of these people, in disembarking goods under such disadvantageous circumstances; and also to convey an idea of the surf itself, which appeared *so threatening* to an old whaler who was considered the best surf-man between Cape Horn and Panama, that he did not deem it worth while to come to an anchor there.

I rather enjoyed my new occupation, for sailing a vessel on that coast was mere child's play; the sea as smooth as glass, and but few hidden dangers. With ordinary precaution, one need never be apprehensive of accident. One serious difficulty which we had to contend against, was the dense fogs which prevail in the winter season, and which I think vie with those that are so common on the banks of Newfoundland, but by exercising great prudence we escaped accident. During my term of service, I met many of the prominent landed proprietors of the interior, and found them men of great shrewdness and exceedingly gentleman-like and companionable, whilst their families were, in many instances, charming, and it was really a great treat, after so long a separation from refined society, to be able to mingle with lady-like and intelligent females once more. Endeavoring to make myself and my ship as agreeable as possible to my passengers, my courtesy was repaid by numerous invitatious to the various estates in the interior; and I now look back with great pleasure to many valuable acquaintances thus formed. Indeed my ability to speak the language was of infinite advantage to me, and brought me in contact with a class of people whom, in my capacity of ship-master, I never could have known otherwise.

The great feature of the South American republics is the revolutions which are continually succeeding each other, and Peru, *par excellence*, is celebrated for her ever-varying government.

No president ever serves out his term of office; and this being a well-received principle, as soon as the incumbent is seated in the presidential chair, knowing how uncertain is the tenure of his office, he commences a wholesale robbery of the public funds, and manages, before the expiration of the first year, to have snugly stowed away in the coffers of some foreign house, enough hard dollars to maintain him for the rest of his life.

The only man who has been able to sustain himself for any great length of time is Don Ramon Castillo, a cholo who rose from the ranks to be the most prominent man in the state.

Old "Boots," as he is familiarly called from his partiality to "Wellingtons," is a rough, unpolished old Indian, but a first-rate general, and a man of great decision of character and great administrative capacity; but, withal, perfectly unscrupulous and extremely avaricious.

Once having the taste of power, he determined not to give it up, and during the last half dozen years has been struggling to retain it, and he has had his hands full. At one time, driven to the mountains, he was for half a year lurking with a handful of followers among the fastnesses of the Andes, until, in pure desperation, he sallied forth against a splendid army commanded by General Echenique, and after an engagement of a few hours, routed them completely. At another time we find him under the walls of Arequipa, laying siege to a band of rebels, who have sought the protection of its walls; and again we hear of him on the quarter-deck of one of his steam frigates directing the operations of his fleet.

It was during his contest with Echenique that my steamer was employed by the latter's government to convey troops and stores from one point of the republic to another.

According to contract, we were obliged to keep steam constantly up, ready at a moment's notice to go off to the point designated. Oftentimes at midnight the watch would awake me, informing me that a man-of-war's boat was alongside, when an officer would announce himself the bearer of sealed orders, not to be opened until we were outside the harbor. Accordingly, we would lift our anchor and proceed to sea, when, after an hour's steaming, our dispatches would be opened, and our destination made known.

The people of Peru are really revolution-mad, and are never contented but when in the heat of a civil war. Elias, Vivanco, Echenique and Castillo, beside a host of lesser luminaries, are always at swords' points upon the subject of the presidency; and no sooner does one of these gentry get comfortably seated in the chair of state, than the others conspire to oust him. A spirit of violent partisanship pervades the whole nation. And as high as party-feeling runs in our own country, we can form no idea of the extremity of measures to which the politicians of Peru resort to attain their ends; libels the most vile, personal assaults and assassinations are common occurrences, while the party in power do not hesitate to employ all the means which their lofty position gives them to silence opposition.

The enormous consumption of guano in every country in the new and old worlds, has given an immense impetus to the trade of Peru within a few years past, and in place of the few coasters and traders that formerly visited her ports, now are yearly anchored in the port of Callao thousands of the world's finest merchantmen, waiting for their cargoes. When I first visited the harbor of Callao, I found it a dull, dirty little shipping town, where no one but ship chandlers, green-grocers and grog-shop keepers thought of living; but now it had undergone a wonderful change; instead of 2,500, we found at least 10,000 people, and in lieu of the mud huts, rows of sightly houses, devoted to business purposes and as dwelling places.

It was anything but dull, the streets swarming with people, and the shop-windows brilliant with everything that could attract the eye *nautical;* indeed, it was a real sailor's heaven—oceans of grog, lots of bright-eyed lassies, horses *ad infinitum,* and, to cap the climax, as villainous a set of sailor crimps as ever robbed poor Jack.

In Callao were gathered together perhaps as "fine a collection" of gallows birds as were ever collected in any one spot on earth, Newgate not excepted; banished from California by the Vigilance Committees, or escaped from Botany Bay and

Norfolk Island, they all centred there, and luxuriated in the utter lawlessness of this delightful spot, indulging the pleasant little excitements of throat-cutting, garroting and highway robbery, so much so, that no one ever thought of moving around at night without having the handle of his revolver in a position to grasp at a moment's notice.

Rascality appears to be epidemic, pervading almost every business transaction, and unless one is ready to stretch his conscience, he had better not undertake to do business there. One principal feature of villainy, on a large scale, is the condemnation of foreign vessels, selling them by auction, and putting them under the flag of the country, thereby placing them beyond reach of reclaim by their foreign owners.

The *modus operandi* is as follows: A fine foreign clipper ship comes into port, and is much admired by a few speculators, who are on the look-out for a "flyer;" these chaps cultivate the acquaintance of the skipper, make themselves extremely agreeable, dine him, and ride him, and take him to the theatre, and in short, show him the elephant in the most approved manner. After sounding the skipper thoroughly, whether or not he is a conscientious man, on discovering the least flaw in his character, they gradually unfold to him their plan of operations, promising him perhaps a larger sum than he ever had in his life, to aid them in the undertaking. Suddenly, from some unaccountable cause, the ship begins to leak; every one is surprised, and most of all the captain, and after in vain trying to discover it, he applies to the consul, who orders the ship to be partially discharged—still the leak continues, and it requires great exertion to keep the water under. Application is again made to the consul, and a survey appointed, and the report is so very unfavorable, that the consul proceeds formally to condemn the ship, and have her sold for the BENEFIT of the UNDERWRITERS; and after a little languid bidding on the part of the outsiders, the *speculators* have her knocked down to them for forty or fifty thousand dollars less than she cost. Of *course* the captain did his best for the underwriters; *he* couldn't help the ship's leaking, and *he*, of *course*, acted for the interests of all concerned in the matter. Of *course* the consul, a man representing a great country, like the United States or England, would not, for the sake of a few thousands, descend to the commission of a fraud—*most certainly not.* Nevertheless, the ship is no sooner hove down by the new owners, than the leak is discovered to be occasioned by some augur holes *bored in her* counter, by whom, *no one knows;* but as the captain goes home by the next steamer, with his pocket full of drafts—and the surveyors are found to be very flush, and the consul is known to have sent home a few *extra thousands* on his own *private account*, the supposition is, that the aforementioned gentlemen *all* made a handsome little operation between them, and that the underwriters were mulcted to the tune of $50,000 to $60,000, while the ship, as sound as the day she entered the harbor, in a few weeks sailed out again under a different flag, and with different owners. Still, notwithstanding the frequency of frauds, of which the above is a specimen, the board of American underwriters do not deem it expedient to pay an agent for attending to their business on the coast. The writer of this thinks he could have saved the New York offices a considerable sum, had he held a commission as their agent, with discretionary powers, when he first appeared on the coast, but when he did receive it, it was too late to act, and with no discretionary latitude whatever.

During the last revolution, Don Ramon Castillo, driven to extremities by his political opponents, put forth a manifesto declaring that all male slaves that should enlist under his banners should, at the termination of the campaign, be freemen. This of course produced an electrical effect upon the whole negro population ; insolent to excess previous to this, and almost useless, their owners lived in bodily fear of their lives ; but now, when virtually freed by government, it was impossible to control them ; and the slave of yesterday became the robber and assassin of to-day—plundering and murdering, not only on the estates of their neighbors, but in their own masters' houses.

About this time I was staying for a few days at the estate of Casa Blanca, in Cañete, and then the planter's house who entertained us was in a completely fortified state. The walls were loopholed, and apertures large enough for a man to creep through were made in them, in order that every room might communicate with each other, and the occupants be enabled to act in concert. During this time a band of the negroes belonging to the estate, choosing the finest animals of their master's stud, made off, and probably became impromptu highwaymen.

In consequence of this iniquitous proceeding on the part of Castillo, the whole country was overrun by a parcel of savage negroes who thought as little of killing a man as they did of eating their dinner, and who would neither work for love or money. The consequence was that the planter was left entirely without means for harvesting his crops, and many were ruined.

At this juncture a wealthy house undertook the importation of coolies into Peru to supply the loss of slave labor; cargo after cargo arrived and were eagerly sought after by the landed proprietors, who infinitely preferred them to the negro. The coolie trade was carried on to a moderate extent, until the Brothers Lomer made their appearance in Lima. They at once succeeded (God knows how) in enlisting the merchants of Lima in their schemes, and with letters from them arrived in Boston and at once made an arrangement with the wealthy house of S. & T., whereby they prevailed upon them to go into an immense coolie business, to be carried on by means of their fine clipper ships. To cut a long story short, the "Westward Ho" and "Winged Racer," and yet another ship whose name I forget, brought over to Peru an immense number of celestials, and the interested parties realized enormous sums by their sale. The prejudice against the coolie trade arises entirely from the inhuman manner in which they have, in some instances, been treated during the voyage, causing the death of many hundreds; but the change for the coolie from misery and starvation at home is a happy one indeed, and his position, morally and socially, either on a Peruvian or Cuban plantation, is far superior to what it was in his own country. By Peruvian law the ship is allowed to sell the coolie for a stipulated sum to the planter—sufficient to cover his passage-money from China, and to yield a round profit to the owner. His term of service is *eight* years, and then he is free for life. During those eight years he is to be maintained in a manner specified by government, with such and such rations, and also receives a stipend of from five to six dollars per month. He is to have feast days and holidays to himself, and in fine, I will venture to say that his position is a thousand times superior to the greater part of the laboring portion of the community of England, Ireland, or of France.

At a later period, while living on a plantation in the vicinity of Lima, with my family, I had a capital opportunity for witnessing the working of this system, and although a northern man, and opposed in the abstract to the extension of any slave system, I must acknowledge that I was very favorably impressed with this new system of labor. On the plantation we had a gang of some twenty or thirty coolies, freshly imported from the vicinity of Swatao; they came from aboard ship enervated by sea-sickness and confinement, and also suffering from the effects of cutaneous diseases from being constantly wet with salt water. No sooner had they arrived than they were marched down to a little river running through the farm and made to bathe and thoroughly cleanse themselves in fresh water (which was repeated each morning); they were then assigned the quarters formerly occupied by the now liberated negroes, comfortable mud cabins inclosed with a high wall; this was their domain and no one interfered with their domestic arrangements. At four A.M. they were roused up and their tasks appointed them; at eleven o'clock they came in from the field, received their (stipulated) rations, of fish and rice, and after resting for three hours, they then went into the field again and worked until seven P.M., when they were again served with their rations, and their daily labors ended. By strict attention to their health, insisting on cleanliness and constant ablutions, in six months they were as stout and healthy-looking a set of men as one need look upon, and as I saw them sitting in their quarters of a Sunday morning, amusing themselves with their national games, I thought how much improved was their condition from what it had been a few months before in their own country, as I myself had witnessed them; in the depths of poverty, without a roof to cover them, or other than the cold ground to lie upon; without knowing where they were to get food to save them from famishing, their existence was one long struggle with gaunt starvation which stared them in the face from their birth to the grave.

Speaking of my residence upon a plantation, I must say that the pleasantest days passed in Peru were while living there. The hacienda, formerly owned by Echenique, the last President of Peru, and from whence he had been ejected by the revolutionists the year before, had been made by his efforts a perfect paradise. The garden, an inclosure consisting of some forty or fifty acres, was devoted to orchards of the rarest species of plantains, oranges, limes, peaches, lucomas, apples, pears, plums and grapes; while an immense space in the immediate vicinity of the house was laid out most tastefully with terraced flower beds, in which were blooming the choicest and rarest flowers, emitting the most overpowering perfumes, while refreshed with bubbling fountains, whose waters, escaping in little rills, encircled the flower beds in their embraces. This lovely little oasis was kept in perfect order by a scientific French gardener, who thoroughly understood his business.

The house was a splendid structure, with broad halls and tessellated court yards, roofed over with colonnades, around whose pillars twined creepers blooming with bright and lovely flowers. Beneath these colonnades were swung grass hammocks, reclining in which, as the soft moonbeams stole through the clustering vines, stirred by the gentle breezes laden with the heavenly breath of the sleeping plants, one indeed might fancy himself in Eden.

Many an evening hour have I gently swung in my capacious hammock, the vesper bells tolling a lullaby, and stirring many a sweet recollection of home and friends, while communing in low tones with one—from whom though long separated—now sharing my voluntary exile.

Our days passed quickly by ; a ride over the fields on our fleet horses, a breakfast off of the luscious fruits of our garden, fresh and glistening with the dew drops, a long siesta, a gallop into town, a sumptuous dinner, shared by friends from the city in search of fresh breezes of the country, a dreamy smoke upon the roof, with the broad Pacific stretching away, rose-colored with the last rays of the setting sun, a good old English song in the evening, with the piano and harp for an accompaniment—this was our everyday life. One drawback, however—being outside the walls, we were liable at any time to an attack by robbers, and a pistol and bowie-knife always lay upon our pillows.

CHAPTER XVII.

CONCLUSION.

The climate of Peru has, until of late years, been considered one of the finest in the world; the temperature one of astonishing equability (seldom varying over twenty degrees from mid-summer to mid-winter), being inimical to those thousand affections of the throat and chest which are so fatal in northern climates, while the absence of rain forbids the accumulations of the stagnant waters and swamps peculiar to the tropics, inducing the poisonous malarias which beget those terrible fevers so much dreaded by the unacclimated.

Strange to say, however, without any apparent cause, that terrible scourge *the peste* (a mild type of the yellow fever), has recently made its dread appearance in the republic, almost decimating certain portions of it in its ravages.

A peculiarity of this disease is, that independently of there being no inducing causes, it does not confine itself to the coast or to the lowlands, but seeks the "Sierra," and is most implacable in its ravages among the hamlets of the hardy mountaineers.

The character of this epidemic is very similar to that of the yellow fever, without the excessively violent symptoms of the former, but the peste is none the less to be dreaded, being more insidious in its nature and leaving the patient generally so debilitated that it is almost an impossibility to raise him.

The occasion of my final departure from the west coast was to me a very sad one, and indeed was most unfortunate in every respect. But a few months previously, accompanied by my wife, I had returned from the United States with business views, and had determined, in the natural course of events, to permanently settle on the coast; or at least to remain sufficiently long to realize enough to enable me to pass the rest of my days in independence if not in affluence; but, as the saying goes, "man proposes and God disposes," and my case did not belie the adage, for I had not been in Lima two months before the *peste* broke out, and after raging with violence, at last attacked my wife, who, being unacclimated, was peculiarly liable to it. Finding that the fever had taken a severe hold upon her, and becoming seriously anxious on her account, with the advice of the physician, I determined to take advantage of the first steamer bound north, and relinquishing my business, to try the effects of the sea air in breaking the burning fever, which it seemed was consuming her, and must prove fatal unless speedily broken; and on the day following my decision we found ourselves an board the New Granada, steaming towards Panama. The cooling influence of the fresh trade winds soon produced a most beneficial effect upon my wife's health, and before we had been three days aboard the steamer, the fever was broken, and the invalid improved by the hour.

I had often heard complaints from gentlemen who, in company with their families, had travelled in the coast steamers, of the perfect indifference to their comfort manifested by the captains of the boats (with one or two *glorious* exceptions), but I had always come to the conclusion that they were probably too *exigeante*, and looked for more attention than the captains could conscientiously bestow; but my experience during this trip led me to believe that those complaints were only too just.

During a voyage of seven days from Callao to Panama, I do not think that Captain W——, of the New Granada, vouchsafed a word or a look to myself or wife, notwithstanding our seats were next his at table. Had this resulted from habitual taciturnity on his part, no mention would ever have been made of it, but when in contrast with his excessive affability and cringing politeness to a large party, the family of Mr. W——, the managing partner of the house of Gibbs & Co., the great guns of the coast, it seemed strange and ill-bred, to say the least of it; and more particularly so when contrasted with the uniform courtesy and really fatherly kindness which Captain Bloomfield, of the same service, had extended to us on a former voyage. And in this connection, although it may be out of place, I must take occasion to acknowledge the extreme courtesy and excessive kindness shown by the ladies of Mr. W.'s family to my wife, performing a thousand little sympathetic offices which the invalid so warmly appreciates when far away from home. On our arrival at Panama, we found that, as usual, the American steamers for the United States had left only a few hours previously, thus entailing upon us the necessity of remaining fifteen days at Panama in the midst of the sickly season, with the option of taking the British and West Indian mail steamer bound for Europe.

This was a most annoying alternative, and doubly so from the consciousness that only a few hours earlier and we might have availed ourselves of the American boat, which we all would most certainly have done, the European passengers reaching their destination *via* New York, in much less time and for much less money than *via* the West Indies.

But the English company having no idea of allowing their passengers the option of the two routes, knowing full well which way their inclinations would lead them, have given strict orders that should their steamers from the south enter Panama bay in time for the passengers to catch the American boat, that they are to be *hove to*, until such time as would render it impossible to make the connection.

Thus, *nolens volens*, we were condemned to be quietly roasted beneath the burning rays of a tropic sun, on board of a nasty, foul little steamer, until our skipper was satisfied that there was not a ghost of a chance of availing ourselves of the American steamer.

After our disembarkation, I found that the fœtid atmosphere of the Isthmus was inducing a second attack of fever, and before I had been two days ashore my wife's situation became so alarming that the physician insisted that her instant departure was the only method of saving her life. So I, of course, at once decided to take advantage of the West India mail steamer that would leave Aspinwall in the course of a day or two.

My determination was a fortunate one, for it was only on the fourth or fifth day after our departure that the memorable "Panama massacre" took place, by which so many Americans lost their lives.

PANAMA RAILROAD.

It would be a positive insult to American enterprise and skill, for any one to visit the Isthmus of Panama, and to pass over that *monument of human energy*, the Panama Railroad, without paying it the tribute of a passing line. On the occasion of my first visit to the Isthmus, in 1849, and on subsequent occasions, I had suffered too severely the inconveniencies of MULE and canoe navigation, over mountain precipices and swollen rivers, not to be fully alive to all the advantages resulting from this speedy mode of transit, and I was always ready to take up cudgels in its defence, when I heard my fellow-travellers complain of the little annoyances to which we were subjected, by an accidental detention, or the like ; but more particularly so, when listening to their groanings over the high rate of passage money, and I sincerely wished that they might be obliged to make the transit, as I had made it, on mule-back and in a bungo, during the height of the rainy season, at a cost of not less than sixty dollars, with a detention of from six to ten days.

I must confess, that when at Panama in 1849, I had conversed with the engineers who were contemplating the preliminary survey, I was very skeptical as to their ability to accomplish even that, and on accompanying one of them to the scene of his labors, and finding him obliged to wade breast deep in a slimy morass to locate his *sights*, I was still more firmly impressed with the impossibility of success ; indeed, a recital of the difficulties which the original survey had to contend against, implies a high compliment to the daring conception of the projectors of this enterprise. And the Isthmus traveller, as his eye wanders over the primeval forest, the impenetrable jungle, the slimy bottomless morass ; as his burning cheek and aching bones warn him of the deadly miasmas arising from them, cannot but concede that Mr. John L. Stephens must have been urged by inspiration when he eloquently pleaded with capitalists for the support they so generously lent him, in carrying out his daring conception.

I leave the task of enumerating the almost insurmountable difficulties which were overcome in the accomplishment of this enterprise to a more eloquent pen than I possess ; indeed, words can give no just conception of obstacles which presented themselves on every hand. A climate as deadly as any that exists on earth, fatal to the white man even when using the utmost precaution ; how almost impossible, then, for the unacclimated engineers to prosecute their labors, exposed by day to the fierce heat of a vertical sun ; wading breast deep in a jungle emitting deadly and overpowering miasmas, and resting by night on the damp, slimy earth, exposed to the seething evaporations, every particle of which atmosphere is a compound of poisonous gases. Under these destructive influences the arm of labor was rendered powerless almost as soon as it reached the scene of action, and cargo after cargo of brawny Irishmen succumbed to the stealthy advances of the destroyer, who fixed upon them his murderous embraces simultaneously with their disembarkation. Still the work did not flag, fresh importations supplied the places of those who had been victimized, and every pile which supports those miles of tressel-work through those dread morasses, points in solemn silence to a victim of the irresistibility of human enterprise.

In a country where vegetation springs up with mushroom rapidity, it was not one of the least difficulties which the engineer had to contend against, to keep open the wilderness which with terrible sacrifices he had been enabled to penetrate, for of such rapid growth and luxuriance is the vegetation of that part of the world, that a clearing now made would, six months hence, be not only not discernible, but absolutely impenetrable.

The excessive moisture, too, acting in concert with the fœtid heat, if I may be allowed the expression, induces the most rapid decay, thus attacking and destroying everything where that most indispensable agent, wood, is concerned. Piles, bridges, sleepers—all give way before its fell influence, and the engineer in dismay recoils before an apparently insurmountable obstacle.

In civilized countries, one great annoyance to be encountered in the construction of a public work, when large numbers of men are employed, results from a spirit of insubordination, so innate in the vulgar and uneducated; but in those countries there is a remedy; men may be discharged and others employed, the police may be called in, and military even summoned to quell a dangerous outbreak; but here, on the Isthmus, the small staff of engineers must rely upon themselves, and it needed more than ordinary firmness to guide with a firm hand a thousand men composed of Carthagenian and Jamaica negroes, the former of whom are noted in that part of the world as being the most turbulent and desperate men in that lawless region.

Indeed the engineers showed great tact in resorting to the only expedient which they could probably have hit upon to save their own lives and prosecute the work.

Taking advantage of a strong antipathy existing between the Carthagenian and the Jamaica negroes, and by organizing the gangs so as to keep nearly an equal number of each nationality in each—they so managed to fan the flame of native animosity, as to keep constantly alive the feeling of antagonism, and thus in case of trouble with one party it was only necessary to call in the assistance of the other.

Although the preliminary surveys were made in 1849, it was not until six years after that a locomotive passed over the entire length of the road, a distance of FORTY-NINE MILES. This fact in itself tells more eloquently than words could do, the overwhelming obstacles which the engineer corps had to contend against; and each and every one of those forty-nine miles, is a NOTE of a grand requiem which chaunts a lasting testimonial to the disinterested energy of Mr. John L. Stephens.

Embarking on board the West India Mail Steamer "Dee," we bade adieu to the Isthmus with thankful hearts, and drew a long breath of relief as we steamed out of the harbor of Colon; and at once felt new life as we inhaled the fresh northwest-trade winds as they came sweeping over the Caribbean Sea.

The "Dee," a fine commodious ship of two thousand tons, possessed all the comforts which one could wish for or expect to find aboard a sea-going steamer; belonging to that powerful and wealthy organization the West India Mail Steam Packet Company, she was well fitted, well officered and well manned, and one might almost have fancied himself aboard a man-of-war, as he observed the heavy gangs of men at work in their several departments, and noticed the strict discipline to which they were all subject; indeed, the marked difference in the manning and equipment between the American and British steamers, gives one a strong predilection in favor of the latter over the former; and I must say, that having the option of making a voyage in an American or an English boat, I should always prefer the latter, from the increased feeling of security the perfect discipline observable in the English steam service gives one who has noticed its entire absence in the American steam marine.

Bravely steaming along the Spanish main and parting the laughing wavelets of the Caribbean Sea, a few days brings us abreast the harbor of Carthagena, once the stronghold of the Spaniards, until a brave English admiral, nothing daunted by the long lines of fortifications which bristled malignantly along the low sand beach at its entrance, swept within it with his fleet, and, driving its defenders from their ramparts, hauled down the proud banner of Castile and in its stead unfurled the English Cross.

These fortifications, perhaps the most extensive and certainly the most scientifically constructed of any in the New World, are now in ruins, and one saddens as he looks upon these relics of departed grandeur.

The city is a picturesque old place, whose moss-grown and mildewed, loop-holed, old wall, hiding all but the tower and steeple of the city, gives it a strangely picturesque appearance. On entering its streets, one sees at a glance a decayed and still decaying city, whose massive store-houses and imposing structures tell in mournful silence of past greatness, but of present ruin.

Taking in a few passengers and a little freight, we once more ripple the quiet waters of this beautiful though deserted bay, and shaving the fortress at its narrow entrance close enough to heave a biscuit ashore, we at once feel the ocean swell and head up on our course.

The next day, we make the port of Santa Martha, with its fine high background of hills and its ruined fortifications, the cradle of South American liberty, the land of Colombia, and of Simon Bolivar.

Santa Martha still possesses some importance in the commercial world, from its position at the mouth of the great Magdalena River, whose waters, swollen by the melting snows of the Andes, bear on its broad bosom the valuable products of Colombia and New Granada to the ocean. Santa Martha, indeed, is the starting point for all travellers who visit Bogota, and more recently a steamboat has been placed upon the river, which will tend to augment its trade.

Standing boldly across the Caribbean, and breasting the stiff trade-wind, we in a few days sighted the island of St. Thomas and entered its snug and capacious harbor.

St. Thomas is a Danish island, but its inhabitants are made up of every nationality under the sun, and the home government being shrewd enough to see that a liberal policy would induce prosperity, exempt not only its own citizens, but every stranger or ship visiting it, from all dues or taxes whatsoever. Custom houses are voted humbugs, and with but a very few salutary restrictions, a shipmaster can do precisely what he pleases without comment or annoyance from prying officials. The change from the Spanish island is very marked; there your every step is dogged, your every motion criticized, while here you can do exactly as you please.

This island has rather an unenviable notoriety as having been for years the rendezvous for slavers, and probably, with good reason, for its lenient revenue-laws invite these lawless gentlemen bound to the coast of Africa, to come in to refit, for often times they are so hard pressed in the United States that they are obliged to escape without taking in the necessary supplies, which they are enabled to do here quite as advantageously.

St. Thomas is a place of considerable importance, from the fact that merchants from the Spanish main, from the coast of Mexico, and oftentimes from the west coast, resort thither to purchase their goods, which, from the absence of revenue-dues can be had almost as cheaply as in Europe, without one's incurring the trouble and expense of making a voyage there.

But what gives it its present notoriety is the fact of its being the depot of the British and West Indian Mail Packet Company—the centering point from which radiate its widely extending ramifications.

One of the company's immense and fleet steamers (for instance the "Atrato," of 4,000 tons, with a speed of sixteen knots), leaves Southampton every fifteen days, and after a twelve days' passage arrives at St. Thomas. Here, on her arrival are awaiting her, with steam up, smaller steamers belonging to the same service, bound (after taking on board the mails and passengers brought out by the large boat), to Cuba, Jamaica, Vera Cruz, Barbadoes, Demarara, and Halifax, and the precision with which this vast scheme of connections is carried out is really beautiful, and entitles the projectors to great praise.

Immediately the signal on the telegraph pole announces the arrival in the offing of the *home boat*, these half dozen steamers make the necessary preparations for taking in cargo and for bearing off, and no sooner is the anchor of the *Parent* boat down than the small steamers haul alongside of her, and receiving their quota, at once stand out to sea to their various destinations.

A more lovely or picturesque spot than the harbor and city of St. Thomas it would be difficult to find. Describing a circle, the bay is hemmed in by lofty hills which secure it from the violence of the autumnal hurricanes. Fronting the entrance, the city nestles under the hills, or goes straggling along their sides, their bright colors contrasting pleasantly with the dark green foliage.

In spite of its lovely appearances, however, it is a real "plague-spot," and in defiance of all *atmospheric* rules is the stronghold of cholera and yellow fever. One would pronounce it, as far as locality goes, to be the most healthily situated city in the Antilles, but, why or wherefore none can tell, yellow fever appears to be an *institution*. In Cuba, yellow-Jack only makes his appearance during the summer months; in winter giving its inhabitants a respite, thus allowing northern invalids to seek with impunity its more genial climate; but in St. Thomas, regardless of seasons, it makes coquettish advances at any time, and killing off a few hundreds, again retires.

Probably the most fatal epidemic that ever visited the island was during the *holidays* at the close of the year 1850.

Passing a fortnight pleasantly ashore, a gun at midnight arousing us told us that the English mail had arrived, and that we must at once repair aboard the Havana steamer. Hastily packing, we reached our vessel, and at daylight steamed out of the harbor.

Seven days after leaving St. Thomas we sighted "Moro Castle," and in a few hours were comfortably located in Havana, whence, after a stay of some ten days, we again embarked on board the "Black Warrior," and on the fifth day the Highlands of Neversink loomed up in the distance.

* * * * * * * * * * *

Surrounded by my little family, who act as anchors mooring me to my home, I hardly permit myself even to look southward ; but oftentimes when hurrying through Wall street, the taunt royal-mast of some dandy clipper, towering over the house-tops, attracts my longing gaze, and an involuntary sigh escapes me as I think of the merry days I have passed floating over the blue ocean, and discover myself making disagreeable comparisons between the past and present.

During the last year of my stay upon the west coast, my attention was directed to the great necessity existing for the establishment of an opposition line of steamers to that of the British company, who, by their extortionate rates and unaccommodating spirit, were curtailing materially the travel, and effectually impeding the development of the resources of the countries along which their vessels coasted ; and, with that idea constantly in view, I neglected no opportunity for the collection of all information which might be of use to me in urging the scheme on my return to the United States.

Upon my arrival in New York, I made use of every effort to induce parties here, interested in the coast trade, to push the matter, but finding others in the field who had more leisure and influence than I had, I awaited patiently until they should bring their matters to a close, either successfully or otherwise.

Within the past six months, however, finding that the efforts of others have been abortive, my attention has again been turned seriously to this subject, and for a time I was sanguine of success ; indeed, I had good grounds for supposing that the organization of an American line was, beyond a peradventure, a fixed fact, for having at my disposal a large amount of subscriptions for South American account, an assurance of lucrative contracts, and considerable subscriptions promised here, I looked upon the matter as settled. When, without any apparent reason, those who had been the warmest advocates of the enterprise, and without whose aid we could not move, became alarmed lest the undertaking should not prove feasible or profitable, and, after hesitating for some time, finally withdrew altogether.

Knowing that there are a large number of mercantile men who take great interest in the trade of the coast, and in its development, I have thought that the introduction in this connection of a prospectus which I prepared a few months since, and which attempts to *make manifest the feasibility of the enterprise,* might not be improper.

It is argued, too, that I have presented the undertaking in a too favorable light ; but I insist that my deductions are in the main correct.

One has only to examine the statistical reports of the trade of our own country with the South American republics, and to note its yearly increasing importance, as the facilities for the conveyance of their products from the interior to a point of embarcation are being consummated, to convince himself of the absolute necessity of a new and opposition line.

It is further urged that, although in the enjoyment of so great a monopoly, even the English company have not been able to divide more than a meagre percentage on their investments. The allegation is untrue, but were it otherwise, the cause would be manifest.

The dividends paid by the British company during the last seven years are as follows—(besides *bonuses*, PRIVATELY paid to the stockholders, in order to keep the public in ignorance of their successful business ; and exclusive of the vast amount of surplus invested in extravagantly built steamers)—viz : Dividends for the year 1858, 4 per cent. ; 1857, 10 per cent. ; 1856, 3½ per cent. ; 1855, 3 per cent. ; 1854, 5 per cent. ; 1853, 5 per cent. ; 1852, 10 per cent.

The *extra* expenditures of this company have been enormous; for their boats being constructed on the most extravagant principles, consume an unheard of amount of fuel ; so much so, that it has been deemed expedient to send them back to England to have them refitted with more economical machinery ;* and no one who knows the cost of sending a large steamer around Cape Horn (not less than $25,000 either way !) would be surprised to learn that a company who had found it necessary

* I am told on good authority, every one of the boats at present on the coast, which has not already been refitted there, must unavoidably return to England.

to go to this expenditure, not in one but in half a dozen instances, were unable, however lucrative their business, to declare such dividends as the trade would seem to warrant.

PROSPECTUS.

Some fifteen years since, William Wheelwright, Esq., an American long resident in Chili, and a man of great energy and penetration, feeling that the immense and growing trade of the South Pacific coast required other modes of communication and transportation than those offered by a miserable class of sailing vessels then navigating it, at once turned his attention to the collection of such facts and statistics as would warrant his appearing before English capitalists and asking their connivance and assistance in the establishment of steam communication from the Isthmus of Panama to one of the southern ports of Chili.

With his accustomed energy, Mr. Wheelwright went earnestly to work, and with the coöperation of others who were interested in the scheme (not only from pecuniary but from patriotic motives, as tending to develop the vast resources of the countries skirting the Pacific Ocean), succeeded in amassing a sufficient amount of statistical proof, and assurance of support on the part of the different governments to enable him to appear before a committee appointed by certain wealthy Scotchmen with such convincing evidence of the increasingly valuable trade of the coast, that they did not hesitate in reporting favorably, and measures were at once taken for the establishment of the "PACIFIC STEAM NAVIGATION COMPANY." This Company has now been established about twelve years, during which time they have been highly successful, and from their profits, besides earning fair dividends, have been enabled to build from time to time several splendid steamships (more than trebling their original tonnage), and also have become the proprietors of some extremely valuable real estate.

Enjoying a monopoly, the British company, like all very successful corporations, have been careless of popularity, feeling that theirs was the only mode of communication or of transportation, and have established a tariff for freight and passage money, which while it filled their coffers, curtailed very materially the business of the coast, and prevented thousands from travelling, who, at a moderate rate, would have availed themselves of such means of transport.

Not caring for popularity, no concessions were made to the prejudices of those travelling on board their vessels, and neither ordinary civility nor a spirit of conciliation has been manifested towards the natives of the coast who, in the absence of another line, are obliged to avail themselves of these ships.

Incapacitated by the exorbitant rates exacted by this company, from availing themselves of the facilities offered by the Panama Railroad Company for a *direct* importation of goods from Europe and the United States, thus avoiding the dangers and delays of Cape Horn ; exasperated by the unaccommodating spirit manifested by all connected with this enterprise, the people doing business on the coast and all those who have been in the habit of travelling by this line, have long since looked earnestly to the establishment of another line, which, while it would be a benefit to the whole coast and a source of great profit to those interested in it, would force the British monopoly to act with a more liberal spirit towards those brought in connection with it.

Spasmodic efforts have been made for several years past by parties in the United States, in connection with merchants on the coast, to get up an opposition line, but as the persons here were, as a general thing, ignorant of the requirements of the coast and of its resources, they failed in convincing capitalists sufficiently to induce their support.

During the past two years, however, an earnest move has been made in this affair among several wealthy Peruvians and Chilians, who, having been ill-treated and injured in business by the arrogance and excessive rates of the English company, have determined to push this matter through, either in England or in the United States, and to give practical evidence of their support by large subscriptions of capital, and lending all their influence in securing lucrative contracts, which would in themselves alone warrant the establishment of a line.

Profoundly impressed with the vast importance of the rapidly increasing trade of the West Coast, and of the utter inadequacy of the present steam line for the transportation of its commerce, or for that rapidity so requisite to an active trade, at the instigation of many deeply interested in, and fully alive to the requirements of the coast, certain parties in the United States, practical men, and who have long resided on the Pacific seaboard and are intimately acquainted with its trade and its resources, have determined to use all their efforts for the establishment of an American line of first class screw steamships, to share the yearly augmenting profits of the English company.

Sanguine not only of success, but of the certainty of large

profits on the investment, the promoters of this enterprise would set forth, as the basis of their operations, some statements regarding the actual trade of the coast, from statistics collected while doing business there, and perfectly authentic (and it might not be out of place here to mention that one of the principals in the enterprise, himself commanded a steamer on the coast, and has likewise traded upon it as master and supercargo of sailing vessels).

THE DIRECT TRADE OF THE WEST COAST, VIA THE ISTHMUS OF PANAMA, WITH EUROPE AND THE UNITED STATES.

The route to be traversed by the proposed line, skirts the sea-board of the republics of New Granada, Ecuador, Peru, Bolivia and Chili.

The foreign exports and imports of these countries, amount annually, in the aggregate, to the large sum of sixty millions of dollars; the entire commerce which these millions represent, is carried by medium of sailing vessels, via Cape Horn, subject of course, to the usual delay of from four to six months in making the voyage, to the deterioration in the value of merchandise in consequence of the constant change of climate, to the damage resulting from being shut up in the confined atmosphere of a ship's hold for half a year, and in fine, to all the casualties to which sailing vessels are so peculiarly liable on that long and arduous voyage; and last, but not least, to the great loss of interest on the money invested, and to the latitude thus given for variation in the prices of goods shipped to a market.

No one felt more sensibly the inconvenience or regretted

more sincerely the loss attendant upon this long and uncertain mode of transportation, than did the merchants on the coast, whose financial operations were so materially crippled by it; *but where was the remedy?*

The completion of the Panama Railroad was hailed by all, as a solution of this problem.

With steam from Valparaiso to Panama; with a railroad across the isthmus, from the Pacific to the Atlantic, and with a regular steam communication from thence to the United States and Europe, who would dream of exposing their more valuable merchandise to the uncertainties of a Cape Horn voyage? Thus they argued, but their anticipations were not destined to be realized.

The English companies with apparently inconceivable blindness to their own interest, not only refused to coöperate with them in their desire for a direct transportation, but actually advanced their rates, which effectually deterred them from making the experiment.

One of the strongest inducements for the carrying out of this enterprise, would be to further the views of those desirous of availing themselves of it, as the means of a direct trade; for although it might seem impossible to those who have not considered the subject, for steamers to compete with sailing vessels on so long a route, still, on estimating the ten thousand miles more of distance, by the Cape Horn route, and in view of the great loss in interest, and the length of time necessary for returns and remittances, one will discover the difference in freight by the two routes would not only not be so great as he had imagined, but in many instances, would be actually in favor of the Panama route.

By way of Illustration—Suppose two shipments of equal value to be made to Peru from New York, the one *via* Cape Horn, the other *via* the isthmus.

"SHIPMENT VIA CAPE HORN."

Cost of merchandise, say 100 tons at $500 per ton	$50,000
Freight to Callao at $15 do.	1,500
Int. on cost of shipment for five months, (rate in Peru), 12 per cent.	2,500
Estimated damage by deterioration from change of climate, etc., etc., etc., 2 per cent.	1,000
	$55,000

"SHIPMENT VIA PANAMA."

Cost of Merchandise, say 100 tons at $500 per ton	$50,000	
Int. on money, 1 month at 12 per cent . .	500	
Freight from New York to Aspinwall, $8 per ton		
Freight by rail across isthmus $12 per ton		
" Steam to Callao 10 "	3,000	
		$53,500
Showing a saving of $1,500 by the isthmus route.		$1,500

From the foregoing we discover that goods could be imported from the United States in *one-fifth* the time required by the Cape Horn route, and at a saving of 30 per cent. in favor of the Panama route, while from Europe the expense would be only at a comparatively small advance, and hence it is but fair to infer that of the sixty millions of imports and exports, that at least one-fifth would take the most expeditious route. One-fifth of $60,000,000 is $12,000,000, representing 40,000 tons of merchandise, which at $10 per ton would yield an annual freight amounting to $400,000 ; this in itself would be almost a sufficient basis for the establishment of a second line.

COASTWISE NAVIGATION.

Only those who have traded on the coast can have any conception of the immense traffic carried on along its shores, from Cape Horn to the Equator.

The states of New Granada and Ecuador exchange their cocoa, their coffee and their fruits ; Peru her sugars, her wines, her guano, and her wool, with Chili for her flour, her metals, her lumber, and her coal ; thus creating a healthy and active trade throughout the whole length of the coast.

Chili imports from New Granada to amt. of	. .	$150,000
" exports to ditto	" . . .	60,000
" imports from Bolivia	" . . .	600,000
" imports from Peru	" . . .	2,000,000
" exports to do.	" . . .	1,800,000
		$4,610,000

Say the amount of the Chilian trade sums up . .	$5,000,000
The local trade of the Peruvian, Bolivian and Ecuadorian coasts will certainly equal that amount : say	$5,000,000
Amounting together to	$10,000,000

which is the usual estimate of the coastwise trade. These ten millions of dollars represent say 50,000 tons of freight, which would avail itself of steam, and which is at present all carried by small sailing coasters, at the very high rate of $12 per ton, while by the contemplated line, the freight (between Chili and Peru) would not exceed $5 per ton—thus certainly securing at least three-fourths, or say 37,500 tons of freight annually, which, at $5 per ton, would amount to $187,500.

Sailing vessels labor under a peculiar disadvantage on this coast; generally of an inferior build, badly manned and expensive in outfit—they are obliged to contend with calms and against head winds which, always blowing in one direction, render the windward voyage uncertain and protracted. No sailing vessels could afford to take freight at less than eight dollars, and while the English boats charge twenty, the new line would take the bulk at $5.

From the foregoing estimates of the coastwise and foreign trade, we may calculate upon 40,000 tons *through* freight at $15 per ton $600,000
(the English rates being $45 per ton),
Upon 37,500 tons *coastwise* freight at $5 187,500

$787,500

Or say $700,000 gross freight money.

PASSENGERS.

The population of the States which border this route, amounts to a total of 8,000,000 inhabitants, a large part of whom are engaged in commercial pursuits.

The postal arrangements of these countries being exceedingly defective, and in the absence of any reliable mode of making exchanges (there being no banks), besides a strong natural propensity on the part of the lower classes to wander from point to point peddling merchandise, all tend to induce a considerable amount of travel, and balsas, canoes, sailing vessels, and steamers go thronged to their various destinations.

Large as the travel is, it would be much greater were the rates of passage on a moderate scale, but notwithstanding their excessive rates the English boats go laden to their full capacity.

By close observation of the passengers travelling in the English boats, a fair estimate of their number, making an average of the "way" and "through" passengers, would be :

For Cabin (through) passengers, 700 at $150 . .	$105,000
" Cabin and second cabin (way) passengers, 4,000 at $25	100,000
" Steerage passengers, 6,000 at $12	72,000
	$277,000

Whole amount of passage money would be, say $300,000.

SPECIE.

A most important item in this connection would be the freight on the treasure shipped between the more important points on the coast, and also the large amounts annually shipped to the Bank of England.

In absence of all banks, and in countries where the governments are in so unsettled a state, exchanges are made entirely in specie, and one need only inform himself of the trade of a locality to approximate to the value of the specie continually in transit.

It is estimated that the English boats receive on board annually $20,000,000 precious metals, at an average freight of ½ per cent., amounting to $100,000.

It would be fair to calculate for the new line, say, $10,000,000, at ½ per cent. $50,000

MAILS.

Notwithstanding the English company have contracts with various countries along its route for the conveyance of the mails, nevertheless the *new line* would enjoy a very handsome income on the freight on the correspondence which it would attract. Running at a speed exceeding that of the English company, and connecting with the fleet steamers plying between New York and Aspinwall, mail matter forwarded by them and thence to Europe, would anticipate by at least *ten* days, the letters dispatched by the English mail, via *St. Thomas*.

The following comparison will illustrate the time and expense saved by the *new line* (as it is proposed to run), in a voyage from Europe to the South Pacific coast over the *old line* (under the existing arrangement):

BY THE ENGLISH MAIL ROUTE UNDER THE EXISTING ARRANGEMENT.

	FARE.	NO DAYS.
From Southampton to Panama, per "British and West Indian Mail Steam Ship Co."	$250	27.
From Panama to Valparaiso, per "British Steam Navigation Co."	290	22
	$540	49

BY THE AMERICAN LINE AS IT IS PROPOSED TO RUN.

	FARE.	DAYS.	FARE.	NO. DAYS.
Amount brought down			$540	49.
From Southampton to New York, per Atlantic Steamers	$125	11		
From New York to Panama. .	80	10		
From Panama to Valparaiso . .	150	17		
	355	38	$355	38
			$185	11

Showing a saving in time, in favor of an American Line, of eleven days, and in passage money of $185 over the English Line, which would in itself secure a majority of the through passengers, who, independently of economizing time would naturally select the route *via* the United States, as offering more variety, and at the same time avoiding the pestilential climate of the West Indies.

The correspondence would *of course* seek the shortest route.

ESTIMATED COST OF A LINE OF FOUR SCREW STEAMSHIPS WITH THEIR RUNNING EXPENSES FOR ONE YEAR.

4 Screw ships of about 1,200 tons each, with duplicate machinery, and complete with all the modern improvements.	$400,000
5 good hulks as coal depots with moorings, buoys, boats, etc.	25,000
3,000 tons of coal placed on board said hulks, at $13.	40,000
Real Estate, etc., etc.	10,000
Cost of putting the steamers in the port of Valparaiso	75,000
Cost of stores for crews and passengers for six months to be placed on the coast. . . .	50,000
Amount required for the enterprise.	$600,000

In order to set on foot this undertaking, it is proposed to organize an association to be known under the name of "The South Pacific Steam Navigation Company." The capital stock of the company to be one million dollars: six hundred thousand dollars to be at present subscribed for, in six thousand shares of one hundred dollars each, ten per cent. to be paid in cash and the balance in instalments, to be determined by the company.

The following is an estimate of the expenses of the proposed line for one year, and of the corresponding receipts:

Provisions for 24 voyages, 48 trips (1 year) for passengers and crews, say	$50,000
Wages, officers and men	75,000
Coal for 12 months, 15,000 tons at $12 . . .	180,000
Salaries of agents and officers, say	25,000
Incidental expenses	10,000
	$335,000
Say	$400,000
Wear and tear, 10 per cent., or say	50,000
	$450,000

RECEIPTS FOR ONE YEAR.

Freight for 48 trips, say 500 tons, (capacity 1,000 tons) through freight per trip 24,000 tons at $15 . . .	$360,000	
(The English Company asking $45).		
Passengers 48 trips, 12 through passengers each trip, at $150, English boats' rates $250, say	80,000	
6,000 steerage passengers at an average of $10	60,000	
2,000 2d cabin passengers at $25 . .	50,000	
Freight on specie, say $10,000,000 at ¾ per cent.	75,000	
Mails, say	75,000	$700,000
		$250,000

Showing an annual receipt over expenditures of considerably more than $200,000.

Assuming the foregoing estimates of the coast trade to be correct, we find that there would be at *moderate rates* a freight movement sufficient to employ treble the amount of steam tonnage, now navigating the South Pacific; and knowing how increased facilities beget an active trade, it would be but fair to look for a considerable augmentation of the coast business, should such a line be established. .

The *English company* has certainly an advantage over any other that may be established, in having contracts for the mails for the republics along her route; but it is not improbable that at the *expiration* of those contracts (some two years hence), the *New Line* (should it prove a popular enterprise), would be enabled to obtain its share of government patronage.

The *New Line* would possess one very great advantage over the English company, which would more than counterbalance the benefits resulting for the mail contracts, which would be in the *immense saving of fuel,* over the Old Line.

In constructing the vessels for the New Line, it is proposed that their models shall be such that while making an average speed of 13 knots they shall not consume over 24 tons of coal per 24 hours; and one has only to examine the propellers, now navigating our coasts, in order to assure himself that vessels combining the above qualifications can be built. Admitting this, four such vessels would consume annually (48 trips

at 17 days each), say 200,000 tons at $12 . . .	$240,000
While four of the English ships at present employed, consuming as they do 60 tons per day, would burn annually 49,000 at $ 12 . .	- 588,000
	$348,000
Showing an extra expenditure on the part of the English company of over	$350,000

THE END.

www.ingramcontent.com/pod-product-compliance
Lightning Source LLC
LaVergne TN
LVHW020059110826
845151LV00001B/22

* 9 7 8 1 4 2 5 5 4 4 9 4 2 *